DAVID DICKINSON

WHAT A BOBBY DAZZLER

DAVID DICKINSON

The Duke

WHAT A BOBBY DAZZLER

This book is dedicated to Christopher Haworth,
a dearly missed friend and partner

And, still working on joined-up writing, where would I be without
Rosemary Kingsland?

Published by BBC Worldwide Limited
80 Wood Lane, London W12 0TT

First published 2003
Copyright © David Dickinson 2003
The moral right of the author has been asserted.

Photographs copyright © David Dickinson 2003, except pictures 16 and 30 Robert
Rathbone/Rex Features; 21 Mark Harrison/Radio Times; 24 London Features International
and 27 Tom Howard/Radio Times.

ISBN 0 563 48724 0

Commissioning editor: Nicky Ross
Project editor: Helena Caldon
Designer: Annette Peppis
Picture research: David Cottingham
Production controller: Kenneth Mckay

Set in Sabon and Trajan
Printed and bound in Great Britain by Butler and Tanner Ltd, Frome and London
Colour separations by Radstock Reproductions, Midsomer Norton
Cover printed by Belmont Press Ltd, Northampton

CONTENTS

·

PREFACE

·

My wife, Lorne, and I have always travelled extensively in the Far East. It is a part of the world we like to visit, with its exotic air of mystique and luxury. Just before I started work on this book we flew into Kuala Lumpur on Air Malaysia to spend Christmas at the Hotel Datai, a five-star island hideaway.

At KMP airport we breathed in the scented tropical air after a long and gruelling flight from Manchester. We had escaped the chill of an English winter but we still had not yet reached journey's end. We had travelled club class all the way, but even so, the first leg had been 13 hours, with a connecting onward flight to Langkawi island which lasted an hour.

It was with a sense of relief that we saw a smiling face greeting us at the small airport on the island. We were ushered away to a Mercedes and immediately given cold damp towels to refresh ourselves and a chilled bottle of Evian each. Driven at speed through a shady forest road, we finally started to relax.

On arriving at the hotel, which is built on an open plan with luxurious villas dotted throughout the surrounding rainforest, we were escorted to the open-air reception area overlooking the main part of the hotel. Cooling fans whirred away overhead and we sank into comfortable chintz-covered rattan seats and were offered chilled champagne in tall misted glasses.

The general manager registered us personally, then showed us to our suite, where our luggage had already been taken. The suite was huge, with a gleaming floor made of some polished local red timber. There were upholstered banquette seats and large glass windows, opening onto a private terrace. All around lay the ancient rainforest, where the moss-covered hardwood trees dripped with lianas, orchids and spreading ferns. There were numerous monkeys and the most amazing birds, some like toucans with yellow beaks.

We stood on the terrace with the general manager, taking it all in, feeling the stress of a hard though remarkable year slip away.

The manager pointed out the private beach below and some of the other facilities, then he said, 'At the moment we have three peers of the realm staying here.'

To which I replied, 'Three peers of the realm – and a Duke!'

We had gone to Datai to spend Christmas; but I had also wanted to go far off the beaten track to have the tranquillity and the space to get my thoughts in order and to summon up the memories of a lifetime in order to prepare my autobiography.

Each day I would go down to the beach and find a secluded spot. I would sit and listen to the waves on the white sand, the breeze rustling the leaves of the palm trees overhead, hearing the strange chatter of monkeys and the call of birds in the forest, and watching the lulling ocean, contemplating both the past and the future. And as I sat there, recording my memories, I realized that my journey through life, with all its twists and turns, had been quite remarkable.

It has been an exciting and interesting odyssey. I was amazed at what I could remember in some detail, things I hadn't thought of for many years. I'm sure that there is a lot I've forgotten, but those days at Datai brought back to me very plainly so much. In some ways I feel quite blessed because I've had an eventful life, a good life. There's been the odd hiccough. Sometimes I've made the wrong decision. But when I look back, it's been a fabulous life. The one thing that stands out is that I've been very fortunate.

I've found the love of my life, a great woman, and this has helped me. It has toned me down, tamed me and given me a great deal of pleasure being married to Lorne for over 30 years. I've had the most amazing opportunities come my way and in grasping them with both hands and an open mind I've had experiences and unexpected career opportunities I would never in my wildest dreams have contemplated when I was a small boy watching another very different sea, in Devon, at the age of five.

And that is where my story opens, in Devon, where I spent part of a magical childhood just after the war. But as you eventually turn the last page, you will see that it is not the end, but the beginning of a new chapter – because who knows what lies around the corner? I certainly don't. But what I will say to you is that whatever it is, whatever fortune and fate have planned for me, the Duke will be there to relish it.

CHAPTER ONE

·

I was born during World War II in Cheadle Heath, part of Stockport. Both areas were rather drab suburbs of Manchester. Like most of England's big industrial centres, Manchester was blitzed in the war. Many families evacuated to the safety of the countryside. But we didn't leave. My family stuck it out with characteristic true British grit, hearing the big bombers flying overhead night after night and watching the flames shoot up from the city centre. Instead, when the heat had literally and metaphorically died down, when I was about five years old we packed our bags and headed for the quaint little fishing village of Brixham in Devon.

Contrary, you might think? Well, perhaps; but I will always be grateful for those almost stolen years by the sea because I had an idyllic time, and I am left with the most wonderful memories. Memories of Brixham's busy cobbled harbour in the early morning sun, full of seaweedy nets, boxes of silver fishes, the giant lobsters that were two a penny back then, and the scream of the gulls. Fishing smacks jostled for space and the old tars seemed to roll along, still filled with the motion of the waves, wearing their thick navy-blue jerseys, their oilskins and high rubber boots.

My family consisted of myself, my mother Joyce and my father Jim Dickinson. Mother was a hairdresser, a bit of a gypsy, who liked to keep moving around from place to place. Or my father got work here or there, and we'd be off again. Mother opened a salon in posh Castle Circus in Torquay and disappeared each day for long hours. Jim was also a very hard-working, decent bloke, who always seemed to have more than one job, so he disappeared for long hours too and I was left to my own devices. Despite my youth, I would get my own breakfast, then would either take myself off to school or race out to play.

Our home for those years was a small cottage just off the harbour. A few steps led up into the jumble of crowded streets that climbed the steep hill of the picturesque village and that was where you would have found us, within sight and smell of the sea. Of course, tourists did go there in the summer holidays, families with buckets and spades, sandwiches wrapped in greaseproof paper, and flasks of cold tea, who usually arrived by train and left, sandy, sunburnt and happy. No coaches or charabancs rolled into the town back then, there were no traffic jams, no crowds, not even on August bank holidays. The narrow streets had a few cafes that served clotted cream teas and magnificent fish and chips. It was only a year or so after the war had ended, so things were still rationed, and there wasn't much choice – but there could be no better feast in the world than the fresh food that was produced locally.

The harbour became my world, where I spent every available moment of the day. I would run along the cobbles, curious about everything, looking with fascination at the fishing smacks crowding the quayside and at large barrels full of steaming water where crabs and lobsters would be bubbling away, being prepared to be sent off to London on the train. Often I saw a basking shark dragged up on the slipway of the harbour. Sometimes it would still be alive and I'd inspect it with awe and great trepidation, in case it suddenly rose up like the monster from the deep and got me. The ruddy-faced fishermen laughed at my antics as they sat on old wooden crates, mending their torn nets. When such powerful fish got entangled and fought for their lives, they caused so much damage the nets were beyond repair. Fishing was a precarious livelihood and these men were habitually poor, so it was their custom to put a plate or a tin out for a collection towards new nets.

It was always a great treat when they allowed me to go on their trawlers with them, chasing the great shoals of sprats and maybe mackerel. The bulging nets were swung over the side above the decks, dripping with salt water and seaweed, and opened up. With a great woosh, thousands of fish flooded out and instantly I was waist-deep in a mass of moving sprats. A strong arm would come down and lift me straight up, little fishes falling from me like streams of quicksilver. Beneath my little shorts and top my entire body, every inch of skin, would be covered in silvery fish scales. Like a sleek little fish, glistening like a jewel, I dashed up the steps to our cottage and in through the door, ready to face the music after we docked.

'Look at you!' mother said in despair. 'How am I going to get all that muck off you?'

Early Sunday evenings was a time when the bells of All Saints Church used to ring out. You'd hear them all round the harbour and out at sea. The tune has stayed with me all my life: 'Abide with me; fast falls the eventide; the darkness deepens; Lord, with me abide.' The words were written by the rector of the church as he lay dying of tuberculosis. He finished it on the Sunday he gave his final sermon. For more than a century since then the bells have rung out across the sea every evening, to give fishermen heart and hope as they set sail on their dangerous work. It was even sung at the wedding of King George VI and later at the wedding of his daughter, Queen Elizabeth.

I was too young then to know this poignant history. To me, as I sat on the steps in the evenings, tired and content after a long day spent outdoors, into everything, the bells represented the depressing thought: school tomorrow!

When I wasn't at school I'd play with other local lads. We were little buggers, I suppose, because we'd often go out seagull's-nesting. Fearless, we scrambled up those huge cliffs – and believe you me, they are high – looking for eggs. Naturally, seagulls had put their nests in the most perilous, unapproachable places, so we were constantly putting our lives in danger but we were invincible. The excitement of the chase was to find these eggs come hell or high water and at times, as we clung to a ledge with the big gulls screaming and battering at us with their powerful wings, it could easily have been high water. How we survived, I don't know. It was such a waste, really, because we never did anything with the eggs, just took them home and put holes in them with a pin and blew them so we could keep the empty shells in a nest of cotton wool in a box. With the pockets of our shorts full of eggs we would scramble down, grazing knees and elbows, often banging into rocks, smashing the fragile shells. On the beach we'd turn our pockets inside out to get rid of the mess but would be left with yellow yolk stains. Once again, I'd get a clump around the ear as mother took my clothes off to wash them.

She'd sigh, 'You've been seagull's-nesting again!'

At weekends we went to local beaches all round Brixham with other boys, to places like Babbacombe, Cockington Village and Cockington Forge. Whenever I see a painting today by the artist Dorothy Sharpe – wonderful pictures of children with handkerchiefs tied in knots on their heads and carrying small nets in their hands, scurrying around rock pools, shrimping or trying to get a small fish to put into a jar – I'm reminded of those salt-scented, sunny days.

The landscape of my childhood in the Forties and Fifties was like the Newlyn School of painting whose pictures are very much the type I've seen for many years in galleries and in auctions, and typify so evocatively those years I spent on that Devon coast. When I stand and look at one of these paintings with those fishing boats, the wonderful weather-beaten characters with their sou'westers, always working, cleaning fish, maintaining their boats, mending their nets, it all comes back to me. The cafes with the clotted cream teas, the jam and the scones are still there today but it's all quite different to what it used to be.

After a couple of years we moved up to Torquay, to be nearer to my mother's salon, and I think Jim had got a job in the town, too. I went to a different school and my memories are no longer as vivid. Eventually we moved back to Cheadle Heath to live with my grandmother, Caroline Emson – or Nanny, as I always called her – at 241 Stockport Road, and once more I experienced the security of being embraced in the large and friendly bosom of the family. This consisted of Nanny and her four daughters – there was Joyce, who was my mother, then came Mary, Peggy and Ethel – and their husbands, and one or two cousins, all girls. Nanny's large Edwardian semi consisted of a spacious kitchen, which was the beating heart of the home, two or three large living rooms and bedrooms, a very large, old-fashioned bathroom, and extensive cellars, which were used for storing coal as well as serving as a laundry and a larder for bottled fruits and jams.

This is a part of my life that I remember very fondly because of Nanny. I had spent the earliest part of my childhood around her, and now I was back again in the fold, to be surrounded by her warmth and kindness. I loved her with a deep and abiding affection that remains with me still. She knew how to treat a small boy. I was given freedom tempered with strictness and she was always there for me when I ran home with a grazed knee or something exciting to tell her. She was kind, comforting, sensible, but knew how to laugh. She represented the heart of our home, the mouth-watering smell of baking, the fresh smell of clean laundry, the cleaning and polishing and making sure that everything was just so. She had a strong sense of morality. She knew that a boy liked to play – but that he also liked to know how far he could go. They call it parameters these days. She just called it being brought up properly. All my table manners came from her.

I can still hear her saying, 'Take your elbows off the table – wash your hands – wash your knees – wear clean underpants every day in case you get run over – '

I smile when I think of that: what clean underpants would do for you if you got knocked down, I'd never know. No instruction was forgotten. When people came to the house I would stand up to greet them; on buses, children were always expected to vacate their seat immediately if an adult got on.

'Lift your cap, Davie, when you speak to a lady. Hands out of pockets!'

Part and parcel of what I became was all down to Nanny's groundwork – and believe you me, I was a rough diamond so there was a lot of polishing, a lot of training.

All Nanny's daughters were married. Ethel was married to Louis O'Neil. With their daughter, Kathleen, who was some bit older than me and out working, they lived further down in Ashmore Avenue on the borders of Cheadle Heath. Uncle Louis had a very good job as the works manager of Fairey Aviation factory, which made aeroplanes. They seemed to be quite well off by standards of the day and had a silver Rover motor car. You didn't see many cars in those days so this was very upmarket. I'd often be down there having teas with them and their teas were special. All manner of things which you didn't necessarily see at Nanny's house were served almost every day.

'I like a good table,' said Auntie Ethel, and out would come the roast chicken or a whole cured ham, the Dundee cake with toasted almonds on the top, or the high Victoria sponge.

Peggy was married to Les Isbister and their daughter was Debbie. Les was very dashing. He had been a paratrooper during the war and was now a buyer at some electronics firm. They lived quite close by but I don't remember spending that much time with them in their home.

Mary was married to John Hayward and their daughter was Caroline, named after Nanny. (Caroline became a headmistress; now she is an inspector of schools.) John, whose job was managing England's shoe shop in Stockport, was very much a man's man. He'd gone through the war as a tank driver in the Normandy invasion, pushed on through Germany, in the thick of the whole heroic action. To a young boy like me, who hung on his every word, he was full of fascinating tales about the war. At my eager urging he would get out his photo album then show me his medals. Like us, they also lived in Nanny's big house. I don't think Debbie was born then. As far as youngsters were concerned, it was just Caroline and me.

Those early years living at Nanny's house have stayed with me all my life, with the routine and the industry that was second nature to women of the time. The lino floors were polished; the doorsteps were rubbed clean every day with donkey stone – a small tablet of sandstone that abraded away scuff marks and dirty footprints; furniture and ornaments were dusted and polished; beds made and tucked in smoothly – none of these Continental duvets existed back then. It was all spick and span and immaculately clean.

The memories of Nanny come crowding in. Like all older ladies she wore a pinny from Monday to Saturday but Sunday was a 'no pinny' day. Sunday was a day for relaxing, for sitting around and chatting, for visiting, for getting out the best china and for having big family meals that were better than usual.

Memories of our meals are so vivid I still savour them. They were good, wholesome and simple, often just mincemeat, mashed potatoes, fresh cabbage or other vegetables, but I never felt we went short of anything. We'd have stuffed sheep's heart, lots of steak and kidney and oxtail. There was tripe as well, which came from the tripe shop and which was so cheap they practically gave it away. You don't see tripe shops much now but back then you could get it boiled, cold with vinegar or hot with white sauce and onions. A sheep's head was always simmering on the stove at Nanny's. It was an alarming object – but intended for our dog, Wagger. Sunday provided a feast fit for a king. A great slab of topside or silverside was put into the baking tin which was so old and well used it was burnt black. Once the meat was cooked and the fat poured off to make Yorkshire pudding, Bisto was sprinkled to turn the remaining fats and juices into the richest, thickest, most delicious gravy, just oozing with flavour. It was heavenly – but today such illicit delights are on the banned list of 'Foods That Are Bad For You'.

Every day there would be a pudding. Nanny was one of those old-fashioned cooks who could make, with no apparent effort, suet puddings, jam roly poly, rice pudding, sago and tapioca – traditional English puddings you don't see much of today. In the summer there'd be a wonderful wobbly thing called junket (a light sort of blancmange) and no end of fruit tarts filled with damsons, plums, whinberries, bilberries, gooseberries, blackberries and apple, redcurrants, blackcurrant – all served with Bird's custard.

Nanny had taught all my aunts to cook; even my rather flighty mother, who wasn't much of a domesticated type, could whip up something tasty when pressed. What they produced from a short supply of money and raw ingredients was quite amazing. Obviously my parents were earning money, as was Uncle John in the England shoe store, so something came into the kitty, but wages were generally low and there was wartime and postwar rationing. However, they made up for it by being so resourceful.

In the summer Nanny and I would head for the countryside, which was just a bus ride away, to spend long contented days in the sun, picking raspberries, strawberries or loganberries that all grew wild in that beautiful part of England. Whinberries and bilberries grew in wooded areas, while farms closer to home would provide peas and beans, apples and plums that we picked in their season. At other times we would tromp up to the local market with our big baskets on Saturday afternoons just before closing time and haggle at the stalls. We scored some great buys. Nanny 'negotiated' for fruit and vegetables which wouldn't last until Monday, or, cheaper still, fruit, like peaches or pears with just a small bruise on one side. Back at the house, aided and abetted by me, Nanny would peel them, discard the small bruised sections, slice and stone them, then bottle the results into large preserve jars. Sometimes she made jam, sometimes chutney. It was all delicious and saw us through the winter in an age when there were no refrigerators or freezers to keep food fresh.

I was a demon for appropriating the empty jars. Down at the local pool I whiled away summer afternoons or evenings after school, catching sticklebacks or little fish. If Nanny spotted me tipping my catch from the precious jars into an old stone sink in the garden I'd get a thick ear. Even though she was in her sixties, she was still very fit and agile. Many was the time when I'd be chased down the corridor with a broom if I'd done something wrong.

I had my designated tasks on different days of the week. As soon as I ran home at three-thirty in the afternoon from the little tin school I attended in Cheadle Heath I would know what job lay in store. But it wasn't a chore; without sounding too smug, I enjoyed helping Nanny because she in turn was a very caring woman.

Monday was laundry day across the breadth and width of the nation and it wasn't any different in our house. Down to the cellar we'd go, where there was one of those big stone sinks with cold running water and a huge zinc boiler to be filled almost to the brim. Soap was added and some soda crystals. In with the wash, whites first. Steam rose, the water boiled, soapsuds frothed and the smell of hot, wet linen permeated the house. I'd climb onto a chair and grab the dolly – which was a kind of wooden object with prongs. With this instrument of torture I'd poke and prod the laundry, beating out the dirt until it was whiter than white.

Big wooden tongs were used to lift the corner of a sheet from the boiler, guiding it through the mangle to squeeze out the soap and then into the stone sink where it was rinsed several times. A magic ingredient was added to the final rinse, one you don't see any more – Dolly Blue – that came in little sachets and that gave the illusion of whiteness. Bedlinen and shirts were stiffened with Robin starch. Back into the huge wooden mangle with rubber-lined rollers it all went. My job as a big strong lad was to turn the handle while Nanny fed in the long folds of the sheets, the towels and the men's shirts, and gallons of water gushed out. By the time the washing was dried and ironed, the sheets and shirts were like boards. You had to virtually tear them apart with a ripping sound. When washing machines came in, those defunct mangles were piled up, two a penny. Now, at country fairs, they're fetching 70 or 80 quid apiece and they're smart objects to stand in the corner of some expensively fitted kitchen or posh restaurant.

Wednesday was Brasso day. Nanny's kitchen was smothered in all manner of brass and copper objects, from military shells to watering cans. There were plaques and warming pans on the walls, coal scuttles in the hearth, hot water jugs on shelves. She was quite a collector, not just of brass but of all sorts of ornaments, many of which went into her 'best' glass-fronted cabinets in the rarely used front room. I think this is where my interest in collectibles and all things old was first sparked. The kitchen table was spread with newspaper, out would come the Brasso and the cleaning rags and the polishing cloths, and on would go the elbow grease and I'd be at it sometimes until seven or eight o'clock at night, cleaning and polishing. After the brass we would move on to the Bungalow range, the massive cast-iron cooking stove. It wasn't used as a cooker any longer, having been replaced by an old-fashioned gas stove, though kettles or big pots and pans were still set to simmer away on the top of the old hob, and tea was constantly on the go. Its open centre section was filled with coals and an open fire filled the kitchen with a warm, comforting glow.

When I think of the ruddy glow of that fire, the shining brassware and the rich cooking smells from that kitchen, Christmases always come to mind. It's Christmas now as I write these words and I'm wandering up and down the beach of a five-star hotel in the tropics, where it's 80 degrees. The sea is peacock blue, little waves lap the sand and palm trees really do sigh in the breeze. My wife and I had a wonderful meal last night on Christmas Eve and we drank champagne. I was togged out a treat in a white silk dinner jacket and Lorne was wearing a little black Valentino number and looked a million dollars – but I still remember those magical, nostalgic Christmases at 241 Stockport Road and a lump comes into my throat after all these years.

Preparation was all-important with Nanny. Every year at November-time she would prepare a cake. All the coupons on the ration cards would be pooled and the ingredients would be bought, the peeled fruit, the cherries, the almonds, the muscovado and demerara sugars, the hard to get lemons and the icing sugar for the royal icing. We didn't keep brandy in, so a small bottle was purchased from the off-licence. I would watch with fascination as it was all mixed up in a great big yellow earthenware bowl.

'Here, David, have a stir and make a wish,' Nanny invited.

Eyes shut, I stirred the heavy mixture with a wooden spoon and wished for something I knew I would never get, such as a bicycle. One of those large tins with a bottom that fell out was buttered and lined with greaseproof paper and the cake mixture was tipped in. I scraped out the bowl and Nanny carted the cake to the stove.

She would always smile with satisfaction as she closed the oven door because now Christmas was well and truly under way. The delicious spicy smells that scented the house for several hours as the cake slowly baked was just the start, a symbol of all the goodwill, the shopping, the eating and the drinking, the singing, all part and parcel of the festive season to come. When the cake was baked it was allowed to go cold and was then put into a large tin in the pantry to mature. There it remained for at least a month. Nearer Christmas it was brought out, marzipanned with ground almonds and iced. Naturally, I got the final scraping of icing in the bowl. Ritually every year, the sacred little plaster Christmas decorations – which today are considered worthless and discarded after a single use – were brought out, wrapped in tissue paper and handled as if they were priceless Fabergé objects, and placed on the top. I can remember that same Father Christmas, the same robins, those logs, that 'Merry Christmas' sign, the elaborate frilly binding that went around the edge, used every Christmas of my childhood. As the cake was cut, the decorations would be removed and carefully rewrapped – often in the same tissue paper – and stored for another year.

As Christmas Eve approached I grew ever more excited. Even though we didn't have a lot of money I went to bed full of anticipation. My pillowcase was hanging at the bottom of my bed, ready to be magically transformed during the night into a bulging sack filled with all manner of goodies. There were cardboard games like ludo and snakes and ladders in boxes, *Beano* and *Eagle* annuals and Dinky cars. Sticking out of the top of the pillowcase I would find a lumpy knitted stocking that crackled tantalizingly with Mars bar selections, crackers, tangerines, nuts, chocolate coins and, if I was lucky, some real money, maybe half a crown (12p) – it was a cornucopia of all manner of exciting bits and pieces.

I would play with my presents all morning and stuff myself with chocolates, while female hands gathered in the kitchen to prepare the dinner. Nanny and the four daughters would have their designated tasks, my mother cheerfully pitching in and wearing a pinny for once like all the others. A large turkey and all the trimmings were prepared and put on to cook. The pudding was put on the range to steam. At about eleven-thirty my uncles and dad would go off to the Farmer's Arms in Cheadle Heath for a 'swift half'.

'Be back by two,' Nanny would warn them. 'You're late every
be back on time for once.'

Everything was prepared; the big kitchen table had been transf
place of work into a festive board with a decorative paper tablec
glasses. The turkey was crackling in the oven, the Christmas pudding was
steaming away on the hob. The women vanished to add a dash of lipstick, a
puff of powder to shiny noses. Two o'clock – and no uncles. Looks of concern
on the aunts' faces.

'Where are those buggers?'

They'd always turn up half an hour late, jostling through the door, red
cheeks, breath smelling of beer, all grinning with that silly grin, clanking a
couple of bottles apiece and maybe holding up a sprig of mistletoe they'd
nicked from the pub.

Auntie Mary and Auntie Ethel would nag, 'We've been waiting, the turkey's
dried up –'

Laughing and talking, the men were urged to the table, the turkey was
carved, vegetables served, bread sauce added, gravy poured – dinner would
start, cooked to perfection. There was no wine but the men would have bottles
of beer. As a special treat I would be allowed a sip as well. We pulled our crackers and everyone giggled as they put on their paper hats and made silly faces.
We'd read the mottoes and guffaw, examine the cheap little plastic treasures
that tumbled out as if we'd found the crown jewels. Nothing was really lavish
or costly but it was the pleasure of pulling crackers, putting on hats, all sitting
down together, one big happy family, all having Christmas dinner, that counted.
At the end, after the pudding had been set on fire and served, licks of blue
flames still sticking to the serving spoon and our plates, the brandy-flavoured
white sauce poured, after the last nut, the last mince pie, the last piece of
Turkish delight had been consumed, we'd go to the hallowed front room where
two large display cabinets held Nanny's treasured belongings; someone would
turn on the radio and we'd listen to the King's message (later, the new young
Queen's). It was a deeply sentimental moment. When it was over, the men
sheepishly stood to attention and saluted while the national anthem was
played, then someone would wind up the gramophone and on would go the
old 78s: 'The Skaters' Waltz', Al Jolson, Vera Lynn, and we'd sing, or perhaps
play charades.

As darkness fell, the women returned to the kitchen to get tea ready. This
time the very best lace tablecloth was brought out, with the best cutlery, serviettes, nice water glasses filled with squash or Tizer for the children, the wedding
tea service and treasured items like large cut-glass bowls for trifles made of
blancmange, jelly and tinned fruit with cream on top, sprinkled with sparkly
little bits. The main event was John West red salmon, which was an extreme
luxury. Several tins of this would be brought out and all eyes focused on it.

There was salad, sticks of celery in celery jugs, all hard to find given the season. There were plates of thin bread and butter cut into triangles and, pride of place on the table, the Christmas cake, heavy and dark with raisins, glacé cherries and candied peel. It seemed like a very grand banquet, the memory of which has never left me.

I have travelled widely, stayed at world-class hotels. I see some lavish banquets but somehow they pale into insignificance when I think of our family's wonderful spreads that they'd saved up for several months of the year to buy, pooling their money to get what seemed to be great luxuries.

Of course, Christmas wouldn't be Christmas without someone disgracing themselves and usually that someone was me. I have always had eyes bigger than my belly and when anyone said, 'Who wants any more?' a little voice from behind the settee would pipe up, 'Me, I'll have some more.' I always ate too much or they'd allowed me to have a drink of beer or port. Invariably, by late afternoon, I was always feeling a bit sick and once, when dressed crab was served, I threw up very publicly, much to my chagrin and everyone else's amusement. But it was all Christmas and it was wonderful.

CHAPTER TWO

My early stimulation by all things old, as well as being an invaluable grounding in buying and selling, originated with my gran, although she probably wasn't aware of it. Often, as I was growing up, we would go bargain-hunting in the little junk shops in the district, and there were plenty of them to choose from. We'd dive through an inviting doorway, the bell on a coiled spring above the door would jangle and some old crone or elderly chap, usually in an old army greatcoat, would come forward and Nanny would smile pleasantly.

'Just poking about,' she'd say.

If she knew whoever it was, they'd engage in a little chit-chat while I wandered around, hoping to find a pile of old comics I could read on the spot, or some of those lead Dinky toys that used to be thrown away by the boxful to spend my few pennies on. When the pleasantries at the front of the shop were over, Nanny would join me and companionably we'd start to root through the treasures on display – or not on display, as the case might be. Many things were piled any-old-how, in jumbled heaps or shoved in boxes, and we spent hours rummaging through them.

'You never know what's at the bottom,' Nanny said. 'The pot of gold's at the bottom of the rainbow, not at the top.'

Apart from the brass and copperware that she loved, Nanny looked for anything small and unusual to put in her display cabinets. Almost anything interesting would do as long as it was small and caught her fancy. Most of her pieces were things she'd brought back from seaside holidays, quirky little mementoes that would remind her of Blackpool, Brixham or Rhyl.

'Oh, look what I've found,' she'd say, swooping upon some small, obscure object in a dark corner of the junk shop.

'What is it, Nan?' I can still hear my voice saying.

'A nice little knicky-knacky,' she'd say. 'It'll look nice in my cabinet. I think I'll have it if the price is right.'

A little shrewd bargaining would ensue and ten minutes later we would carry whatever it was triumphantly home to join the 50 or 60 knicky-knackies already in the display cabinets. These were not like locked museums where treasures never saw the light of day again but were the source of much pleasure on a rainy Sunday afternoon. I'd sit with her while she told me all about them, their history and where they'd come from and so forth.

My favourite object was a small replica of the legendary Liberty Bell of Philadelphia. I was very taken with the romance of the story, as told to me by Nanny, and with the words engraved on it: 'Proclaim Liberty thro' all the Land to all the Inhabitants thereof.' She said that the bell had been made to celebrate the American War of Independence in 1776. A century later it had famously cracked. This little replica, Nanny said, had been given to her as a child by her Uncle Cyrus, who was a learned don at the university in Philadelphia. She earnestly believed, and told me, that it was a part of the original bell.

'The slaves cracked it, ringing it too hard after the abolition of slavery,' she said, 'so they melted it down and made another one. This is made from leftover material.'

I was enthralled to be holding a piece of history in my hands. I would examine the crack and then ring the bell, listening to the flat thump of the clapper.

That little bell represented so many memories to me that many years later, before she died, when Nanny asked me, 'Is there anything of mine you want, David? Now's the time to have it,' I immediately said, 'The Liberty Bell!'

She gave it to me and I've still got it. In later years I came to realize that this wasn't made from bell metal, it was lead. However, when I showed it to people knowledgeable about Americana, they said it was contemporary and would have been issued shortly after the cracking of the bell. And the most famous crack in history? Well, it wasn't made by excited slaves but occurred while the bell was being rung for Washington's birthday in 1846. Also, it had been made in London at the Whitechapel Foundry in 1751, a quarter of a century before the Declaration of Independence, to hang in Philadelphia's State House. I wasn't in the least bit disappointed on learning the facts and none of this diminished my pleasure in the piece. Finding out the truth about things is fascinating to me and the Liberty Bell is something I will never part with. A million pounds wouldn't buy it, believe me.

I never tired of hearing Nanny's stories. She was an old-fashioned, quite strict old stick but she knew what pleased a young boy's imagination. I always enjoyed her tales about growing up in the London district of Wembley Park in the Victorian era of the late 1800s, of gadding about in her little sulky – akind of racing carriage – but best of all was the story of the Great Blondel, the Frenchman who had walked over Niagara Falls on a tightrope many times, and had even cooked an omelette that he lowered to the amazed passengers in the *Maid of the Mist* below. He fell in love with London when he came to perform his feats at the opening of the Crystal Palace at the invitation of Queen Victoria's husband, Prince Albert. Eventually he bought a substantial house in Ealing, still a rural village just outside London, which he named 'Niagara Villa'. For some reason, late in his life, he came out of retirement and went to lodge with Nanny's family while he practised for a daredevil walk over the Thames at the Tower of London. He put up a low wire in their back garden – it was perhaps three or four feet high – for practice. Usually, he wheeled his daughter, Adele, in a special barrow, but sometimes, when Adele wasn't there, he used my young grandmother instead.

'It was so exciting,' Nanny recalled. 'I felt that part of his fame rubbed off onto me. Of course, after that, I took an interest in his career.'

Blondel gave his last public performance in 1896, in Belfast, when he was 72. The following year he died a very rich man at his Ealing villa; he is buried in Kensal Green cemetery, next to his two wives.

Another one of Nanny's lessons that I won't forget was to take nothing for granted.

'Always count your change, David,' she instructed. 'People will cheat you if they can get away with it.'

I had my first lesson in the art of fiddling when dealing with the men who delivered our coal. Within the range of cellars in Nanny's house was a large room we called the coal-hole. Above this, at ground level, there was a metal grille that could be opened to allow the coalmen to empty their sacks of coal through it. You would hear the flatbed lorry draw up and the melodic cry 'Co-al!' resonating from the street.

Nanny was a wily old bird. 'Quick!' she urged. 'Get down to the cellar, David, hide behind the door.'

From long practice, I knew exactly what I had to do. As the bags were tipped into the coal-hole from above, I was to ensure that they were full of lumps of coal, not slack. Slack was dust and rubble which didn't burn and was good for nothing. Apparently, when they bagged up at the coalyard, down by the station, they would fill a few sacks with slack and hope to get away with it. Often they did, because coal was cheap in those days and we regularly ordered a ton (20 sacks of a hundredweight each) so when you came to look at the mountain of coal in your cellar it was hard to tell what was what.

I would race down the cellar steps and position myself just out of sight as the coal came hurtling down. Sometimes I'd catch them out. There would be a few sacks of proper lumps of coal crashing down with a roar like the sea on a shingle beach, then suddenly a stream of dust and useless little chips descended, with an entirely different sound, and I'd nip upstairs.

'Nanny! Bag of slack!'

'Right!' she'd say and then she would be outside, giving them a real old chinwagging.

'Oh no, missus, we'd never give you slack,' they'd protest.

Those cunning men were so full of coal dust themselves they were as black as the ace of spades. They looked a tough bunch. Strapped on their backs and hanging over their shoulders were ridged rubber mats to help carry the sacks.

They wore heavy, steel-bottomed boots that rang sparks onto the cobbles. Their trouser legs were tightly tied with twine.

But Nanny would stand firm. 'You get another bag of coal down there or you're not getting paid!'

And knowing when they were beaten, they would haul a heavy sack off the lorry and tip it down the hole.

'All right now, missus?'

'Yes, and don't do it again,' she would say as she counted out the cash into their horny, blackened paws.

It was a good lesson for me to absorb. 'Never take anything for granted. Use your eyes and inspect, inspect, inspect.' I can hear myself saying it now when I tell people how to go about the business of buying antiques, and that, I'm sure, is where it originated: with my wily grandmother and the coalmen.

I was preparing for the eleven-plus but for some reason, before that happened, I was transferred from my familiar little tin school to another one closer to Stockport in an area called Brinksway. The school was near to some pretty rough housing estates, the worst of which, Gorsey Bank Estate, was notorious. It was filled with rough, tough families of eight and ten kids who used to take the doors off their houses and chop them up and burn them. They'd keep coal in their bathtubs and had old mattresses and rusty junk in the front gardens. We called them the 'Gorseys'. They were feral, the kind of people I was warned against when I went out to play. Thrown defenceless amongst them, I befriended a little lad who belonged to the Dolan clan, which was as rough and tough as the best. Eddie Dolan looked half starved with his skinny little legs and gaunt-eyed look. I used to bring him back after school to Nanny's to be fed. He'd demolish her big doorsteps of bread and jam then he'd put out his plate wordlessly for more. He was nice enough but I know she would sometimes look askance at his manners.

I had always earned money as all boys do, by running errands, working as a paper boy, getting the odd pennies any way I could to buy a few extras for myself. My life as a wheeler-dealer, of trading for myself, really started in earnest after I failed the eleven-plus. My destiny for the next few years lay at Avondale, the big secondary modern. There, it was a matter of dog eat dog and the survival of the fittest and I very quickly learned to look after myself. The biggest lesson I learned early on was that nothing was free and that if I wanted anything it was up to me to provide it.

I became the boy who was always able to swing a few deals. I'd buy and sell marbles, old roller skates, things that other boys wanted. When conker time came round I'd search out the biggest and harden them up with special remedies, like baking them in the oven or soaking them in vinegar for a long time. At school one of our main pastimes in the playground was to play marbles for military cap badges – there were plenty of those around just after the war. You would dig a little pit next to the wall and bury the badges upright, revealing just the tops. The idea was to stand back so many paces and aim alleys (big marbles) at them, listening out for the clink of metal to indicate that you'd scored a hit. If you won, the badge became yours – if not, you forfeited your marbles. Then would come the cry: 'OK – put it up again!' and you would have to replace the badge and let the loser have a go at winning it back. If you were successful you could win a lot of alleys in this way and perhaps sell your excess. You stood further back for the rarer badges; the most prized one of all was the cap badge of the Black Watch, a famous Scottish regiment. It was a beauty, about four or five inches in length, hard to get hold of. You'd have to dig a really deep pit for this one and stand about half a mile away – well, 25 or 30 paces. Boys rarely hit it from that distance and you'd soon be pocketing everyone's alleys.

Fights would start, over accusations of cheating, because disgruntled boys would resent losing all their badges and alleys, and the bigger the boy, the more likely you were to get bashed. As you got older, the fighting got harder and rougher. There were always tough boys in school who were physically stronger. Perhaps they came from hard areas where it was necessary for them to be stronger than the other kids. There were always bullies and I'm sure that things haven't changed today. The only way out was to fight. There would be a dispute over something, then came the dreaded command: 'The park at four o'clock!'

Some of these boys had such terrible reputations that your knees turned to jelly at the prospect of meeting them in the park, or anywhere else, at four o'clock. You had the choice of scurrying home and hiding or going to the park and fighting. But the threat didn't go away; it was with you the next day and the day after that, so effectively there was no choice. You had to go to the park at four o'clock and fight.

All afternoon in class you didn't work; fear gripped you. Then the moment was upon you. You had to get up from your desk and leave the safety of the school buildings. It was a bit like walking that 'green mile' to your execution. Your friends went along with you to act somewhat like seconds in an eighteenth-century duel. They would hold your blazer and urge you on to valour and victory. When you arrived at the park the big tough lads were waiting. Jackets came off, fists were raised. No messing about, no warning, they knocked you down and you got up with a bleeding nose or a swollen cheek and that was the end of the matter. It was over in a flash of time. Nobody jumped on you, nobody kicked you. There wasn't the viciousness kids have to deal with today. You were even proud that you had gone and faced the moment.

Often these very tough lads begrudgingly even gave you a hand to pull you up from the dirt. 'You're all right, Dickie,' they'd say. And you suddenly felt all right, you could walk home with a swagger – until the next time. Because there was always a next time.

Standing up to bullies takes tremendous courage. I always say to young people when they ask, not everybody can do this. It's hard facing up to bigger boys or more vicious boys and there's no doubt that it is worse now, but that's the way we had to handle it when I was a boy.

Bullying came in many different shapes. Discipline was ferocious. Some teachers were quite soft and I got on easily with them, but some were feared. The maths and science teachers were extremely strict and never let up the pressure. You'd be sent home to learn your times tables and were tested at school the next day. If you didn't know the answers, a hard board rubber, one of those wooden blocks with a green baize edge, would hurtle down the length of the class, straight at your head. Their aim was unerring. If they'd bowled for England they couldn't have done better. You'd sit there nursing a massive bruise the size of an egg and then the questions would be fired relentlessly again. Sometimes you'd be marched out to the front of class and a bamboo cane or yardstick would be produced from under the desk and you'd be struck four or six times across the hands. If you moved you had to put your hands out again.

I was always in some scrape or another and was quite regularly sent to the head's office. You knew it would be the cane but they made you wait outside the door until the head was good and ready. Often there would be two or three quaking boys waiting there. We were too terrified to speak, too apprehensive to do more than stand and squirm. Sometimes we'd wait as much as an hour, then the door would open: 'Dickinson!'

Out came the cane, your hand was stuck out, down swooped the bamboo so fast and hard you could hear the whistle. Back would leap your hand. A silent wait while you stuck it out again. *Whack!* Three times on each hand. It was fierce. You could not flinch or show weakness. The head would ask you to thank him. 'Thank you very much, sir.' You walked out of the room, clenching your hands, eyes crying, then you'd run to the boys' toilets, put hot water in a bowl and immerse your hands. Those men would hit you so hard that the joints of your fingers were puffy, too swollen to bend. We accepted it as part of the everyday discipline of school, for not doing our homework or whatever the case may be. If you had gone to your father – in my case, my mother or Nanny – and whined that you had been caned, he would have told you, 'You must have deserved it.' But, of course, you never complained, never told your parents what had happened, it just wasn't masculine or 'laddish'. When I look back on it now, it didn't seem to do us any harm. It drew the line in the sand to tell you just how far you could go.

There were many watersheds in my first year at the secondary modern. My first bicycle was one of them. I had wanted a bike for a long time, with little hope of getting one since they were very expensive and my parents didn't have a lot of money, despite being extremely hard-working. To my initial delight and amazement, when I came down on Christmas morning, a bike was waiting for me. I stared. It was a little bit of a horror, although it *was* a bicycle. My father had gone out, got second-hand parts together, dipped them in the factory degreasing plant where he worked, then painted everything black. The family were all smiling as they waited for my reaction. Dad was always a very caring man and it was obvious he had gone to a great deal of trouble over many weeks to produce this bike. I knew he had put a lot of love into it, so I hid my disappointment and received it in a very joyous way.

But deep in my heart, when I saw the other boys on their dashing Raleighs I did feel a little bit like a second-class citizen. Sadly, I was a little bit ashamed of this black, old bits, painted parts bicycle, but I never said anything. I'm glad that I didn't because Dad died of cancer shortly afterwards, when I was 12. I don't think I was even aware that he was poorly. He was taken ill and rushed to hospital one day and never came out. Perhaps it was kept from me a little – terminal illnesses and death were treated more discreetly in those days. It all seemed so fast. I do my recall my distress when Uncle Louis and Auntie Ethel came to see me in the afternoon. I was as usual playing in the backyard with my bits when they broke the news: 'David, your father is dead.' It was a blow.

Things must have been said afterwards about 'managing'. I must have absorbed some of the discussion about money and finance, or their reduction, because it was from about this time that I increased my wheeling and dealing activities. But part of my desire and motivation to do well also came from seeing how others lived and wanting the same.

Opposite to where we lived at 241 was a large semi-detached house, which was more substantial in every way than ours. In it lived a very nice family, Mr and Mrs Johnson and their sons, who were around my age. Harry, the eldest, was a pal of mine so I was often invited round for tea or to watch television. To have a television was an amazing thing. It was quite a rarity in our street, possibly in the whole of Cheadle Heath, and their set was quite a large one. We certainly didn't have one. Mr Johnson was a second-hand car dealer and obviously business was booming because they seemed to have everything. Their house was quite lavishly decorated; it had nice furnishings, some works of art hung on the walls and the carpets were thick to walk on. As I lay on one of those luxurious rugs with Harry, watching television of an evening, I would look around me and think, 'This is very comfortable. I'd like some of this.'

Perhaps my thoughts weren't quite as obvious as that at the time but it's in those early years that you decide you want to get on, and think, 'I want nice things, I want a house like this, I want nice furnishings.' I think the motivation, coupled with a background I didn't yet know I had, sparked something in me. There was a secret ingredient that gave me a flair, a natural ability, that extra little bit of nous, to achieve what I wanted. I didn't even realize it but I had the tools to fulfil my ambitions. These forces start to build within you: 'I want a new bicycle, I want to have things like other boys, I want to make something of my life.'

Having the biggest marble collection in school was no longer enough. I started to look seriously for other ways to make money. At the time boys had a mania for making little orange-box carts on wheels. We called them bogeys or trasher carts. They had a kind of seat to sit on, large wheels at the back and smaller wheels at the front. We had no trouble getting the orange boxes but wheels were a problem. I managed to find a source, at an old type of scrapyard-cum-shop, where they bought and sold all manner of second-hand goods. It was like something out of *Steptoe and Son* and the man who ran the place, a Mr Dalziel, was as wily as old Mr Steptoe. He had a load of old prams piled up at the back of the yard. These prams were really ancient wrecks but they all had one thing in common: they had wheels and, magnificently, these wheels were attached to those wonderful, old-fashioned undercarriages with long-leaf springs.

Following Nanny's example, I haggled. I managed to beat Mr Dalziel down to five bob (25p) a pram and then, not caring how I looked, I would wheel them back to my workshop (otherwise known as the backyard) to dismantle them. I would dump the carriage part of the prams and keep the rest to sell on. These spare parts could be turned into Rolls-Royces of bogeys and I didn't even have to go to the trouble of constructing them myself. I always had three or four sets of wheels available and word spread. All the local boys had pocket money or paper rounds or ran errands for ladies so they were quite flush. They would come round to buy from me. I resold my five-bob wheels for ten – a lucrative little earner, as they say in the trade.

Making money is a funny thing. Once you start, the bug takes hold of you. It's very enjoyable to have it but it's the crack of making it that's the real excitement. I have spoken to a lot of self-made men over the years and they all have this driving force to have something better – but most of all, like me, they enjoy the crack. I always was a little bit of a daring bugger and they do say that fortune favours the brave.

I started to get a little more daring, a little wilder. I found out that people would take their empty bottles, 'empties' as we called them, back to the Co-op for a refund. Lucozade bottles were worth thruppence or sixpence (1–2p) – I can't remember exactly – but the biggest score of all was to get your hands on a soda siphon. These produced the princely sum of half a crown (12p). Armed with this information, I was always looking for bottles in the backyards of the houses where I ran errands.

'Can I take your rubbish out, missus? Any empties to return?' I'd cheekily ask.

Often housewives didn't want to bother with returning these empty bottles and so I scored heavily. Soda siphons were very rare because usually people would trade them in for a full one themselves.

I soon found out that the local Co-op had cases and cases of empties stacked up in the yard round the back. The temptation was too much. I climbed the high wall, a precarious thing to do given that there was jagged glass along the top, and peered over. I was rewarded with an eyeful. The sight of dozens upon dozens of all kinds of empty bottles, including soda siphons, was like stumbling across a cache of buried treasure. I stacked up several cases to make my getaway but, on the point of climbing back over the wall with one, my nerve failed. Taking so many at one snatch and grab seemed a big step. So I retrieved only a couple of soda siphons and half a dozen Lucozade bottles and scarpered.

Returning them at the front of the shop was another matter. I decided on a test run by walking in with just the Lucozade empties. No problem at all. But on coming back a few moments later, clutching just one of the soda siphons, I was met with suspicion and interrogated by a member of the Co-op staff.

'I'm bringing it back for my auntie,' I fibbed, and stuck out my hand for the money.

Eagle eyes bored into me and I felt my nerve giving. On the point of fleeing, I heard the chink of coins and a small pile of silver landed in my outstretched palm. I have to admit that I threw the other siphon away in the local woods. In future, I decided, I would stick to less stressful ways of coining it in.

Perhaps something Nanny had once said had made more of an impression on me than I realized. I used to keep my money in a tin, my kitty box as I described it. I was always quite open about it and took no pains to hide it. One day Nanny happened to pick up the tin to dust under it. Perhaps she was curious about its weight. At any rate, she glanced inside the tin and was astonished by the sheer quantity of cash that met her eyes.

'Where did you get this money from, David?' she asked.

I told her it came from my wheels, my marbles, roller skates, empties, running errands, the paper round and so on.

I'll never forget her words: 'You know, you will have to be careful, David. When you grow up, if you're not careful, you will be a spiv.'

A spiv to my gran was a man who sold butter and nylons on the black market, items that were hard to come by during the war years. I don't think Nanny knew of such a thing as an entrepreneur, a businessman who would make his money living on his own wits and enterprise. She knew a few white-collar workers but most men of her acquaintance were blue collar.

At the same time, Auntie Ethel, whom I visited nearly every day, supported me in everything, regardless of what it was. She had a lovely daughter, Kathleen, but perhaps she also saw in me the son she never had. She was the typical motherly type, a large, cuddly lady with all the love to give. Whenever anyone said, with a hint of reproof, 'David's selling this, or doing that,' there was always that wink from Auntie Ethel, that encouraging smile, that whisper in the ear that summed up her total faith in me: 'You go for it, David, you can do it.'

CHAPTER THREE

There was a secret hidden at the heart of my family that I had no idea about as I'd merrily gone along my way through childhood. I'm not sure how I found out. At the age of about 12 I was either rummaging through a bureau and found some papers or a local playmate may have mentioned something to me. Whatever the way it came about, I asked, and was told: 'Yes, David, you were adopted.'

I don't know why but it didn't come as a heart-rending shock. Even the news that I had come from a Dr Barnardo's orphanage for waifs and strays (as it was then called) wasn't that much of a blow. It didn't leave a huge hole in my life nor any sense of desolation. Everyone told me how much they loved me; my mother described how she had first seen me in the orphanage as a tiny baby and had chosen me. Auntie Ethel said she had known my mother – my blood mother. My ears pricked up at this – this was tangible, something that did pique my immediate curiosity.

'I didn't know her personally,' Auntie Ethel explained. 'She lived in Cheadle so I used to see her about. She was a foreign lady.'

This sounded exotic enough to appeal to my sense of individuality and made perfect sense to me. My adoptive family, the only one I had ever known, were lovely people, the salt of the earth, but in a way I can't explain I had always felt just that little bit different. You only had to look at photographs of Joyce and Jim to think, 'He can't be their kid!' Looking back, this may have been obvious to other people but it certainly wasn't to me as I grew up. The difference I felt showed itself in more subtle ways than my olive complexion and dark, curly hair. I felt different from the other boys. It revealed itself, more so as I grew up, in a desire to stand out from the crowd and do well so I could acquire a more comfortable way of life.

I sat up and paid attention when Auntie Ethel mused, 'Their name was Gulessarian. I believe she was Armenian, though it was rumoured that there was some French connection.'

In later years I would learn that my mother had been brought up by her Armenian father – my grandfather – after his wife, a Frenchwoman, had run off. I was told that Joyce and Jim had snapped me up – wisely, I thought! –

from Dr Barnardo's, where I had been lodged from my birth on 16 August 1941. It took a few months for proper checks to be made and the paperwork to be completed before I was carried home to become part of the extended family at 241 Stockport Road.

You hear of children going to pieces when they find out that they have been adopted. Some of them never get over it, they become bitter, go into therapy, say they feel somehow diminished. Some spend their lives searching for their roots and are never happy. While not making light of their feelings, I have to say that the discovery and aftermath of growing up within a family that I hadn't started off in never really worried me. It was not because I have no feelings or heart but I strongly believe it was because I was brought up in such a way that I was happy. I was surrounded by love and affection, made to feel totally secure and confident about my position within the family. I knew that my parents loved me, that Nanny and Auntie Ethel, especially, adored me; and I in turn loved them and would have done anything for them. Possibly another reason for my sense of security was that I was adopted as a very young baby. I didn't go through the rigours of an institutional background like many of those youngsters you see on television who have perhaps spent several years in a home and become so mortified by their background they feel despondent with life.

Once I had absorbed the information I just got on with my everyday life. At school, after a rocky start academically, I had settled down and was doing quite well. I was an average scholar in most subjects but was particularly interested in history and geography, subjects which stood me in good stead in later life. I was also doing all my wheeling and dealing and adding to the little stash of money in my kitty box. I had no plans to spend it on anything in particular, though I did have dreams of possessing a shiny new bike, perhaps a car later on. Saving became a habit I would maintain for the rest of my life, wanting to have a little cushion, just in case.

My school was co-educational, so girls had always been there, but in the background of my consciousness. But when I became a teenager I started to notice them. Music was part of the trigger – and raging hormones, of course. 1955 was the year we suddenly moved from ballads like Rosemary Clooney's 'This Ole House', Doris Day's 'Secret Love', or 'The Happy Wanderer', 'Stranger in Paradise' and 'Three Coins in the Fountain' – to the sudden sensation of Bill Haley's 'Rock Around the Clock'. This was the sensational-for-the-times song featured in the film *The Blackboard Jungle* that captured the heart and soul of teenagers everywhere. We flocked to the Theatre Royal, Manchester, where on one memorable night I and my pals, along with a thousand other teenagers, got up to dance in the aisles. I felt wild and exhilarated in that heaving mass of flying arms and legs, starched crinolines and ponytails, with boys and girls grabbing each others' hands to jive almost deliriously away, as we expressed ourselves with total abandon. As always, a few loonies caused problems. They grabbed some fire extinguishers and set them off. The police were called and the crowd was ushered out.

At the Plaza Ballroom in Oxford Street, Manchester, where a youthful Jimmy Savile was the manager, they had great rock'n'roll nights with fantastic jiving competitions. We all caught buses and trams into the city centre and let ourselves go under the revolving mirrored lights. It was all pretty innocent stuff. Even when we walked a girl home afterwards, she would giggle goodnight, take her leave with a swift peck on the cheek if you were lucky, and dive indoors, where more often than not her dad would be sitting watching the clock. Homework, naturally, went to the wall. What was homework when we could rock around the clock and tried to get away with creeping in after midnight? Adults, and particularly our teachers, weren't impressed. Our parents, grandparents, aunts and uncles looked at us as if we were alien creatures. They said they didn't understand it and asked where it was going to lead us. It was a tidal wave and there was no holding back, not even in the working class areas of Cheadle Heath and Stockport, where traditions died hard. The badges of our rebellion were tight blue jeans and American-style white T-shirts. The anthem was rock'n'roll.

My mother's remarriage came as something of a shock, not because I didn't expect it, or resented it, but because it looked as if I would be uprooted from my comfortable home to live elsewhere with her and her new husband. It sounds sad and cruel to say this but from my early teens my mother started to lose my affection, though through no fault of her own. She was so busy working I rarely saw her, but Nanny and Auntie Ethel were always there. Auntie Ethel in particular had a real motherly instinct and she and I had a strong connection. While this largely went unsaid, I knew I could count on her whatever happened, and so she came to replace my mother in my heart.

Joyce was the smallest and most delicate of Nanny's four daughters and she was the least home-loving and dependable. She saw herself as more of a Bette Davis type, with her little half-hats and fashionable clothes, her careful make-up and lavish use of perfume.

One of the aunts said, 'Oh, Joyce does like to trip the light fantastic!' and that really summed it up.

After my father died, although she continued with the hairdressing, she started going out more in the evenings. Nanny and I would be sat in the kitchen with me doing my homework or drawing, Nanny knitting or doing a little baking for the next day, when mother would pop her head round the door to say goodnight.

'Are you going out?' Nanny would ask, although it was perfectly obvious that mother was not going to sit in the kitchen with us, glamorously dressed to the nines as she was in a frilly blouse, pencil skirt, pearls and high heels.

'Well, I've got a life to lead,' was mother's defensive response.

Nanny, who was very old-fashioned, would ask with that slight edge to her voice, 'You're not going down to one of those pubs, are you, to meet people?'

That always stuck in my mind. I'm not implying any immorality on my mother's part; I realize that she was a woman who was lonely and wanted to meet someone else. It was Nanny's tone when she said 'one of those pubs' that made me think that there was something rather sinful and scarlet about those kinds of places. In her eyes it was not done for a single woman to go on her own to a public house. Unconsciously, this put a sense of morality into me, an acceptance that ladies are ladies.

Ironically, mother's new husband was a publican, a nice enough fellow. I just didn't fancy living with them, so off they went to their new life and, to some extent, out of mine. All this coincided with me coming up to leaving school, which in the Fifties was set at the relatively green and tender age of 14. You could stay on longer, of course, and would if you were destined for university, which I was not. The matter was discussed amongst my grandmother and aunts and they decided, 'Young David should have a trade in his hands.' It was widely considered in blue-collar land that all young men needed a trade or a skill in order always to be able to earn a living.

Word was passed out to Uncle Louis, who, in his capacity as works manager at Fairey Aviation, was able to enrol me in the apprentice school at the plant at Heaton Chapel. It made sense for me to move in with him and Auntie Ethel so that I could go with him in his silver Rover motor car to the factory in the mornings, returning under my own steam on the bus in the evenings. I took to life in their household like a duck to water. Nothing was too much for 'Our David' and I luxuriated in the comfort of their home.

I was in the apprentice school for some nine months and found it very interesting. Even today I can recall quite clearly the metalwork lessons in the tool shop, where we worked with files and saws to produce six or eight individual pieces to display in order to show that we had acquired a solid grasp of the subject. These apprentice pieces were deceptively simple to look at, just blocks of metal which had to be sawn or shaped precisely into cubes, squares, double squares and so on. The examiner would come along, carefully inspect your work and, if it passed muster, you'd go on to the next piece. I will always remember the flat plate that was used to check the smoothness of the metal surface. A kind of viscous red liquid called razzle was spread over the plate and it was pressed against your sample of work. If you hadn't smoothed the metal enough all the high spots stood out through the razzle and you had to do it again. Being a bit smart, as I thought, I soon found out that mixing the razzle with oil made it thin out and flow over all these high spots. But the examiner was no fool. He gently touched the surface of the razzle, held up his finger and inspected it, then looked me straight in the eye.

'Do it again,' he said.

In such a way, through trial and quite a few errors, it was amazing how much skill I acquired in my hands, and eventually I was judged ready to go into the main factory. The idea was to send you from department to department until you had a basic knowledge of many engineering skills. Whichever skill you showed the most aptitude for determined where you would eventually be sent, perhaps for the rest of your working life. My first stop was the tool shop, which produced the component parts for the various jigs and tools used in aircraft manufacture. In this area all the men wore white coats, not the blue overalls seen elsewhere, and displayed astonishing skill at precision work. I found it absorbing.

In due course I was moved to a small specialist tool shop, where I worked with Len Wade, a lovely old guy, who took a deep pride in his work. Our job was to repair the pneumatic drills that ran on compressed air to drive in rivets on aeroplane bodies and so forth. Men came to the little window of our room and I'd take their drills, check them in, then learn from Len as he repaired them. Unfortunately, I had a great deal of freedom and that, coupled with my modest wages, was my downfall.

At apprentice school the pay was 15 shillings (75p) a week. That increased to 22 or 24 shillings in the tool shop, hardly a king's ransom if, like me, you craved nice things. I had already bought my first brand-new bicycle, a King-fisher, from a bike shop in Edgeley. Although I had amassed some £50 or £60 in my war chest even before leaving school, more than enough for the bike of my dreams, I wanted to put only half down and pay off the balance over 12 months. I asked Nanny to stand guarantor and showed her my savings.

'Why don't you just buy it outright, David?' she asked.

'Well, you never know when you might suddenly need some cash, Nanny,' I explained.

She understood that because having to manage, juggling her finances and making ends meet, was always with her. For many years the weekly tally man had been a regular part of our lives. Annually, I was outfitted by Prescott's, a shop in Stockport that allowed credit to be paid off at so much a week. Every Friday evening, for about ten years of my life, the tallyman would come round at about six or seven for the shilling due on the card for my clothing, park his old boneshaker of a bike and come in for a cup of tea, his bicycle clips still around his trouser legs. He was such a fixture he became like an uncle. I don't know how many cups of tea these men had on their rounds; it was always a cup of tea and a digestive biscuit. Each week Nanny also paid him sixpence or ninepence (2p or 3p) insurance towards her funeral.

'You've got to leave enough money spare to be buried,' she always impressed on me.

That, along with clean underwear in case you were run over, was a part of her class, a part of her generation and a sign of those times.

When I started at Fairey Aviation I wanted to buy nice things for myself that didn't come from Prescott's old-fashioned emporium, like the despised gabardine trousers and tweed jacket for best or the grey flannels and blazer for school. Instead, I spent my money on pairs of tight blue jeans, white T-shirts and a kind of heavy boot not dissimilar to a Doc Marten's that was all the rage amongst teenage boys. I also had my eye on a black leather bomber jacket so I could turn up the collar and strut my stuff like my heroes, Marlon Brando in *The Wild One* and James Dean and Sal Mineo who starred in *Rebel Without a Cause*. Going to the cinema in Stockport as often as possible with your friends, to slouch in your seat and soak up 'the look' – which included the lip sneer – was crucial.

Becoming a teenager could be quite expensive if you wanted to keep up with the crowd and as my interest in girls developed I certainly wanted to look the part. The dance halls and academies of my schooldays, where you learned to do the two-step and then rock and roll, were just starting to give way to coffee bars, where we fed the jukebox and drank frothy coffee and where all teenage life was played out. Every time I hopped on a bus or a tram to go downtown I needed some money in my pocket to buy the latest 78 or to take a girl to the pictures, and my weekly wage didn't seem to stretch far enough. Once again my inbuilt enterprise came into play and I decided to run a raffle at the works.

I asked Len Wade if he thought it would be all right. He said he didn't see any reason why not so I tested the water with quite a few men who brought their pneumatic tools to the tool-shop window, received many votes of confidence and put my money where my mouth was. One Friday pay day I went out and bought a bottle of whisky that cost maybe 30 shillings (£1.50) and two raffle books. One book would cover the cost of the bottle, the second book would be my profit. On Friday afternoons wage packets were delivered to the men's benches and I'd be going along behind to sell sixpenny (2p) raffle tickets. I told them the raffle was quite genuine and showed them that there were only two books, which gave them good odds. When all the tickets were sold I went back to my little store and, at 3 p.m. on the dot, held the draw. Watched by Len and a few men who came along out of curiosity, I put the stubs into a bucket, stirred them around, called one of the men from the shop floor to pull a ticket out – and announced the winner.

I went along to the man's bench and said loudly so that everyone within earshot could hear: 'Bill Robinson, congratulations, you've won this lovely bottle of whisky.'

It was a nice little diversion to the week. The men saw that the raffle was bona fide and above board, and after a while they trusted me enough to stop coming to watch the draw and let me get on with it. It was a lucrative little earner, too, doubling my weekly income; but, as ever, my eyes were bigger than my belly. I decided to expand into chocolates, cigarettes, crisps and soft drinks.

I had noticed that the men would have to go out at lunchtime if they wanted a snack or ran out of cigarettes so, like all good traders, I decided to supply a need. I went out and found a small wholesaler who would supply me with the small quantities I initially required, and set up my business under the counter. Word went about that young David Dickinson had chocolates and cigarettes available and soon the queues to buy my wares stretched so far that often men coming with tools to repair couldn't get to my window. I was pumping up my income by the grand sum of £6 or £7 a week and probably making more than my uncle. Well, of course, it didn't go unnoticed. The supervisor in charge of the apprentices called me in one day.

'I've heard about your business activities,' he started.

'Yes, sir.'

'Well, lad, it won't do. You're obviously not cut out for this job as a tool-maker, are you?'

'No, sir,' I was forced to agree.

'Your uncle is the works manager. It would be embarrassing to have to sack you but if you push us we'll have to go down that road. You wouldn't want that, would you?'

'No, sir. Shall I hand in my notice, sir?'

'Good lad. The world's a big place and I think you're going places, David. Good luck,' he said.

I shook his hand, said goodbye to Len, and headed home to tell Auntie Ethel and Uncle Louis that toolmaking was not the career for me.

'Whatever suits you, David,' Auntie Ethel said, comfortably. 'There are lots of good jobs out there for a bright boy, aren't there, Louis?'

Uncle Louis didn't say very much but I think he knew how my career at the factory had concluded. It was up to me to find my next job. I decided that I would put my skills as a salesman to use and found work in a large furniture shop in Manchester. I did well and enjoyed advising people on what to buy for what room, taking their orders for the G-plan furniture and studio couches that were the coming thing in the Fifties, and earned good commission along the way.

My evenings were still spent trawling the coffee bars and the pinball arcades, widening my social circle. I began to meet and befriend a different class of boy from those I had known at Avondale Secondary Modern and the streets around my home, boys like Christopher Haworth, who became lifetime friends.

Chris went to a private school in upmarket Heaton Moor. He was a lovely lad with a frank and friendly attitude, a bit quieter and more serious than me, but we clicked. The attraction of opposites, I suppose; we each saw something in the other that appealed. And we almost shared the same birthday, being born within a week or so of each other, so there was that closeness. I also got involved with some Syrian lads, whose father was a Manchester textile magnate by the name of Lababidi. Samir was the elder brother, Ali the younger. Their background was very privileged, as I soon discovered when they invited me to their huge home in Bramhall to listen to records. Not only was the house in affluent Bramhall Lane exceptionally luxurious, but the furnishings had an exotic eastern influence that I much admired. Parked outside in the drive were several cars, including their father's Cadillac and a small estate car that Samir had the use of. In Cheadle Heath it was unheard-of for a lad of our age to drive his own car and I was suitably impressed.

After I'd been working at the furniture shop some six months or so, Samir told me that at his father's wholesale textile warehouse in Princes Street they were looking for a hopeful young lad to start learning the business. He'd mentioned me to his father and would I like to go along for an interview? Well, I'd seen at first hand, at Samir's home, what luxury the textile business could produce so I was down there like a shot in my best gear, shoes polished, nails clean and wearing a crisp new white shirt to be interviewed by Mr Lababidi himself.

'How does £4 a week sound?' Mr Lababidi asked after he'd grilled me and decided I was the kind of keen young fellow they were looking for.

It sounded very good to me and I was quite the cock of the walk as I left the premises of R Lababidi & Co. to hand my notice in at the furniture shop. However, I decided that I had been working hard for a couple of years and would take a break first. It's possible that the fact that I believed that my mother was connected with France in some way was in my mind and inspired me to want to know more about the country. Whatever the reason, I took £30 or £40 out of my kitty box and went on a hitchhiking holiday to France with a pal. We joined the Youth Hostel Association in order to have cheap places to stay in, took a ferry from Dover and headed towards Paris, our sights set on the south of France, where all the beaches and sun-kissed girls in bikinis were to be found. At first, lifts were easy to obtain, despite our limited French, but we hit a bad patch south of Paris. For 24 hours we sat despondently by the side of the road as Citroëns and Fiats whizzed by, ignoring us. In the end my friend suggested we might do better if we split up. I felt a little insecure about this, but finally agreed.

'How will we link up again?' I asked. 'I don't want to be spending all my time wandering about the Mediterranean looking for you.'

'We'll meet at the hostel in Fréjus in four days from now,' he said with a confidence I didn't really share.

With that, he walked away from me and stuck out his thumb. I was disconcerted when he got a lift immediately and, with a wave in my direction, disappeared from view down the long and suddenly lonely road. I waited and waited. I walked a bit and got one or two short lifts. I could see myself walking to Fréjus. Then inspiration struck. My last lift had dropped me off in a small town, outside the railway station. I walked in, consulted a map and timetable and counted my money. The fare to carry me 50 miles or so towards my destination seemed a good investment. In next to no time I was ensconced in a carriage, watching the scenery flash by.

No one came for my ticket, the scenery continued to flash by and gradually the penny dropped that this was an express. I had the money ready in case an inspector showed up, even though I would have been left with pockets to let. Broke in the middle of France, on my own, was not a happy prospect; but still no inspector popped his head into my carriage and I started to relax. I was always a little on the wild side so I took my chances and put my money away. Hours passed. Eventually the train slowed and then stopped. I was in Lyons, gateway to Provence and the south.

Carrying my rucksack, hat pulled down low, I waltzed off the train, along with hundreds of people, through the barrier and onto the street beyond, and not a soul stopped me. Easily obtaining two quick lifts, less than 24 hours after I had parted company from my pal I was in Fréjus, with three days to spare.

The youth hostel, an old stone building plastered thickly in faded terracotta, was surrounded by stone pines and olive trees which cast a welcome shade after the heat of the day. It was a buzzing hive of different languages and cultures, filled with young people from all across Europe; suddenly one of them, I felt my spirits lift. I had used my brains to get here, I had done it smoothly and efficiently. I felt quite worldly and cosmopolitan as I checked in and took my bearings.

Fréjus is an ancient Roman port founded by Julius Caesar and it lies on the Riviera, between Cannes and St-Tropez. Above the town a dam had formed a large artificial lake. (This dam would collapse some three years later, the flood water killing over 400 people and destroying everything in its path.) Left to my own devices while waiting for my friend, I explored the numerous monuments, including the Porte d'Orée – a golden door – still standing amid the ruins of a third-century Roman baths, and a first- or second-century amphitheatre, one of the largest to be found from that period. It was all fascinating to a young lad from Cheadle Heath, whose horizons for some years had been shaped by downtown rainy Manchester.

When my friend eventually arrived, hot and dusty from the road, I was quite the suave tourist as I welcomed him. He looked very surprised to see me, even more so when I appeared so relaxed and settled in.

'When did you get here?' he asked.

'Oh, days ago,' I replied airily. 'What kept you?'

We hitched along the Riviera, through the small fishing villages and stretches of the wild and rocky coast of St-Tropez, St-Raphaël and Ste-Maxime, Antibes and Cap Ferrat to Cannes, and beyond to Nice and Monte Carlo, seeing all the locations where *To Catch a Thief* had been filmed a couple of years before. We stood outside the casino where Cary Grant had dropped a gambling chip down the front of Grace Kelly's *décolletage* while admiring her lavish diamond necklace; and we travelled along the Corniche, the dangerous road that zig zags above the azure sea, and admired the fairy-tale pink-washed royal palace, idly imagining that we might catch a glimpse of Grace Kelly, who had just become 'Her Serene Highness Princess Grace'. The palace was built spectacularly on the edge of cliffs above the circular harbour and was hung with flowering vines. In those days there were no billboards or placards along the winding roads, the beaches were clean, the sea full of fishing boats and the white sails of yachts. Even the air smelled different from Manchester. It was scented with flowers and oranges and the intensely salty tang of the sea.

In Cannes' main drag, the fashionable Croisette, we stood outside the gleaming white wedding cake of the magnificent Carlton Hotel, with its black-tiled pepper pots at each corner, and watched expensive cars driving up to be greeted by uniformed concierges. Successful-looking men in white linen suits and women in silk frocks with large sun hats glided in and out of the main doors, perhaps to cross the street and promenade along the front beneath the umbrella pines and palm trees, and I thought, 'Wow! That is some place. One day I'm coming back here and I'm going to stay in that hotel.'

We crossed the road to have a swim in the sea but found that the beach immediately in front of the hotel was cordoned off and out of bounds to the hoi polloi like us. Rich people could sit on one of the outdoor terrace restaurants and order seafood and cold champagne but we couldn't – even if we could have afforded it, we weren't members of that exclusive club. Instead, we walked for a few hundred yards to the relatively crowded public beach. After a cooling dip we lay on the unraked sand in the burning sun. By turning my head I could look along the shore to the fenced-off area where, on the carefully raked sand, banquettes were laid out under shady umbrellas at discreet distances from each other. Waiters scurried about carrying drinks. Mixed with the scent of sun oil, you could smell the wealth. Again I thought, 'That's for me. I'm coming back here.'

A week later, back in Manchester, I started my new job at Lababidi's warehouse under Mr Kodadad, who was in charge of gentlemen's suitings. We sold very high quality silks and worsteds and lightweight mohair from the Yorkshire mills direct to the trade, either on the shop floor to men who dropped in to select their lengths of fabric in person or shipped to customers, many of whom were in the Middle East where expensive lightweight fabrics were much in demand.

I had never seen such fabulous rolls of fabric before, never seen anything with such a sheen, such a fine silky finish, such perfection. For the first time I realized what quality was and it was nothing like what I'd been used to from Prescott's. I learned the names of these top-notch manufacturers woven in along the selvedge – names like Holland & Sherry and Dormeuil. Lababidi's would buy complete rolls, about 60 yards in length, but the secret of their success was that their prices were exceptionally low. The rolls they bought were perfect except for some minor flaws; that is, in one or two places – not more than that – there would be a distinct line where the weaving machines had dropped a warp or a weft. However, on a full roll you could easily cut the fault out and still be left with almost the maximum number of perfect suit lengths. A standard suit length of three yards normally retailed for £12 or £14 but we were able to sell it wholesale as seconds for £3 or £4, a huge reduction for exactly the same fabric. After a while, through conversations as I served on the floor, I discovered that traders known as commission agents were buying these suit lengths and taking them to London to sell directly to smart Savile Row tailors or to private customers at a mark-up.

Being a commission agent appealed to me because I would get out and about and make extra money. I made the request and Mr Lababidi allowed me to give it a go. Soon I found myself dealing with other shippers in Manchester's garment district, men who were mostly Lebanese, Iranians or Armenians. What I didn't know at this stage was that my real grandfather had worked in this same Princes Street area, dealing in fabrics, mainly silks. I thought I knew as much as there was to know about my blood mother's background, such as her name and the fact that she was Armenian-French and had lived in Cheadle Heath. Some time later I came to realize that my Armenian grandfather had been retired from business for a few years and so we had never connected. It is strange to consider how I was drawn not only to the same district but also to the same kind of field as him: luxury textiles. Textiles were to dominate my life for the next few years and, in a major way, to change it.

CHAPTER FOUR

By now I was 17 and still living at Auntie Ethel's. I was going out and about, not only in the evenings with Chris and Samir, but also occasionally during the day, learning how to be a commission agent. I decided that I needed a car. I already knew how to drive. Samir had taught me in his estate car and I took to it like a duck to water. For me, there was only one car. I went to a motor house in Stockport and ordered a brand-new Mini, in red, of course – what other car or colour could it possibly be for a dashing young man who wanted to make his mark on the world? It was a bold step for a 17-year-old.

My war chest held quite a substantial amount at this time, some £400 or £500 but, following my usual pattern of not wanting to end up with nothing to fall back on, I put down a 20 per cent deposit of £100 for the car against a purchase price of £485, putting the balance on finance. The heater was £14 extra and there was no radio. When I took delivery I almost burst with pride. I drove it straight home and showed Auntie Ethel.

'Ooh, that's lovely, David, very nice,' she said, coming outside to admire it. 'It's just what a smart young man who's going places in the world needs.'

She didn't ask me any awkward questions about how I was able to drive on my own with only a provisional licence. True to form, Uncle Louis didn't say a lot, beyond making sure that I had road tax and insurance. When the time came and I was finally old enough to take my test, he drove me to the test centre. I was a skilled driver by then and passed with flying colours. The Mini was to make its mark on a new age as the trendy little car driven by the Beatles and models like Twiggy – and there I was with one of the very first, hot off the production line. That little car was sheer delight to drive and opened up an exciting new world. I was mobile and independent, and as I set off every morning to see what that day would bring I really thought I could fly.

I'd been at Lababidi's warehouse for about a year or so and work was going really well. I had learned so fast that Mr Kodadad said that he thought I could have been born into the textiles trade. Well, he wasn't far wrong at that, when one considers the grandfather I was yet to learn about. It really was as if I was treading unknowingly in his footsteps, as if it was in the genes and was intended to be.

As well as selling in the warehouse and learning about quality – that a light-weight fabric was described as having a weight of 10 or 12 ounces or that you could mix silk with mohair, cashmere or vicuña – I was also being allowed to take two or three suit lengths into the street to sell. Not that I set up a stall in a shop doorway to flog my wares, but in that district, peopled by the cosmopolitan type of merchant traders you'd find in the Middle East, a lot of business was done in the street, much as it would be done in Cairo or Baghdad, as well as in little tailoring establishments up three flights of stairs. It was a busy, frantic way of life and I embraced it with energy.

It wasn't long before I displayed the usual tendency of my eyes being bigger than my belly. My war chest was looking healthy, I had many contacts in the trade, I had learned a great deal. It was time, I thought, to go out on my own. Once I'd left school and started work I had grown used to having a regular weekly wage coming in. It was a strange feeling to depend entirely on myself. There was no safety net, no source of income unless I generated it. But that appealed to me. Once I got started, the excitement of going out, putting deals together, seeing money flow back, was fascinating, not only for the financial reward but also for the thrill of completing a deal on my own.

I started to go to the big wholesalers who supplied the finest textiles to buy suit lengths on my own account. Working the garment district, I'd run in and out of little tailors' workshops and show them what I had available. I would have a sample book with Dormeuil or Holland & Sherry and so forth printed on it and would show the customer that my fabric was identical – but at a vastly reduced price. I knew that these tailors would buy their fabric for £4 to £6 a yard, maybe a little bit more, which meant a suit length would cost them between £14 and £20; I showed them that they could buy exactly the same thing, an entire suit length, for £6 or £7. Everyone likes a deal, if they can pass the deal on to their clients. It makes them more competitive, and I sold a lot. Naturally, I didn't tell them that these lengths were costing me only about £3.

My interest in fine suits started at that point. I was developing the 'look' that in many ways I would have from then on: sharp, elegant, refined – and expensive. The best is costly but it's more than that, it's quality, and I wanted to look, and to feel, the business. With me, it was not a case of 'never mind the quality, feel the width' but the reverse. With me, quality counted then, and always has done.

Seeing these tailors at work, measuring, cutting, making and trimming bespoke suits out of the quality fabrics available, made me appreciate the oceans of difference that lay between an off-the-peg garment both in cut and quality. The price was higher but what you had was something unique that not only looked good but also felt good. I wanted what other men had. I also worked out that the best advertisement for my wares would be me, wearing what I was sell-ing, putting my own money where my mouth was. Maybe it was also a bit of the boy from the working-class background wanting to do well for himself.

I found a tailor just starting out in Britain, a Greek Cypriot called Chris Nicolaou. I blagged him a bit, in an honest way.

I said, 'Mr Nicolaou, as you can see, I'm a young chap who hasn't that much money. But I'll wear your suits and tell everyone who made them if you give me a deal.'

He was eager to succeed and offered me a very good discount. I think I was his second or third customer but he did well and 40 years later he's still my tailor. These days he does a little better out of me.

True to my word, whenever I showed someone a length of fabric, I would stand up in my suit and ask them, 'What do you think? This is the fabric – and this is the man who made it.'

And I'd hand out Chris Nicolaou's card.

People noticed. I gained in confidence, I was expressing myself in my own way. I really felt someone in a tailored silk and mohair or a lightweight worsted. Girls looked at me and I could see them thinking, 'Hey! Bloody hell, look at Dickie. He doesn't half look sharp!'

My first impoverished trip to France, as an outsider looking wistfully in on those glittering hotels and Riviera people, had changed my perception of what was 'normal' or acceptable. Coming from a working-class home I saw for myself the flair that Continental men had. I couldn't help noticing the quality of some of their clothing. Not only was it slick and elegant but people in drab, rain-washed England would never have used some of the colours that those Continentals dared to choose for their shirts, their ties and their casual wear. I might not have started to take the plunge right away with brighter colours and slightly more flamboyant styles, but I was certainly absorbing it all and storing up ideas for later.

Oddly enough, all this coincided with a new look coming in from Hollywood via the 'beefcake' boys you'd see pictured in *Photoplay* magazine. Elvis had been king since 1956, of course, with his sneer and his blue-black, slicked-back hair, but now Tony Curtis, an Italian from the Bronx, was the hero of the day, with films like *Johnny Dark*, *Trapeze* and *The Sweet Smell of Success*. Reflecting this, fashions got a little slicker, a little more Italian. His celebrated hairstyle, the DA, could have been made for me, with my thick, dark, wavy hair. For nicety's sake we didn't call it the 'duck's ass', but the 'duck's anatomy' or the 'duck's tail'. I was quick off the mark, in there at the barber's shop, where the walls were plastered with black and white photographs of Tony Curtis, Rock Hudson and Rory Calhoun, to have my hair razor-cut with the characteristic feathered parting down the centre of the back. The final touch was to drag a comb down the back dead centre to exaggerate the duck tail look. The barber slapped on the Brylcreem to sculpt it in place and I emerged, quite the bee's knees.

Soon, all the boys were walking around with a cute quiff at the front and combing it slickly back at the sides to make a DA. Boys were never supposed to care all that much how they looked then. Even with the Jimmy Dean–Marlon Brando turned-up-collar look, we had always ignored our hair. But suddenly, narcissistic youths were spending hours gazing into mirrors or looking into their reflection in plate-glass windows as they sauntered by, wide-toothed combs sticking out of the back pocket of their jeans, with the girls in their poodle skirts and Leslie Caron elfin haircuts hanging on their arm.

Always at the cutting edge of style, rock and roll bands were moving away from the blue jeans image and starting to dress in snappy suits. They'd shop in the little boutiques that were springing up here and there, the forerunners of London's Carnaby Street and the King's Road shops of the early Sixties. I started selling lightweight silk and mohair suit lengths to the Toggery, a really trendy little place that sold Continental menswear in Stockport, where I shopped for shirts and ties. The manager, whom I came to know, managed the Toggery Five, a group that I believe later changed their name and went on to become the Hollies. I'd often bump into the boys in his shop and stop for a chat. It was seeing them in my fabrics that gave me the idea I could cast my net further afield to cater to the rock and roll shows going around the country from theatre to theatre.

One show in particular on the circuit was produced by London promoter and impresario Larry Parnes, who was about ten years older than me. Like me, Larry had left school young and started off in the textiles and clothing business. By the age of 18 he was running his own clothing shops. It was a chance meeting – and too much Scotch – that got him into showbiz. He went to a West End of London club one night, drank spirits for the first time in his life in a whisky-drinking contest, and discovered the next morning that he'd invested in a loss-making play called *The House of Shame*. He brought in a hotshot publicist who changed its name to *Women of the Streets* and the female cast were somehow persuaded to flaunt themselves outside the theatre during the interval. They were promptly arrested, splashed all over the newspapers the next day – and the show was a smash hit.

In quick succession Larry Parnes signed up the unknowns who used to perform in the coffee bars and small clubs around London, singers like Tommy Hicks, Reg Smith, Roy Taylor and Ron Wycherly. Never heard of them? You'll know who I mean when I tell you that Larry changed their names to Tommy Steele, Marty Wilde, Vince Eager and Billy Fury and almost single-handedly started the rock and roll revolution in the United Kingdom. Larry didn't always get it right, though. He turned down Cliff Richard. He used the Silver Beatles to back one of his stars, Johnny Gentle, on a tour of Scotland, but twice declined the chance to manage and promote them exclusively – Brian Epstein did so, and the Beatles were born.

I got some cards printed and went along to the local Odeon theatres in my car, loaded down with samples. On Sunday nights they used to put on live rock'n'roll, with Larry Parnes's stable of talent in shows like *Idols on Parade*. I would breeze up to the stage door, a couple of samples tucked under my arm, having first glanced at the front-of-house posters or the names in lights over the marquee, and ask to see whoever was performing that night. Over a period of two or three years I got to see them all, stars like Cliff and Adam, Billy Fury, Marty Wilde, Joe Brown, Dicky Pride, Joe Sampson, the John Barry Seven. The list is long and encompasses the rock and roll history of the late Fifties and early Sixties. I can remember selling the John Barry Seven seven pieces of silver-grey silk and mohair and then, the next time they came around on the circuit, seeing them on stage wearing suits made up in the same stunning fabric. It gave me a buzz, I can tell you.

I branched out to all the local big revue theatres where theatrical stars and artistes were on every night, places like the Palace or the Opera House in Manchester. I met the late great Tommy Cooper, a huge, fascinating man with a deep, booming laugh. He was very warm and welcoming and immediately invited me into his dressing room.

'Well, Dickie – can I call you that? – let's see what you've got,' he'd say jovially, holding out his massive paw to take my samples.

He was very canny and tried to talk me into letting him have the lengths free of charge.

'I'll stick a label on the back,' he joked, 'saying, "Supplied by David Dickinson, clothier to the stars".'

'I can't do that, Tommy,' I'd protest. 'I have to make a living.'

'But I'd be your best advertisement,' he would cajole. 'You can't say fairer than that.'

To further persuade me, or perhaps because he liked my company, he would take me off to the little chophouse near the theatre and we'd have a grand evening over a meal, while I listened agog to some of his stories. I think I might, in my modest way, have entertained him too. At least, he would break into a great guffaw of laughter now and then and clap me hard on the back. Eventually he bought – and paid for – half a dozen mohair and silk lengths, mainly in blues and greys, with a very nice sheen to them.

'Always show me plain fabrics,' he'd say. 'None of those posh pinstripes for me, I'm not a banker or a solicitor.'

He was a nice man, a real gentleman.

The Mersey Sound was starting and I jumped in my car and headed for Liverpool. Armed with my samples, I dived into cellars where it was all happening, places like the Cavern and the Iron Door. I met Freddie Garrity of Freddie and the Dreamers, Gerry and the Pacemakers and Billy J Kramer among many others, some of whom fizzled out, others who became, and still are, legendary. I didn't meet the Beatles then but some time later bumped into them in London at the Ad Lib Club, the 'in' place to go.

I had been getting my suit lengths from wholesalers, who were able to afford to buy the 60-yard rolls direct from the mills. To protect its reputation, a mill would sometimes cut the selvedges off the material in order to remove its prestigious name; this didn't make any difference to the quality but it made it harder to sell to the customer so I always insisted on buying lengths with the name still on them. This cost me a little more but it was worth it. As I got more customers and gained in business know-how, I was soon able to go direct to the big Yorkshire mills. I would buy entire rolls and divide them into suit lengths myself, thereby cutting out the middleman and making more of a profit. In such ways I was always on the lookout to do better, to increase my turnover.

I'm not sure where I got the idea from, but I decided to go to Paris to see if I could break into the textiles business there. This was another bold step for someone whose French wasn't all that good, but perhaps at the back of my mind was the thought that, with a mother I believed to be partly French some-where out there in the world, I should soak up some of my heritage and also familiarize myself with the language. I'd been before when I hitchhiked. That had turned out all right in the end but this time I decided that I would go there in style in my car. The plan was that I would pack the boot with samples, sell the lot (of course) and on the proceeds head for the south of France to enjoy a free holiday in the sun, watching all the Brigitte Bardot lookalikes strolling by in their bikinis.

I felt quite adventurous as I set off on my own one morning in the early summer. The boot of my red Mini contained about 40 suit lengths, my suitcase contained my own very stylish wardrobe for all eventualities and I was ready to make my mark on the streets of Paris. I didn't know a soul on my arrival and didn't speak much French but that didn't deter me. I went to cafes and got into conversation with people, asking where the various tailors were and so forth. They were more than willing to chat and I started to make friends and contacts in this way. The language wasn't that much of a barrier; I learned a few useful words, like *tissu* for fabric, and progressed from there with a kind of Franglais, or a mix of pidgin.

Prices were higher in Paris, thanks to the export duty and taxes they paid, so I could easily get £12 or £14 for a suit length, where I'd been getting £7 in England. I hadn't been there long when I met a young English guy in an outdoor bistro. We took to each other and he invited me home to his tiny apartment to meet his French wife. The apartment, in the heart of Paris, was expensive and very small, and they were hard up but idyllically happy. Over wine and bread and cheese he told me that he worked part time in the post office.

Then my ears perked up when he said, 'I also work in a film studio. I'll take you along if you like.'

'Can I try to sell my fabrics there?' I asked.

'No reason why not,' he replied. 'I'll introduce you to a few people.'

It was a generous offer and I resolved that I would compensate him if I made a few sales. We arranged to meet at the studio the next day. As we entered, a small, dark-haired man was coming out. I didn't recognize him at first. He was a big star in France (though he was much less well known in England), having appeared in many films, including *Atlantis* and *The Lost Continent* and the one that launched Brigitte Bardot's career: *And God Created Woman*. His name was Jean-Louis Trintignant. Formerly a lawyer, he was the son of a world-famous racing driver, and often drove racing cars himself in films. (He was to survive a 200 mile an hour crash in Le Mans in 1980.) My friend and I went through into the studio, where I was introduced to the actors and production crew. In no time at all I had sold my entire stock of 40 suit lengths.

With my nice little profit tucked into my pocket, I zoomed off to the Riviera in the style I told myself I could easily grow accustomed to. This was far better than hitching. In St-Raphaël I checked into a nice little hotel on the beach, at about 15 shillings (75p) a night, showered and changed and went for a stroll. In those days St-Raphaël, which lay off the main coastal road that ran from Marseilles through Cannes and on to Nice and Monte Carlo, was virtually deserted. It had charm and character and I felt alive and carefree and totally at home. I could lie on quiet, clean beaches or I could jump into my car and go off to find some nightlife. True to form, I met girls, went dancing and had a wonderful time. When my money ran low I went home.

Needless to say, I was itching to go again the following spring. This time I asked Christopher Haworth to go with me. With Chris and me, girls always seemed to be the centre of our life. We were always chasing some sweet young thing or another at the local nightclubs or, more especially, Bredbury Hall, a quite posh country club in the Stockport area that had a nightclub attached. We'd go there to meet girls, have a drink and jive until dawn. It was all very hunky-dory and life really was, as they said back then, 'a gas'.

I was telling Chris about my experiences in France the previous year and added, camping it up a little, 'You'd love it. The girls – ooh la la!'

Chris laughed: 'Yeah, sure, why not? We'll have a ball.'

I explained how I had financed my last little vacation by selling fabric in Paris and told him how easy it had been.

At once Chris said, 'Can I chip in? You could buy more lengths and we'll both have some spending money. I like the idea of a free holiday.'

I saw that he was very much up for the trip and agreed that between us we would invest the princely sum of £450 in suit lengths, which, in order to make our task easier, I would ensure had the recognizable bona fide brand names printed along the selvedge. Thanks to Chris's private education, he had rather more inkling of French than I had and I thought this would be a bonus. By now I had traded in my Mini for a larger, more upmarket Ford Consul convertible, albeit a second-hand one. It was a powder-blue, two-door model with a hood, and really looked the business.

When I went to France the year before I'd driven off the ferry and kept going, not stopping at customs. In fact, I hadn't really known if I should have declared anything and, besides, my 40 lengths didn't seem all that much. But this time we had 150 lengths. We dithered a bit as customs loomed up, knowing that if we got it wrong we could lose our stock and, my pride and joy, the car. We knew, too, that the gendarmerie did spot checks on any car with a GB plate.

In the end, imbued with my usual devil-may-care attitude, I grinned and said, 'Let's run the gauntlet, Chris.'

We drove straight through, weren't stopped, and went on our merry way.

We were in Paris a few hours later and headed straight for the slightly seedy bohemian Montmartre area, which really was filled with artists and musicians and wine, women and song every night until dawn. Sadly, these days, it's more commercial and there's a whole generation of young people who don't know what they've missed. After checking into a reasonable hotel, at my usual rate of 15 shillings a night, on rue Geoffroy Marie, near the Folies-Bergère, we changed and had a meal; in the evening we went clubbing. This was to be our pattern every day: clubbing at night and eating in a local restaurant used by office workers and therefore cheap. Breakfast consisted of coffee or hot chocolate and croissants and the restaurant did a special three-course lunch: soup, a main dish and pudding, with a carafe of rough *vin ordinaire* thrown in, for a few francs.

Once again, business went smoothly. With his reasonably good French, Chris started chatting to people at the tables over breakfast the next day and almost immediately we sold our first length of *tissu anglais*.

Our first weekend in Paris we sauntered off to the Champs Elysées to watch the fashionable crowds go by and to look in the shops, which were like costly Aladdin's caves. Some day, I vowed, I would be back, and shopping here with the best of them.

We explored the streets off the main thoroughfare and found that they were trendy hangouts for young people, many of them students from the nearby Sorbonne. We adopted two places in particular; one was a large drugstore-cum-coffee shop and the other was the Scotch Club. When we first discovered the Scotch Club we thought we'd arrived in heaven. The first drink was very expensive but worth it – this place was wall to wall with the most fabulous girls we had ever seen. To give some idea of how stylish it was, the hat-check girl was Régine herself, just starting out in the business that would make her famous and take her to clubs in London, Rome and New York.

Mostly, though, our life revolved around Montmartre, the Soho of Paris. That very seediness and sense of sinful decay made it all the more tempting and exciting, and ladies of the night paraded sensuously in provocative berets, dangly hoop earrings, tight sweaters and skirts split virtually to their thighs. Great as the temptation was to two young men who really did fancy themselves as macho, these women were too much for us to handle.

Our suit lengths were going, but slowly. We had found that nightclubs were a good place to sell in. One night we pulled up in front of the Folies-Pigalle, in Montmartre. After parking the car we walked up to the front door and confronted the huge bouncer, who had shoulders like a barn door and hands like hams. Chris asked him if we could see the owner.

'Allez! Allez! Go away! Vamoose!'

He shooed us off, his huge hands inches from my nose.

We were on the point of leaving when a car drew up right outside. Some elegantly dressed men – Arabs, perhaps Algerians, judging by their appearance – got out and came to the entrance.

I've always been a cheeky bugger and in my broken French I asked the doorman, 'Are they connected with the club?'

One of the Algerians rapped out in French to the doorman, then turned and asked me in English, 'What do you want?'

He sounded courteous enough, so I smiled back and said, 'I have something to show you.'

They all smiled. You could see them thinking, here was a right cheeky bugger. Quickly, I explained that I had some fabulous *tissu anglais*, would they like to see it? It was available at a very good price.

'Sure, we'll have a look,' the boss agreed. 'Come to my office.'

Chris and I returned to our car, selected eight of the best lengths and were ushered all the way though to the inner sanctum. The boss was very pleasant, smiling and assured, surrounded by a gang of the biggest toughs I have ever seen. I let him feel the quality and made sure he saw the respected names on the selvedge.

Finally he nodded: 'OK. How much?'

I suggested £16, he bartered me down to £12. In the end he selected five lengths of the finest quality silk and mohair and sent us off to his tailor with them. It was an interesting way of doing business. I didn't realize it at the time but all the clubs in the Pigalle area were run by Lebanese or Algerian gangsters like Monsieur Dudu – the name I always knew him by. He seemed to like my cheek and we got on well. When his tailor gave the word that we were honest, I sold more lengths to him, and to his tailor, and he passed us on to other people.

Sometimes, when I dropped by, he would pull out some card or another and say, 'Go and see Monsieur Jacques... or Charlie... or Henri...'

In the clubs and bars we were now going to all the men resembled Alain Delon, all the women La Lollo, Gina Lollobrigida. At the time, France had big problems with the *pieds noirs*, the Algerian freedom fighters and Foreign Legion dissidents who wanted to make Algeria (which was a French colony) independent and tried to achieve their aims through terrorism. It was all very much like *The Day of the Jackal*. We heard bombs going off and were often stopped by police doing spot checks, but never really saw much ourselves.

Near our hotel was the Café Bergère. Chris and I first went there when we were directed to sell to M. Charlie. When we discovered that the dancers from the Folies-Bergère would come in for a coffee and a nightcap after the show, we would stay. With their long, spiky eyelashes and full stage make-up the girls always looked evocatively 'Parisian' even when they were dressed in their normal street clothes. Chris and I were always trying our luck but they weren't interested in us. They wanted richer, older men.

On one occasion I had been called in by M. Charlie to sell to some of his friends. I was busy showing them my wares when out of the corner of my eye I saw one of them slip a length under his overcoat before walking away towards the rest rooms at the back. When he returned I went up to him discreetly and asked if he wanted it.

'What? What do I want?' he blustered.

'The material.'

'What material?' His voice turned nasty.

'The material you took,' I said plainly.

He denied it, I persisted. He started to shout. M. Charlie called me over and asked me what was going on. I explained. Breaking into a fast Arab dialect, M. Charlie and the man got into a heated argument. Then M. Charlie turned to me.

'David, are you sure?'

I nodded. M. Charlie opened his jacket, revealing an enormous gun in a shoulder holster. My eyes widened in shock, I was suddenly feeling distinctly uneasy. Was I about to be embroiled in a gangster shoot-out? The man went to the back, returned with my fabric, threw it down and walked out. That was when I became aware for the first time that these men, as charming and as generous as they were with me, always paying me promptly, were gangsters. It didn't deter me. I got to know them well and always respected them.

I met another fascinating man by chance, who approached Chris and me in the street to ask about our material. A Polish Jew, his name was Samson Chatasville. He said he was in the same line of business and thought our fabric was interesting because it was different. His apartment was close by and he suggested we talk there. We took some of our samples up and he bought them. Over a drink I noticed that on one wall of his sitting room several prestigious awards were prominently displayed, amongst them a framed *Croix de Guerre* and the *Légion d'Honneur*.

He noticed my gaze and said softly, 'I was in the Resistance.'

He was a most unusual, exceptionally courageous man, who would have had many stories to tell but chose to keep them to himself. Samson and I remained friends for many years and I would return to do business with him on other occasions.

For Chris and me the exciting time in Paris continued. At times it became too exciting. One of the places where we would drop by to do business with M. Dudu's associates was on the boulevard St-Denis, an area amazingly full of call-girls who actively worked the street. It was pure Shirley MacLaine in *Irma La Douce*, all of them strikingly beautiful, with striped Breton tops and the traditional berets. Going into a cafe in the early hours I noticed one particularly stunning girl, whose name was Gabrielle, and we fell into conversation – only conversation, though maybe, it being Paris and the spring, there could have been a little bit of infatuation. Being a normal, red-blooded 18- or 19-year-old, I didn't need to pay for girls. I suggested to Gabrielle that we went dancing. We did, and had a wonderful time. But word gets around. The next time I went into the Café Bergère, M. Charlie pulled me to one side.

'David, someone mentioned to me that you've been taking Gabrielle out.'

'We've been dancing,' I agreed.

'Well, David, back away. Her minders are not happy.'

He looked at me meaningfully. I backed away. It was almost July and everything was due to shut down in Paris for the long summer closure – *la fermeture annuelle*. It was time to head south.

CHAPTER FIVE

·

We had the hood down, our sunglasses on and the hot wind of summer blowing through our hair. It was with a sense of excitement that Chris and I bombed down the road that followed the Rhône valley, straight as a die for hundreds of miles all the way to the Côte d'Azur. The scenery was fabulous, the weather perfect. We stopped here and there to eat at some little wayside bistro but otherwise kept going. As we approached the South, and passed through the coastal mountains, the scenery grew more spectacular. Then we were in Provence, with scented fields of lavender as far as the eye could see, and zooming towards the coast.

'This is the life!' Chris said fervently, breathing it all in.

'This is just the start,' I assured him. 'Let's meet those girls!'

After all, I thought, we were both young, attractive and healthy, with plenty of money burning a hole in our pockets, what was the point if we didn't have fun? That old cliché, 'You're only young once', comes to mind, but it certainly summed up our mood.

We checked into the place I'd stayed in before, the pension right on the beach in St-Raphaël. The lady owner, *la patronne*, recognized me at once and her face broke into a welcoming smile.

'Monsieur David,' she cried, bustling forward. 'It's good to see you again.'

'Thank you, Madame. This is my friend, Christopher Haworth,' I said. 'We want to stay a couple of months, until the end of the season. Do you have a room?'

Her face fell. 'Not until tomorrow. It's the season, you know, and we're booked right up, but tomorrow you can have a very nice twin room with a view of the sea. Why don't you try the agency in Cannes for a room for tonight?'

Disappointed, we had to go along with that. The accommodation agency looked through their books and said all they had was a room in a hotel in Mougin, for £4 a night. I knew our room in St-Raphaël, right on the beach, was only 15 shillings (75p) a night, so protested that it was too much.

'But, Monsieur, Mougin, it is a very fashionable little village,' the agent said. 'A famous restaurant is there, le Moulin de Mougin – the Mill – where everyone goes.'

There wasn't much we could do and after such a long drive we were tired.

'Hell, we've got pots of money, £4 won't break us,' Chris muttered to me. 'Let's go for it.'

The small hotel in Mougin certainly looked smart from the outside but when we got into our room we looked around in dismay.

'This isn't up to much,' I said, taking in the general air of decay, the musty smell and the narrow, uncomfortable-looking beds.

'It's just for tonight. Let's get changed and go and find some dinner before everywhere closes,' Chris suggested.

We both showered and changed then Chris got his razor out of his case. He plugged it into the light socket and – *bang!* There was a flash and we were pitched into darkness.

'That's it – I'm not staying here,' I said.

We went to the front desk and told them we were leaving, explaining why. The manager wasn't at all happy. He went to investigate, returned quickly and said we'd blown a fuse. I said the wiring was in a terrible state, like our room, we wanted to go and could we have our passports back? He refused and said we had to pay for the room and the damage. The row escalated. Someone must have called the police because they turned up, screaming to a halt outside the hotel and running inside as if a murder was being committed. We tried to explain the problem but they didn't listen and we were carted off to the police station, sirens going.

'Do they still use the guillotine down here?' Chris asked me.

I had to admit I didn't know. Things weren't looking good and I was hungry. At the police station they gave us the third degree. Chris told them what had happened when he plugged in his razor. They nodded, talked amongst themselves and went off to get the villain of the piece – the electric shaver. They handed it to Chris.

'Plug it in,' the inspector said, indicating a light socket.

'What happens if it blows your lights?' Chris asked, nervously.

'Then you'll have to pay to fix it,' the inspector said smoothly.

I closed my eyes while Chris plugged the shaver in. Amazingly, it worked and I opened my eyes in disbelief. 'Blimey,' I thought. 'It's a miracle!'

After some more hand-waving and excited discussion they threw us into the back of the cop car and back we shot to the hotel. The inspector himself rattled off some furious French to the manager for wasting his time and demanded our passports back. We had won the war but not a victory. We drove down into Cannes and parked right outside the splendours of the Carlton. But it was still way out of my reach. As Chris and I bedded down for the night in the car I gazed at the bright lights of the hotel, up at the rooms where rich people were sleeping in comfortable queen-sized beds, and said to myself, 'In your dreams, David. But some day –'

The next day we installed ourselves in the pension in St-Raphaël and our holiday proper started. We lay in the sun by day, topping up our tans, and danced each night away with a succession of beautiful, carefree girls. After a few days spent in this hedonistic manner the old trading instinct kicked in when I saw a pretty girl walking about the beach with a bucket from which she was selling bottles of Coca-Cola, Fanta and so on. No one else was selling drinks so she was doing very nicely, thank you. When stocks ran out, she vanished for a while, before returning with a fresh supply. When she came round to us I sat up and bought a couple of drinks for myself and Chris. We chatted a little and I saw that the bucket was filled with cold water to keep the bottles cool. Pocketing her money, she smiled, said 'Ciao' and carried on with selling to the next customer.

Not one to hold back, I started flirting a little with her each time I saw her and eventually I invited her out one evening. Over a few drinks she chatted quite artlessly away, telling me that she had a good little number going, buying crates of drinks from a wholesaler around the back of the town and walking a mile back to the beach to sell them.

'How many crates do you sell a day?' I asked, as we jived away.

'I double up, two in the morning and two in the afternoon. It's enough,' she said.

'You make money?'

'Oh yes, enough to stay here for the summer.'

I needed no more information. Chris and I had the car, so we could load up, and there were miles of crowded beaches to cater to so we wouldn't be treading on her toes. So we got a couple of buckets and were in business.

'Orange! Coca-Cola!'

The only problem we had then was the weight of all the centimes and franc coins rattling in the pockets of our shorts. Feeling quite the high-fliers we decided, since it would be Chris's 19th birthday the next day, that we would take some time off to go to a bullfight. In the evening we would do a spot of gambling at the very posh Palm Beach Casino in Cannes. All we had to do was to sign on 24 hours beforehand, show our passports and register as members.

I had seen posters announcing a bullfight at the amphitheatre in Fréjus, the little town where I had stayed in the youth hostel two summers before, so we bought tickets and joined the crowds flocking into the ancient arena where gladiators had once fought with lions. Without question, bullfighting is a very brutal sport and not for everyone. The glamour, the pageantry and the spectacle were stirring, even though the bulls were all eventually despatched by the matadors. Part of the spectacle, of course, is the danger and the skill displayed by the matadors. I noticed that when something especially dangerous was about to occur the crowd sensed it and either grew very quiet and tense or started to explode with a mighty roar.

As far as I was concerned, the real highlight was the sight of two celebrities sitting quite close by in the presidential-type box, which was hung with the French flag, the tricolour. One was Anthony Perkins, who was enjoying an unexpected success in France with several records in the pop charts. After his 1957 cover of Pat Boone's big hit, 'Friendly Persuasion', Perkins had launched himself onto the French hit parade, singing (in French) such songs as 'On Ne Meurt Pas Pour Ça' and 'Ne Dis Plus Rien'. These were a smash on the Riviera that year, played over and over in every club and bar. But the major star in my mind was Pablo Picasso, who was there with his wife and his ten-year-old daughter, Paloma. My eyes kept straying from the spectacle in the ring to the rotund, brown-faced, bald-headed man. Despite his almost insignificant appearance there was nonetheless something fiercely powerful and magnetic about him. Paloma looked like a dark-haired Spanish doll. Her father had named her 'Dove' in Spanish, after the symbol of peace he had designed for Europe.

That evening, dolled up in a couple of powder-blue suits, very nice shirts and bow ties, Chris and I looked the James Bond business and felt fantastic. As we parked the car and strolled towards the bright lights and glitter of the lavish casino foyer we saw the girl of every boy's dreams at that time, the young 'sex kitten' Brigitte Bardot, being helped out of a car by her current boyfriend, who was in a white silk dinner jacket. BB, or 'Bébé' as the French called her, was tiny and extremely glamorous in a low-cut evening gown, her blonde curls tumbling about her bare shoulders. I think the man with her was Sammy Frey, the man for whom she had left Jacques Charrier, her new husband of only a year. There had been a great deal about it in the papers and here was the scandal come to life before our eyes. As we followed in BB's wake Chris and I grinned at each other. 'This was the life,' we both thought. We were definitely moving into jet set circles now!

But just a few weeks later, at the end of the summer, Bébé found life so unbearable that she attempted suicide. It just goes to show that even in Eden things aren't always what they seem. But that was in the future and in the here and now everything in the garden looked rosy indeed.

If we had thought we were James Bond lookalikes earlier as we dressed in the room of our pension, without a doubt we were on the set of *Casino Royale* now – not only on it but inside it. All the men wore the white silk evening jackets and black bow ties I had admired the first time I had wistfully stood outside this very casino as a lowly hitchhiker a couple of years ago, and all the women looked like movie stars. And as for the glittering jewels draped around their throats and on their wrists, well, I instantly thought of the casino scene in *To Catch a Thief* and the river of diamonds about Grace Kelly's slender neck. Then I thought of the humble income we were earning on the beach by day and laughed. My life seemed full of wild and improbable extremes.

We sensed the buzz of excitement emanating from one table. A gambler was sitting behind a stack of white chips, or 'plaques' as they called them, not a flicker in his eyes, and quietly smoking a cheroot.

'How much are the white chips worth?' I asked the woman next to me.

'One thousand pounds each,' she replied in perfect English.

'Blimey, this is too rich for us,' I said to Chris, as the pile of chips grew ever higher and the atmosphere at the table palpably throbbed with tension.

Not daring to sit at a table, we spent an hour just wandering about, soaking up the atmosphere. Finally, I thought this is Chris's birthday – he should do something to remember it.

'Righto,' I said. 'Get your money out, Chris. We'll have a bit of a go.'

We cashed in £50 each, which gave us a stake of £100 between us. Counting our pile of red chips – no white ones yet for us! – we agreed we'd be careful.

'We leave when this lot has gone,' I cautioned.

Chris nodded, though from the gleam in his eye I could see he was eager to hit the tables. I had been watching carefully and saw that, while it wasn't the most exciting way of gambling, on evens we'd have a 50–50 chance of winning something. They paid out virtually double on odds, evens; black, red; high, low. So if you laid down £10 you'd get it back if you won, plus another £10 on top.

Much to our amazement and joy we started winning at once. Each time, we increased our stake.

Five wins later, Chris said to me, 'This can't be happening.'

'Happy birthday, kid!' I said, betting again.

By now we were the ones creating a buzz, the centre of attention. We won an incredible 16 times in a row without a loss. The last time, we had £800 riding on the table. As the wheel spun we were so hypnotized we could barely breathe. We lost.

Without hesitation, I said to Chris, 'That's it. Let's cash in.'

We carried our pile of chips across to the cash desk and in return received a bundle of francs worth £1,200. It was a lot of money for those days – the price of three cars or half a nice little house. In fact, we could have bought a vineyard up in Provence with our winnings and retired to the easy life. It seemed astonishing and we were wildly excited as we went to the bar to celebrate. We ordered two glasses of champagne and I raised my glass.

'Blimey, what a way to earn a living!' I said.

'It's been the best birthday I can ever remember,' said Chris, 'and it's not even my 21st.'

I noticed someone at the bar eating a chicken sandwich. It looked delicious so we ordered a couple. They duly came, full of white meat, the crusts cut off and one of those little twizzle sticks stuck through them. The waiter presented the bill. My eyes opened wide. It was 15 shillings for each tiny sandwich; that was how much it cost to stay for two nights at our hotel. Suddenly the sandwiches didn't taste as delicious as they looked any longer.

'Let's get out of here,' I said to Chris, 'or they'll have all our winnings off us at the bar.'

Outside we breathed in the clean night air, watching the reflection of the moon on the water, with yachts gently bobbing on the waves. It seemed unbelievable that we were on the Côte d'Azur, our pockets full of money. Somehow, when you're young, everything is bigger, brighter, more invigorating. At that moment I really think we felt as if we could fly.

We heard music floating on the night air. Across the road, on the opposite side to the casino, was a nightclub, the Whisky-a-Go-Go, which lay partly open to the stars. In we went and, still flush with money and success, decided to do it properly this time by ordering a bottle of champagne. All the girls looked like Brigitte Bardot, their hair piled up, dressed in bikini-style costumes of flowered chiffon, displaying bronzed midriffs and more than a hint of bosom. One song in particular I remember from that evening was 'Ya-Ya'. They kept on repeating it and we kept on dancing. Anthony Perkins was someone else whose records they played constantly that night. I felt it was such a coincidence to have seen him in the flesh that afternoon in the bullring in Fréjus.

Chris and I returned to the pension in time for breakfast, still exhilarated. *La patronne* smiled at us as she set the tables on the terrace.

'You are enjoying yourself in France, eh, *mes amis*?' she said.

We couldn't contain ourselves. We flaunted our money and told her about our amazing success. She warmly congratulated us, then uttered a warning:

'But be careful. There are many gold-diggers looking for good-looking young boys like you. Not all thieves are pickpockets.'

We laughed as we hungrily tucked into our eggs and croissants.

'Don't worry, Madame,' I said. 'We are thinking of residing down here for six months a year and becoming professional gamblers.'

She winced: 'No, no, you'll lose your money for sure!'

I stood up and bowed.

'Madame, we are gentlemen of the world.'

I said it jokingly but I really meant it. At 19 we thought we could take on the world. Nightly, from then on, we tripped off to the casino. After a run of four or five nights of continuous losses we had not only squandered our £1,200 winnings, we had also gambled away the £450 profit we had made in Paris.

It was the end of our much-vaunted debut as professional gamblers. We had to go back to the pension, tail between our legs, absolutely drained, and tell *la patronne* we would have to cancel the remaining five or six weeks of our stay and return home.

Dismally, I said, 'You were right, Madame, a fool and his money are soon parted.'

'Ah, *non*, I didn't say that,' she protested.

'Perhaps not, Madame, but you thought it,' I said.

She was sympathetic and asked if we had the cash get us home. Fortunately, we had had the sense to keep enough money back to pay our hotel bill and basic travel expenses, though it would be a hungry drive. She made us a picnic for our journey, gave us some bottles of mineral water and sent us on our way.

We were so low on funds by the time we reached Paris that we called on Samson Chatasville to loan us another £30 or £40 to get us back to England on the ferry. Fortunately, he was pleased to see us. He said he had some interest from his clients in Germany for my suit lengths.

'Bring them next time you come,' he said.

The next time I returned to France I was on my own because Chris couldn't get away from his job in a car showroom. I took the materials that Samson had ordered and we drove in his powerful car to the German city of Baden-Baden, close to the French border, not far from Strasbourg. The Black Forest scenery was spectacular, with thousands upon thousands of acres of dense, dark pine forest stretching away as far as the eye could see. Baden-Baden had long been famous as a spa resort and the city was immaculately clean; every house looking freshly painted, with flowers blooming in all the window boxes. It seemed incredible that war had so recently raged back and forth over this border.

We drove up to the Hotel Brenner, an imposing pink-walled building like a French château, with small spires and a grey-tiled roof, set in the middle of a spacious park. Mentally, I wondered if I could afford to stay here. To my astonishment, Madame Brenner herself came bustling forward, arms outstretched, her face wreathed in welcoming smiles, to greet Samson. And, of course, as I very quickly discovered, my stay in this luxurious five-star hotel was to be gratis because Samson Chatasville and Madame Brenner were friends, whose working relationship went back to the war. I'm sure that theirs was a fascinating and heroic story but unfortunately it was one I wasn't made privy to.

In many respects my stay in Madame Brenner's grand hotel was to be in marked contrast to my stays in far different establishments in the months and years ahead.

CHAPTER SIX

.

I had been living for some time with Auntie Ethel and Uncle Louis. I was happy there, I adored Ethel and we got on incredibly well. I told her most things, chatting with the ease born of a great deal of respect and affection. Uncle Louis was slightly different in that I knew he was sometimes a little jealous of the attention I was paid, and it caused some conflict between him and Auntie Ethel. I was very much master of my own fate by now, coming and going as I chose, travelling around England and popping across to Europe from time to time, but, having reached the grand old age of 19, I decided the time had finally come to fly the nest. Naturally, Auntie Ethel was upset but I reassured her that I was taking a flat quite close by in Didsbury and would be back often to see her and Nanny.

'Well, look after yourself, David,' she said, waving me off.

'You too, Auntie,' I replied.

I wasn't exactly going off with a spotted handkerchief tied to a stick, though I have to say that however independent you are as a young man leaving home for the first time can cause a bit of a pang, even when it's mixed with a great deal of anticipation. There's no doubt that the first place of your own is one you always remember. Didsbury then, as it is now, was a bohemian, rather avant-garde area close to Manchester, full of flats and bedsits occupied by students from the university, which had a campus there. It had once been a rural village on the Wilmslow Road, and even though it had been built up considerably, there was still something of that leafy, country atmosphere about it. It was the kind of friendly place where you could hear music until midnight from open windows on summer nights and where there were many cafes and small shops selling anything from groceries to hardware.

I quickly settled in and enjoyed life on my own, more able to take friends home, to entertain them to all hours, to come and go as I pleased. I had a large circle of friends, business was going very well, and I was proud of the fact that I was supporting myself and was fully independent with a nice car, nice clothes, my own flat and a healthy war chest. But, like many young men, I wanted to run quicker than I could walk. I am aware that I always had this vulnerability, that sense of running the gauntlet, as I had through customs that time in France, of wanting to take that slight risk.

When some people approached me to do a little tricky trading on the side it seemed almost like a game at first. In this case the game I was sucked into was slightly more than risky: it was seriously illegal. I make no excuses. I knew in my heart of hearts that what I was involved in was a scam. I don't want to go into too many details because there were others involved and it's not up to me to spell out their names. These men, more senior than I, convinced me to go along with them in a mail order business. We bought goods on credit and sold them, at a slight loss, to wholesalers, recycling the money back into the business in order to gain a better credit rating, in order to buy even more goods. I was a bright young man who could count. I knew that if you bought goods at one price and sold them on quickly at a lower price, then bought more goods on credit in order to feed the beast, the end result would be a deficit. And that's exactly what happened. The only way you could continue was to keep buying more and more, taking on more and more credit that you had no hope of ever paying off. Such a scam even has a legal name: it's known as long firm trading. If I ever paused to consider, to wonder where it was all going to end, by then it was too late. I was trapped in a whirlpool that was taking me down.

I was still doing my legal textiles business, still ducking and diving, perhaps hoping that I could keep ahead of the game, outwit the law, come out from under the mess. It wasn't to be. The sums of money involved were too large. Eventually I was charged with conspiring with others to defraud several companies. After some considerable time on remand, I duly took the punishment, which was a severe one. I was packed off to prison for four years.

It was a terrible shock. Perhaps today, a young man facing a first offence, involved with older, more experienced people, might get probation. The courts were very severe then. But when you want to play with the big boys you have to stand up and take the consequences. I knew I had done wrong. I resolved I would take my punishment like a man, not complain, and do the time. Trying to be brave is one thing; arriving in Manchester's notorious Strangeways prison is quite another matter.

I was devastated when the grim walls of that old Victorian horror loomed above me after the trial. Driving through the huge gates was a terrifying moment. By the time I was processed and the iron door of my cell slammed shut on me, I was numb. 'David, what are you doing here?' went through my mind as I sank down hopelessly onto the hard bed covered by the harsh wool blanket. It didn't seem real. In those first days, shock was my overriding emotion. Then gradually I accepted this was my own fault. When I embarked on the venture I knew it to be wrong and I thought I might even get away with it. I had been greedy, I wanted too much and wanted it fast.

In my head I could hear Nanny saying, 'David, if you're not careful, you'll end up being a spiv.' I groaned. I had ended up in a far worse situation than I could ever have dreamed of when I was a young and carefree boy playing in the backyard with my wheels and deals, my conkers and my marbles, and I had let everyone down. With my ability I could have stuck to the right path, worked that little bit harder and eventually achieved all I wanted without getting into this mess. I swore to myself that I would never get into trouble again, that when I eventually got out I would turn my life around and it would never happen again. I meant it then, and I've stuck to it ever since, to such an extent that I've even overcompensated. If anything looks the slightest bit dubious I will walk away from it. It took me many years to rebuild my reputation and 40 years on I can put my hand on my heart and say I have never since knowingly taken a wrong step or done the wrong thing by anyone else. Young people ask me about this today and my answer is always the same: the quick illegal fix is not the road to go down. Be straight in your life and in your intentions. You'll feel better and you'll do better.

Because it was my first time in Strangeways I was sent to a wing for first-timers that was intended to keep you away from harder, tougher criminals. I hated it, every moment of it, but I knew I had to get through. The only way to survive each day was to get my head up and take it on the chin as best I could. It was like facing the bullies at school, but far worse. Every day there was a new dragon to be defeated. The biggest ones were despair and fear. Prison is a very dangerous place. There are men in there who have nothing to lose by hurting, maiming or even killing those around them.

After six months I was transferred to Walton jail in Liverpool. It was pretty tough there, too, in those days. There weren't the drugs around then that there are today but the place was run from within by men who were so hard it was like an island where warlords ruled, adrift from the rest of the world. At the top of the prison hierarchy was the criminal elite, who were either notorious gangland figures or the traditional hard men of the day, men who didn't rely on guns as they do now on the outside, but fighting men who used their fists and feet, or weapons they shaped from any material they could get hold of, men with fearsome reputations who fought each other like gladiators. Oddly enough, it was against their code to pick on weaker men. In their language this was a liberty. The star players always seemed to be professional criminals such as bank robbers who had wielded pickaxe handles, or armed robbers who had attacked mail cars with sawn-off shotguns. There were quite a few London gangland criminals in Walton, including some of the Great Train Robbers.

Locked away in that world you change. Within the prison environment these hardened men get your respect. It's a bit like being the 11-year-old at a tough city school on the first day and seeing the big boys approaching you. Maybe it's the animal instinct in us all to be scared of bigger animals; even puppies roll over and pee themselves when a big dog looks at them. Not that that is what I did. I just learned to mind my own business and didn't pretend that I was one of them.

As a white-collar criminal I was sent to work in the prison canteen, where the men could spend their earnings of three or four shillings (15p–20p) at the end of each week on small treats like bars of chocolate or stamps. My job was to do the books and prepare all the pay slips. When the men lined up to receive their pay they often engaged me in a little banter and conversation, which is how I got to know them.

There were a lot of lifers in Walton. Many were gangland figures, enforcers and the like, who went about their criminal enterprises by working together in a strict pecking order. They lived and died by a certain code because even in their topsy-turvy world – the Underworld – they needed an outlaw kind of law and order. Some were clever and astute, and went about planning a robbery in a meticulous, military way. Many of them didn't actually look like thugs and would have done very well in the Special Forces, where such brains and clinical detachment would have been useful. They were violent men but there was also another side to them. Many had come from generations of criminals who had always lived outside society. A few couldn't read or write very well; a small proportion were completely illiterate. These were the men who would approach me to write a letter for them to their loved ones, and in turn they would befriend me, keep an eye out for me so that some of the younger, thuggier elements wouldn't have a go at me for any particular reason. Any younger, thuggier elements who stepped out of line and had a go at them in the hopes of coming out on top would be very quickly despatched.

However, not all of the men I was locked away with were professional career criminals. Obviously, I wasn't the only first-timer there; quite a few others had been led astray and were basically decent blokes. The types of crimes they had committed were quite varied. I was surprised to learn that most of the killers in Walton were not cold-blooded murderers but men who had attacked someone close to them in the heat of the moment. True, they had taken a life, but it had been in anger, a *crime passionnel*, usually as the result of some domestic crisis. The number of men who had killed for money was surprisingly low, though you wouldn't have thought so considering the coverage they got in the papers and the public's perception of them and their crimes. But gangs of armed robbers always did make for much more dramatic headlines.

The prison chaplain came to my cell one evening at about eight-thirty. This was unusual. We were always locked away in our cells quite early until the next morning, and for me to hear footsteps approaching, then the key in the lock, made me apprehensive. When the chaplain entered my cell, he sat on my bed next to me, with an expression of deep concern.

'I've got some bad news for you, David,' he said. 'Your Aunt Ethel has passed away.'

That was the biggest blow I had taken so far in my life. It was the hardest thing of all to bear, far worse than facing up to such a long sentence. Here was this woman who had always been such a great support to me. She had been the pillar and pivot of my life, someone who understood me and always gave me the benefit of the doubt. Her love for me and her loyalty were without question. Even when this dreadful thing, prison, had occurred, she had visited me regularly, often struggling to walk with a stick. A heavyish lady, she had circulation problems and very bad varicose veins. She'd recently had one of the first hip replacements. In those days there were no anticoagulants and I think a blood clot had killed her after the operation.

I was not very religious, though I had gone to Sunday school and done all the usual things as a child, but after the chaplain left I was actually on my knees wondering why a woman as good as this should go, while I was a little sod and still alive. I was so devastated, so deeply upset, that if I could have struck a bargain there and then for me to go and her to come back, no question, no question whatsoever – I would have made that deal.

I can say in all honesty, even after the distance of all these years, that losing Auntie Ethel was the hardest thing. It made it worse that I was inside when it happened, unable to visit her in hospital beforehand, but that was nothing compared with knowing that she was gone for all time. It made me see things even more clearly. Nothing was ever certain, nothing was for ever. Being a young man with no ties I realized that what I had missed most were selfish things, like my own freedom. I knew that I would emerge one day and get through this. I was determined and had made a promise to Auntie Ethel that I wouldn't let prison ruin my life. I could almost hear her saying with a comforting smile, 'I know you won't, David. I know you've learned your lesson.'

They liked to move prisoners around the country so they wouldn't get too comfortable and settled in one place, and perhaps to prevent them getting too close to, and influencing, the warders. About halfway through my sentence my next port of call was Wakefield jail in Yorkshire. It was another grim Victorian prison, built into the 15-foot-thick old town walls. My time was spent in the weaving shed, making some kind of coarse material for uniforms. This was especially ironic, though I wasn't laughing much, considering the mohair and silk fabrics, as soft as a dream, that I was used to handling. If only I'd stuck to my business, I thought ruefully, as the rough serge cloth emerged from the loom I had learned to use.

Like Walton, Wakefield was also full of lifers and armed robbers doing seriously long sentences. These were the criminal elite. Despite myself, I found something fascinating about these men. Films such as *The Godfather* romanticized gangsters, which is very wrong. Coming into daily contact with them, though, I did feel that they had a certain amount of charisma. Maybe 'charisma' is not quite the right word; it was more the fascination of a cold and ruthless snake that has you trapped by its unblinking eyes. Their style, their code was unique. The worst thing one of their fraternity could ever do, for example, was to inform or talk about themselves to others. It was not done, never tolerated, and the consequences were severe. If you ventured into that pool you had to take the consequences. While not wishing to be any part of them, I did want to be an adult, to be responsible for my own actions. Why be a snitch or an informer to lessen your own burden and put it onto someone else? It was quite apparent that men who had done that were the lowest of the low. There were special wings where the lowest form of life, sexual offenders, had to be placed under guard for their own protection; and those who had informed were also put there for their own safety.

Locked away, trying to survive, has a way of clarifying your thoughts and focusing your mind. 'Stay strong, survive,' I told myself anew each day, 'and you'll get through it.' I wasn't interested in mixing in a criminal way with criminals. I didn't want to become one of them when I left, as others did. When I got out, I vowed, I would leave all this behind me. I went to the library, got books, started to study. In the library I met some colourful and interesting characters and I enjoyed talking to them because their minds were so sharp; men like Peter Kroger, who had spied for the Russians. He had been in prison for about three or four years by then and he appeared to me to be an elderly man with greying hair. In fact, he was in his early fifties, so obviously spying ages you.

No one knew much about Peter Kroger in those days. It was said that he came from Canada or America and had made his way to the UK – again, no one seemed to know when or where. He was perceived as the professional master spy and spy-minder who had sent Gordon Lonsdale, the James Bond-type KGB operative, out into the field. Much of this was wrong. Kroger was born Morris Cohen, in the Bronx in 1910, the son of Russian-Jewish parents. After university in Illinois, where he had met and married his wife, Helen Kroger (real name Leona Petka), he went to Spain to fight on the Communist side against Franco in the civil war, under the name of Israel Altman. Back in New York, he worked for the Russians, then joined the US Army in World War II. After that he and 'Helen' became part of the New York Soviet spy ring, along with the Rosenbergs, who stole atomic secrets. They fled just before the big arrests of the early Fifties and somehow wound up in London as the Krogers in 1954. In fact, Lonsdale was the spymaster who operated them. Their home was used as the UK-based Soviet communications centre for sending information back to Russia.

Kroger was in charge of the library at Wakefield jail and during our many conversations I got to know him reasonably well, as well as it is possible to know someone from that clandestine world. He was a deep, clever man, who never said a great deal about his spying work. Talking one day about this and that, I asked him what he felt about imprisonment, knowing he was doing what he believed in, for his country. He nodded slowly.

'Well, that was just the way it went,' he said. 'I was lucky.'

'Lucky? Why?' I asked, surprised.

'I was arrested in a blaze of publicity and came before the courts in an open trial, with the press there, and was duly sentenced. It was all open and above board. It could have been a lot worse.'

I asked him what he meant and he smiled enigmatically. I think he was saying that – as in Russia – with the way the secret services operated in England he could simply have disappeared. He didn't say that outright to me but there was something about his expression which said a great deal.

He was still serving out his 20-year sentence when I last saw him. Some four or five years later he and Helen were exchanged for the British lecturer Gerald Brooke, who had been visiting Russia and was seized by the KGB to be used as a bargaining chip. The Krogers vanished a few years later and have not been seen since. Lonsdale was also exchanged, for Greville Wynne, but unlike the Krogers he received public acclaim and many medals in Moscow. He died of a heart attack in 1970 (the year after the Krogers went to Russia) while picking mushrooms in the back garden of his Moscow apartment.

About halfway through my sentence some realistically good news arrived. I was called into the governor's office and told I would be transferred to Leyhill in Gloucestershire. This didn't mean a lot to me. I was informed I was going there because of my good behaviour and attitude, all of which had increased my status as a model prisoner. When I discovered that Leyhill was an open prison my relief was palpable. I thought that at least I would now be getting out of these enclosed prisons, these dreadful, draconian places where every moment of the day you had to walk a very narrow line, watching your step, careful who you spoke to.

Going to Leyhill was like stepping out of a dark and gloomy way of life into the brightness of a new day. The difference between the old-style prisons and Leyhill was quite an eye-opener. Leyhill is deep in the heart of the Gloucestershire countryside, in Wotton-under-Edge. As we drove through trees and fields and past the traditional golden stone houses in the Cotswold villages, I was deeply moved. I had forgotten how wonderful, how simple and beautiful the English landscape could be. I had got used to cells with old paint, high, barred windows, thick walls and a narrow view of the sky. Clouds, hills, flowers, trees, birds – even sheep and cows – seemed fresh and vivid to my starved eyes.

The transit vehicle drove through the gates of Leyhill into a compound of army-style barracks, to a reception area. The first surprise was the reception committee itself. This was a group of half a dozen blokes, prisoners like myself, not prison officers. A tall, grey-haired man greeted me with a posh though pleasant voice. He was a sophisticated city type – later I found out he had been a bankerwho had helped himself to the bank's funds. All the men in that welcoming committee were similarly well-spoken men from privileged backgrounds, such as banking, insurance or the law. All had one thing in common: despite their advantages they had gone astray. Like myself, they were all paying the price. It was such a change to see these men. It was like re-entering civilized society. Perhaps it sounds odd to say they were normal but in most respects they were. They were the kind of people who admitted they were foolish to have wound up in this position, unlike the hardened professional criminals and lifers more commonly seen in the enclosed jails, for whom criminality was a way of life, often the only way of life.

After a brief welcome, and having read from what was obviously a copy of my record handed on from Wakefield, the senior man, whom I'll call the Banker, said, 'Dickinson, this is still a prison, don't kid yourself. There is a certain amount of freedom, though, and it's up to you to respect that.'

'Yes, sir,' I replied smartly, standing to attention.

'No, don't call me sir. We're all on the same level,' the Banker said, indicating the others. 'We are all serving time. None of us are saints.'

I was surprised, and showed it. The Banker smiled slightly.

'I know how it might seem. But the best of us can fall from grace. It's up to us to pay the price to society, take it like men and not repeat the same mistakes again.'

This was just the kind of language I understood because it was exactly what I had been telling myself almost every moment of every day during the previous two terrible years. The Banker continued, telling me the rules, that I would be allocated a job of work, some of which would be paid. I'd have a certain amount of free time.

'There are sports fields, you can go for walks in the countryside, as long as you stay within the perimeter of the prison,' he said. 'There is no fence but there are hundreds of acres here, so you shouldn't feel the need to stray.'

I could hardly believe it. It was like a breath of fresh air.

'I can go anywhere? What about an escort?' I asked.

'No escort. But if you do go beyond the perimeter you'll be put in handcuffs and transferred back to a closed facility, no question about it. Only a bloody fool would do that, don't you agree, Dickinson?'

'Yes, sir – I mean, yes,' I quickly agreed. 'I know what's expected of me.'

'Good lad,' he nodded.

There were 20 or 30 corrugated iron Nissen huts, set in serried ranks. As I was taken across to the one I had been allocated I learned that this place had originally been set up as a hospital during the war. In each hut there were 40 metal-framed beds, 20 to each side, each with its own little locker. I was given fresh bedding and left to unpack and get on with it.

I spent a long time gazing out of the window behind my bed, which faced on to the playing fields. I couldn't get used to the fact that there were no walls, no bars, and the door of the hut was open for me to come and go as I chose.

I just had to step outside, walk off the path and I could lie down in clover, literally and metaphorically. It was almost scary.

The area right outside my hut was a rugby pitch. If I craned my neck a little I could see a cricket pitch and – blimey! – there was even a pavilion with a scoring board.

Once I got used to all this space I settled in relatively quickly. I think anyone who is imprisoned, especially in a maximum security establishment, as I was, goes into shock; and as you start to emerge you suffer from delayed shock. It can take a long time to shake off. Of course, I was still in prison, but for the first time in a very long time I could see the light at the end of the tunnel.

There was a different type of prisoner at Leyhill. Most of them were what I call 'white collar'. Yes, they had done something wrong, but they were not violent. What was noticeably different was that there were none of the tough fighting men, the gangland types I'd been surrounded by for two years. At Leyhill there was a handful of men who were serving life, who had done eight or nine years already and were being prepared for release in perhaps two or three years, on licence. All of them had been carefully selected as being rehabilitated and suitable for this open environment. A few, a very few, abused it and escaped. It did them no good. They were always caught and then they had to serve the rest of their time in a closed prison. To me it just wasn't worth it – in fact, I didn't even remotely consider it.

I settled into the routine. I won't say it was leisurely because I don't want to make light of this, but compared with having lived on the edge of my nerves for two long years, of always having to be careful and watchful, this was heaven. I've heard it described as a country club but, frankly, that's ridiculous. How can it be a club when your liberty is taken away? Other than that, I have to admit it was bearable and even, at times, pleasant. Perhaps it was a bit like being in the armed forces. We could forget where we were when the conversation was good or when we were eating the fresh food that we ourselves had grown. (It's worth noting that Leyhill won a Silver Medal for its flower garden at a Chelsea Flower Show recently – and a film, *Greenfingers*, has even been made about the gardening contingent there.)

I soon fell in with groups that appealed. There were debating societies, we had televisions in the recreation rooms which could be used after tea when we had finished work. I even enjoyed my work. Previously, at the enclosed prisons, I had been allocated to workshops, which were generally rather grotty. At Leyhill I was told I was to be a waiter at the prison officers' training college, which was within the grounds. Together with several other prisoners I was to serve breakfast, lunch and the evening meal on weekdays, when the college was open. Some of the young men being trained as prison officers were extremely rude and arrogant. Perhaps they thought it was expected of them. Mostly, we inmates would look at each other and ignore their behaviour. It certainly altered my attitude to waiters. To this day, every time I walk into a restaurant, I remember the training college at Leyhill and am reminded that a waiter is a man who is there to do a job. I never talk down to him. I'm pleasant and polite. If he gives me good service, I give him a tip.

Overall, the work at Leyhill really was a cushy number. When the officers had finished their meal the waiters were allowed to take and eat what was left over. It was a far cry from the truly atrocious, stodgy rubbish we'd been fed in the enclosed prisons. Gradually I started to get some self-respect back, I felt like an individual again. As the fear left, I was able once again to indulge in light-hearted chat and banter. I know that others felt the same. It was as if we had been walking around with a lump of ice inside that at last was beginning to melt.

I particularly remember on Sundays, when I didn't have to work, going to the canteen for breakfast and seeing the governor with his wife, and sometimes his daughter, queuing up with his prisoners to have breakfast. It struck me as something special. I thought, 'This is quite a man.' He treated us in a civil way and always said 'Good morning' when he walked in with his wife. To a woman we'd stand. This was nothing to do with rules or regime, and wasn't done for him. This was us showing our respect to a lady. There were lots of gentlemanly men there, who remembered who they had been. I was there at Christmas, always a difficult time for men away from their families. The governor shared Christmas dinner with us and the men stood and applauded him.

Many of the men, as I got to know them better, proved to be fascinating individuals. Some were embezzlers – solicitors or stockbrokers who had raided their clients' accounts; some were bank managers who had done something fraudulent; some were scam or con artists. Many were intellectual, well-travelled, cultivated men, from the middle or upper classes. I learned a great deal around them. Summers were particularly pleasant, with cricket on the mowed green and strolls through the spacious grounds. We could have been at boarding school. I was even in the cricket team, something I had never achieved at my old secondary modern. Many of our chaps had been at public school so we put on a good show. Visiting teams from the surrounding areas regularly came to Leyhill to play cricket. Dressed in whites, you couldn't tell the difference between us and them. They were allowed to bring their supporters and on visiting days the families of the inmates would come too, and though the two groups were segregated it was discreetly done. At the end of the match the players from both teams would all troop off to the pavilion and sit down together for tea. Over social chatter we'd consume sandwiches and fresh scones, home-made Victoria sponge and fruit cakes and even our own strawberries and cream. Being around normal, friendly people from the outside who treated us as human beings brought us into contact with real life and prepared us to go out into the world again.

Three years after I had first been arrested I was released, with time off for good behaviour. I think I came out a better man, one with more worldly-wise experience and understanding. I don't judge people. I get on with all types because we all have failings and stories to tell. Whoever I meet, whether it's a Mrs Mop the cleaning lady, or His Grace the Duke of wherever, I will always find a level where we are both happy to have a conversation.

I vowed I would never do anything to put myself back in this position again. I had brought shame on my family, I'd been a cocky young thing and I knew it was now up to me to get on with the job and restore myself to a good position in society and do well. I felt no bitterness. I had brought this on myself and no one else was to blame. I like to feel I took it on the chin. I respected the rules, conducted myself in an orderly manner and didn't go around crying.

Determined to do well, but in a proper way, I marched out, head high. I felt no stigma. They say that many men in prison become institutionalized but I didn't – and that is largely thanks to my mental attitude when I first went in, determined to get through it, and to the decent way we were treated at Leyhill. I walked out of there proudly, shook hands with the blokes I'd billeted with and made friends with. I'd never done National Service but it seemed like that. I was deeply moved when they turned out at the gate to see me off. It was quite an emotional thing.

CHAPTER SEVEN

.

I wanted to get away, to fully understand and then forget, all that lay behind me. I wanted a fresh start and perspective. I had some money put away in the old war chest, my own money, honestly earned, enough to last a long time if I were careful and went somewhere inexpensive. I decided on Ibiza, the third largest of the Balearic Islands. It was still almost unknown. The Summer of Love, 1967, was still a year away from exploding on the scene but in the spring of 1966 a few early hippies were starting to drift across from San Francisco, with their beads and flowers, their kaftans and their bags of pot – illegal but hardly the biggest problem in the world.

We became one small, happy community, living on next to nothing, spending our days on the beach, swimming, cooking over driftwood fires, making music and talking. My new friends were fantastic young people, my age. It was all peace and love, man. Don't make war, make love. It was a simple ideology. I often look back and think of the peace demonstrations that came later, the flowers thrust into the barrels of the National Guardsmen's guns and compare all that with the violent youngsters roaming the world today. I know they're in the minority but their aggression seems to dominate. Those young hippies were no threat to society. Their beliefs were very cool. It was a marked contrast to the toughness, the violence, I had known for the past three years, and I allowed their peaceful, happy ways to wash over me and heal me, like the waves washing the beach. Day after blissful day I felt my tension ease away and I started to get back some of my old joy of living.

Six months later I was revived and refreshed, ready to get on with my life and to pick up the old threads again. Some threads were gone for ever. I still missed Auntie Ethel and often thought of how I had always promised myself that some day I would shower every form of luxury that I could on her, to repay her in some way for the love she had always given me. It will always remain a regret that such a promise could no longer be kept. But in the peace of Ibiza I was finally able to mourn her properly and come to terms with her passing.

With the approach of winter I returned to Manchester and found another flat in Didsbury. I bought some suiting lengths and started to sell again to my old contacts, making some new ones along the way. It was almost as if I'd never been away, as if the previous years had been a very bad dream. But nonetheless, a dream that had changed me for ever. Chris Haworth was there, of course, my stalwart old friend, who was like a rock. He greeted me warmly, didn't blame or accuse me of anything, and we continued as we always had, working hard, going out in the evening to all the old haunts, meeting girls, thinking we were in love, spotting another pretty girl and realizing we weren't in love at all.

The great love of my life, Lorne, happened purely by accident. I was in a nightclub one evening, chatting with friends, chewing the fat about this and that over a few beers, as young men do, when I looked across the room and saw this startling-looking woman. She was tall and slender with auburn hair. Her face had a timeless, classic beauty that was very different from mere prettiness. She resembled Sophia Loren a little. I'm not sure how we met, if I was introduced, or if I went across and introduced myself. We talked for several hours and exchanged telephone numbers. Within a day or so I telephoned and asked if she would like to go out. She agreed and I said I'd pick her up.

Now here, our versions of what happened next vary. According to her, I stood her up. My recollection is slightly different. I was convinced she hadn't meant it. I didn't want to drive up only be told, 'Oh, sorry, David, I'm washing my hair tonight.' I knew someone who lived in the same street as her and asked them to tell her I couldn't make it. They forgot, so Lorne didn't get the message. Instead, she got ready to go out with me and waited... and waited.

So why didn't I go? I really don't know. It remains one of life's little mysteries, what it is that makes young men and women tick and react the way they do when romance is in the air. I won't say I got cold feet because I was never shy in coming forward. But I got this feeling that she wouldn't be there, I'd be the one to be stood up. Perhaps I was protecting myself a little because I knew she was the one for me and I was terrified she might just be in it for a fling. She was exotic and very beautiful. In fact, after I had spent the evening talking to her, when I returned to the group of my pals and told them I had a date with her, they starting jibing me. 'Ha ha, she won't turn up, David. In your dreams!' and so forth. So perhaps all that had registered.

I went out with my pals that night and carried on as normal, though I'm sure at the back of my mind a regret lingered. Meanwhile, Lorne was seething. She said to herself, 'Right, I'm going out!' She telephoned a friend and they set out to paint the town red. I'm sure she probably knew where I'd be because I was casually leaning against a bar when I heard a voice in my ear.

'What the hell are you playing at?'

I turned round and saw Lorne. I made some kind of a lame excuse about being delayed. She pretended she didn't really give a damn anyway – you know the way it goes when boy meets girl. For six or eight months we started going out, courting. They were wonderful days, the start of a great love affair that has lasted for over 30 years.

It wasn't long before I became aware that Lorne was a cabaret star, head-lining shows up and down the country in all the top clubs. She was with what was probably the top agency, London Management, where Billy Marsh was the big impresario of the day. The famed brothers Nat and Cyril Berlin were also agents there, while Burton Brown, a former American act, handled all Lorne's business. London Management had been a part of the Delfont-Grade empire and many of the stars, such as Morecambe and Wise, Norman Wisdom, Laurel and Hardy, and Bruce Forsyth, came across when Billy Marsh bought it out. I knew none of this background, little of Lorne's day-to-day life in the public eye when we started our relationship. She would come and go, while I was still living at my flat in Didsbury and doing my textiles.

Over the months, as we got to know each other better, Lorne's story unfolded. She was from the Tiger Bay area of Cardiff in South Wales. Her father was a seaman from the French Cameroons; her mother, Ida, was Welsh. They got married and had seven children – five girls and two boys. Life wasn't easy. Ida did a remarkable job, bringing up seven children on little money, with her husband constantly away for large portions of the year, but it was a very poor existence. The memory of this has always lingered with Lorne. As Christmas approaches, especially Christmas Eve, the time of the year I remember with nostalgia and affection, Lorne gets a sad, doe-eyed look in her eyes, as if to say, 'Oh my goodness, I'm not going to get anything again.'

As a little girl she would wake up on Christmas morning, like other children everywhere, but there would be no presents piled on the end of the bed, nothing in her stocking, perhaps no tree, and often very little indeed to eat. It has taken years to bring her out of her shell. I've always tried to make a special effort to give her a nice Christmas – and myself as well, of course. I try to think of everything possible, to give that Christmassy feel, something she never had as a child.

Lorne had always had a natural talent. It was that which won through for her and took her away from the poverty of her early life in Cardiff. She started singing young, in church choirs, in the Salvation Army, in amateur talent and dramatic shows. Always, there was this burning desire to sing and entertain. Gradually she progressed, in her teens, to seaside amateur shows, where she was spotted by a London agent. Phyllis Rounce and her partner in International Artists, Colonel Alexander, were well-known agents who handled many major stars, including Rolf Harris and Charlie Drake. Phyllis told Lorne that although she didn't look like Shirley Bassey, another girl from Tiger Bay, she certainly had her strong, powerful voice and delivery. She said there was only ever going to be one Shirley Bassey but Lorne had the talent and potential to be a major star in her own right and she wanted to take her off to London to groom her for stardom. Of course, Lorne agreed. She packed her bags and headed south.

Initially, Lorne lived for some six months in the Theatre Girls' Club in Soho, along with actresses, singers and dancers, many of whom became famous names. Her days were filled with training and she was doing a few shows in nightclubs and theatres to prepare her for bigger things. She was often sent out with major artistes like Frankie Vaughan, Norman Wisdom, Rolf Harris, Lonnie Donegan and Bruce Forsyth. Suddenly, Lorne started to grab headlines. Auditions with major television and theatrical impresarios followed, designed to build up her image and profile. Cilla Black was at the height of her pop career, appearing at the London Palladium. One night she fell sick and Lorne was rushed in to cover for a few days. She packed them in and again made headlines.

To paraphrase, articles said things like: 'She has a Welsh accent like Shirley Bassey but there is something different about Lorne Lesley. What makes her so individual and stand out from the crowd is her body language and sense of fun. She has a great voice, but more, she is a natural comedian.'

Things were really looking up. But, as so many young women have done in the past, and no doubt will continue to do in the future, Lorne fell for a young bloke who saw her potential and wanted a slice of it for himself. He took her into Europe to the clubs, theatres and concert halls there, away from the agents who believed in her, who were grooming her for stardom. She started headlining in Belgium and Scandinavia, building something of a reputation as a very powerful international cabaret star, but she was away from the limelight and the musical explosion in Britain, where it counted. This liaison produced her two delightful children, Robbie and Catrina, but sadly, the fellow didn't turn out to be a very gentlemanly chap and, disillusioned, Lorne returned to England.

She signed up to Billy Marsh's London Management and got back into the UK cabaret circuit. When we met she was at the stage where she was very well established. Our love affair developed from there. At the time Lorne was renting a very nice town house, while I had my flat in bohemia-land. We moved into a large family flat in Wilmslow, a very posh area in Cheshire, where the kids attended a local school. Looking in the papers one day I noticed a house to let in Bramhall. This immediately attracted my attention because as a boy this was where I had gone to visit my pals Samir and Ali, the Lababedi brothers, who lived on Bramhall Lane. To me, Bramhall summed up success in life. It was also a very pleasant, leafy place to live and I wanted to live in a nice house in a nice area because Lorne and I had decided to get married and I wanted everything to be perfect for the start of our new life together. We were married on 10 November 1969. I adopted the kids and gave them my name. Like many children of that young age – four and six – they didn't remember their previous life and I became the only father they loved and have grown up with.

I was still continuing with my own work but was finding myself getting interested in Lorne's career. When you live with someone and share everything, things rub off. I began to pick up on the names Lorne dropped into conversation, the people, the places, the rules of engagement. It wasn't long before we realized that unless we were together more we would never see each other. It seemed a natural progression that I should get more involved in her work. I had never been in show business before but it's like any other business – you learn the basics and carry on from there. Lorne was the artiste but business was something I'd known all my life. While she continued with London Management as her agents, I started going out with her to learn all I could, to find out as much as I could from the ground floor up so that I could take a lot of the pressure off her, as her personal manager.

I travelled with her, seeing to her needs, making sure that everything with the shows was to her liking. I checked lighting with charts and electricians. I watched and learned all aspects of presentation of the business. Lorne had a musical director who rehearsed the musicians. She would go to the clubs and rehearse tirelessly, going over the music until she was entirely satisfied. From her, I learned, 'You're as good as you were the night before.' You do everything to make sure it's as good as you can make it, then you go out and entertain the public and sock it to 'em. There are no excuses as far as the public is concerned. If the sound or the lighting or the orchestra are wrong, nobody turns around and says, 'It's OK, we understand these technicalities.' If the orchestra plays at the wrong tempo, the audience doesn't want to know the reasons why. All they want is to see and hear that everything is perfect and gels together and is to their liking.

The first time I ever saw Lorne perform I understood at once what was so special about her, what made her stand out from all the others. She was tall, very beautiful, very dynamic, she had the glamour and the voice, but there was also this very personal sense of humour in her that made her connect immediately with the audience. In particular, I noticed, she always developed a rapport with the women. They instantly perceived that she was no threat to them with their boyfriends or husbands. She'd come on stage and catch her heel in the hem of her gown, then pretend to trip and recover, throwing an impish look out at the crowd, laughing at herself. She was warm, not aloof, and audiences loved it. Long before people like Marti Caine came along, Lorne had that natural style and voice. There was something that Lorne did that would stop the shows. I remember watching her once when one of her false eyelashes came loose during a number. Without missing a beat, with a mischievous glance at the crowd, she peeled both eyelashes off and placed them on the piano. The audience roared with laughter. From the women there was that sense of recognition that here was a glamorous woman daring to take off her false eyelashes. It caused such an appreciative reaction that Lorne would often build this into her nightly programme, knowing what the reaction would be.

I don't know why, but after I met Lorne a ghost from the past returned to haunt me. I have always said that I had a very happy childhood, and it's true, I did, for which I will always be grateful, but different things were starting to assume importance for me now. Getting married and establishing a nice little family unit with Lorne was one of them. And knowing who I really was, was another. A desire to find out more about my mother and my background grew stronger and began to prey on my mind. I don't know whether Lorne spotted this (she is a very intuitive woman and I have always taken notice of that) or whether it was she who first put the idea into my head. Whatever the reason, my curiosity became more conscious. What was she like, my real mother? Strangely enough, I never particularly wanted to know what my father was like. Maybe, instinctively again, I knew that my strongest genes were on the Armenian side. I always knew that I was a Gulessarian through and through. If I ever found my Gulessarian relatives I knew I would look like them and be like them.

I decided to trace her, this unknown, shadowy figure. I wasn't sure where to begin. I started to dig deep to bring back little facts that I'd pushed to the back of my mind. From conversations with Auntie Ethel I knew the family name. Once she had mentioned to me that she had looked it up in the Cheshire telephone directory we had used when we lived in Cheadle Heath.

'There is a Gulessarian listed in Weaverham,' she had said.

This was 20 or so miles away, southwest of Manchester, towards the Mersey. It was somewhere to start from. I approached my solicitor and asked his advice.

'Are you sure about this, David?' he asked. 'She might not want to know.'

'I know that,' I replied. 'Perhaps, if this Gulessarian in Weaverham is a connection, you can ask discreetly.'

My solicitor made the phone call. I don't know exactly what he told the man who answered the phone but I believe he said it was over the matter of a will. Without giving away any secrets he very quickly established that he could be on the right track. The man he spoke to turned out to my mother's brother, Jack Gulessarian. As soon as the solicitor told me that Jack Gulessarian said his sister's name was Eugénie, I was enthralled. Was that my mother's name?

'They call her Jenny,' the solicitor replied. 'He gave me her address. Her married name is Moss and she lives in Jersey.'

'Jersey,' I repeated slowly.

My solicitor continued, saying he had traced her through directory enquiries and had rung her. He had spoken to her, then got onto the subject gently.

He had said, 'I believe you had a child in Manchester, in 1941. Is that correct?'

I listened as he told me this, not realizing how tense I was.

My solicitor said, 'There was complete silence for about a minute. Finally, she said, "Yes." We had quite a long conversation. I explained that you would like to contact her.'

'What did she say?' I asked.

'She hesitated. She said it was a long time ago, nearly 30 years. She said she felt so conscious of the thing that she had done she wasn't sure that she had the right to speak to you.'

I nodded slowly. 'So she didn't say she wanted to see me?'

'No, she didn't. But she didn't forbid you to get in touch,' my solicitor said. 'I'll give you her address and telephone number. It's up to you to decide what you want to do.'

I thought about it for a little while longer. I didn't attempt to contact her by phone, thinking it could be too big a shock. Instead, I wrote to her. I don't remember exactly what I put in that letter. I think I expressed my desire to meet her and told her a little about myself. I stuck on the correct postage and sent the letter off.

She in turn wrote a very sweet letter, which I have kept all these years. As I read it I was deeply moved, wondering how she must have felt to have given me up. Your mother is a very special person and for me to be holding a letter she had written in her own hand, for us to have made this contact, even in a tentative way, meant a great deal to me.

Villa Olga
Jersey, C.I.
26.1.69

Dear David,

Thank you for your letter. It was thoughtful of you to write me. I appreciated it very much.

As you will have gathered, Bert was not terribly pleased about my receiving a letter from you, but then I suppose I couldn't really expect him to be.

I did tell him all about my 'past' before we were married, I thought it best to start with a clean slate so to speak. He said very little at the time, and has never brought up the subject during all the years we have been married.

I am not going to tell him that I'm writing to you now because I know it will only cause tension between us, but I cannot let your letter go unanswered.

You must not feel embarrassed about trying to find me, I understand perfectly, you did what you feel you must. It is I who am embarrassed, that you should have been put in this position. I hope you can forgive me, because I can never forgive myself.

At the moment, the only thing that matters to you is to see me – but you could be hurt. You may or may not have a picture of me in your mind's eye... and you could be terribly disappointed.

You have half opened a door that has remained closed for over 28 years, now we both feel that we should like to see what is on the other side. But would it really be a good thing? I'm wondering if too much time may have passed. I honestly don't know. There is much I would like to ask you, but I haven't the right. Perhaps in time and circumstance.

I know you will understand it is not going to be possible for me to write to you – or for me to have any letters from you.

I'm truly sorry about this, but I do have a duty. Please forgive me any sorrow I may have caused you.

Yours very sincerely,
As always,
Jenny Gulessarian

I read the letter many times. Her name – Jenny – made her real and brought her closer. She had said I mustn't write but she didn't say I couldn't telephone. She said there was much she wanted to ask me. I read again the line: 'You have half opened a door that has remained closed for over 28 years, now we both feel that we should like to see what is on the other side.'

To me, that was a clear invitation to get in touch. I picked up the telephone, held my breath and dialled the number.

When she answered the phone, I asked, 'Is that Jenny?'

I heard an indrawn breath. There was a pause. I could almost hear her heart beating.

'This is David,' I said.

I sensed her searching for words.

'Yes, I know,' she said, with a break in her voice.

I knew instantly that she had been expecting this call.

'I'm sorry to ring out of the blue like this,' I said. ' I just had to speak to you.'

'Yes, David, I quite understand.'

It felt very strange to have my mother say my name after all this time. She had given me my name. It was on my original birth certificate: David Gulessarian. She still sounded hesitant, as if unsure what to say to me. I tried to make it easy by sounding happy and breezy.

'It's lovely to be talking to you,' I said.

'I'm delighted, too –' then she hesitated, as if still feeling her way. 'I feel I don't have the right to speak to you. Not after what I did. I feel so terribly guilty.'

I could sense the tears were very close to the surface. My thoughts then were to reassure her that I was a confident young man at ease with himself.

'Jenny, let me assure you, you have nothing to reproach yourself about. I had a very happy childhood with a wonderful family, who loved and cared for me. Never doubt that for a moment.'

'Never a day went by when I didn't reproach myself,' she said. 'You were never out of my mind. I thought of you every single day. I never forgot you.

When your birthday came around each year I would think of you with such pain and guilt for what I had done.'

In a way, our roles were reversed as I sought to put her at her ease, to reassure her, to make her see that guilt was the last thing I wanted to lay at her door. I knew how much she must have suffered down the years and I wanted to alleviate this if I could. As I spoke to her I could feel quite a weight lifting off her shoulders. She was eager to talk, she wanted to hear more about my childhood and my life as a young man. Once the conversation started, it flowed. We talked for a very long time that day as we caught up on a lifetime. She was intensely curious about my life and seemed as if she wanted to absorb every detail. Before we hung up I asked if it would be all right to call her again. She agreed but said it would always have to be at a prearranged time.

'I'm sure you understand this, David,' she said.

'Yes, Jenny, I do,' I assured her. 'I don't want to make any difficulties for you in any way at all. I just want to get to know you.'

After that I called her regularly. She went into detail, not a lot, but some, about the circumstances of my birth. She told me very little indeed about her private life. I asked about my father. She was very hesitant, reluctant to discuss this, but eventually she did.

'I met this man, he was very nice...' she started. Then she paused a while before continuing. 'He was a pilot in the war. He died – '

Then her voice petered out again. That was all she would ever say on the subject. I could only visualize how it must have been for a young woman, a nurse, as she had been, to have fallen in love and have had one of those intense wartime romances with a dashing young pilot who perhaps flew a Spitfire or a big Lancaster bomber, to have got pregnant and then, before they married, for him to have gone down in a blaze of glory in the early days of the war somewhere in the skies. It must have been doubly tragic for her, a single girl who had lost her sweetheart and who had the stigma of expecting a child in 1941, a more puritanical age than today.

My mother told me often that having to give me up had haunted her all her life. She had met her husband two or three years later and before they were married she told him about this liaison and that she'd had a child as a result of it. She then told me that she had another son, born shortly after her marriage. He was some three years younger than me, his name was Ken. He still lived on Jersey and wasn't aware of me. Apart from that, she told me nothing else about him.

I was very curious about what she looked like and we exchanged photographs. When I opened the envelope and took the picture out I was absolutely stunned at the very strong physical resemblance between us. I was 28 then and I suppose she would have been in her mid-forties but we could have been clones. I don't think it's possible to describe what I felt as I sat gazing at her face.

For many years we spoke on the phone on a regular basis, perhaps once a month. It sounds clandestine but we arranged the calls for when her husband was not there. It was easier for her like that and I'm sure it caused less conflict. Sometimes, during our conversations over months and then over years, I would say, 'Look, I'll come over and see you.'

She was always very hesitant. She had told me that her husband was a very difficult and jealous man. I think also that she couldn't face telling her son.

She said, 'This is a very small island. It might get around.'

I knew exactly what she meant by that. Obviously, I wouldn't go to her home. I would check into a hotel suite so we could have some privacy, but having seen her photograph and knowing how closely we resembled each other, the cat would soon be out of the bag. Someone would notice and put two and two together. Our meetings would not remain a secret for very long. But I don't think those were the real reasons she put me off. If push came to shove, I think she would have been a little embarrassed to meet me in the flesh. Here was a boy she had given away as a tiny infant. She didn't know how my life was going to turn out. It could have been a dreadful life, an unhappy life. Fortune landed me in the lap of a kind and loving family but, equally, fate could have gone against me. You read of children who remain in homes and are abused. While I was growing up many children were being shipped off to Australia to harsh conditions in work camps and on farms. Perhaps over the years she had anguished over that. I don't know.

Jenny often used to say that maybe I had a certain picture of her in my mind's eye and I'd be disappointed. Well, frankly, that would not have been the case. I was not expecting a society hostess or a glamour queen. I was just expecting an average lady. From her photograph she looked lovely but it wouldn't have mattered if she didn't – she was my mother.

CHAPTER EIGHT

I started to get more involved in Lorne's career. She was still with London Management, who fixed her some fabulous shows up and down the country, accepting only the major nightclubs in England. At the same time I was looking into the kind of huge clubs she had previously appeared in on the Continent. I made some good contacts and we started to mix new Continental bookings, which I set up, with the English ones booked by Lorne's agents.

The first enquiries came in from Portugal. Lorne was invited to top the bill at a glamorous big casino in Estoril. This was a lovely part of Portugal that many crowned heads of Europe retired to. Lorne continued to appear there every season for many years. The casino was very stylish, having been built in the Twenties or Thirties. Madame Bluebell had a contract to bring a troupe of Bluebells from their base at the Lido in Paris to dance at the casino. These famous long-legged dancers, all of them over six feet tall, were stunning with their ostrich plumes, their bugle beads and their silver-sequinned-corset costumes. They performed in three places in the world only: at the Lido, at the casino in Estoril and at the Hotel Orient in Las Vegas. In those days there was always a big variety show before the headliner came on, with acts like faro singers and flamenco dancers in traditional costumes, as well as speciality acts – conjurers, jugglers, escapologists, pickpockets, coloured dogs and doves, troupes of local singers and dancers, a whole host of unusual turns you don't see any more because a lot of the old-style venues, large cabarets and theatres with vaudeville have gone.

Lorne was always in demand for these shows because not only did she have an established name and was highly professional, she could also introduce her songs in four or five languages and perhaps sing one or two in the local language – Spanish or Portuguese, French or German – which always went down very well.

Things were going well and we were busy. While our rented flat was nice and quite spacious we had decided we would like to buy a place of our own; we had a deposit put away in an account and I had already arranged the appropriate credit checks at the bank to facilitate a mortgage. However, we hadn't had a moment spare to actually go out house-hunting. One day I was driving down

Bramhall Lane south on my own when I saw a 'for sale' sign posted outside a handsome detached house. It was Edwardian, built some time between 1910 and 1915, with a black and white mock Tudor facade consisting of black beams and white pebble-dash which was a bit dirty at the time. 'That would look a lot better with a lick of paint,' I thought, then realized at the same moment, 'This is a cracking good house. I want it!'

I turned around and drove home. I picked up Lorne, hustling her out of the house before she had time to change, and drove back down the lane. We went up the garden path and knocked on the front door.

A pleasant-looking elderly lady opened it and I said, 'Excuse me, madam, but I'm really excited by the "for sale" notice outside your house. May we have a look around?'

Her rather startled glance took in Lorne and me. I had long hair down to my shoulders and we were both casually dressed, perhaps a little in a flower-power way, Lorne in a crocheted jacket and carpet slippers. I could see the woman thinking, 'These two hippies can never afford to buy my house.'

Sounding a little doubtful, she said, 'You should really book an appointment with the agent –'

'I know this is not the correct procedure,' I agreed, 'but we are very serious people.'

She smiled at that and was kind enough to say, 'Well, you'd better come in, then.'

Her name was Mrs Thornley. She was a retired schoolteacher with nice manners and refinements. She made us welcome, showed us everything and said she had lived in the house for very many years. Every room was in its original condition, with fireplaces, coving and cornices, wainscotting and solid wooden floors exactly right for the period. I didn't know this at the time, of course – I was very ignorant of such things – but it just felt right. Everything belonged together. Everything fitted. Perhaps Nanny's early passion for her little knicky-knackies and our hunting through junk shops had rubbed off on me more than I appreciated. But almost instinctively I found myself liking what I saw because it hadn't been messed about with or altered in any way. The rooms were spacious, there was a large garden that was mature and well tended with mowed lawns and flower beds.

Lorne and I looked at each other and I said, 'We'll have it.'

Somewhat taken aback, she said, 'Are you sure you can afford it? The asking price is £8,650.'

With my usual confidence I assured her, 'You bet your life we can. Don't sell it to anyone else – I'll be back.'

I was so eager to close the deal I went straight into it and for once I didn't haggle over the price. I went down to my bank, where, with my usual foresight, I had already arranged a mortgage just in case we ever found a house. In a remarkably short space of time the deed was done, the house was ours. I don't know who was the more surprised, Mrs Thornley or us.

The house was filled with all manner of beautiful antique furniture and objects and was very tastefully decorated. Offering us first refusal on whatever took our eye Mrs Thornley told us she would be getting in some house-clearers, it was all to be sold. I think we bought one or two pieces of furniture and some silverware, porcelain and glass, but much as we would have liked it all we were not in a position to buy more. All the rest – tables, chairs, sideboards and bureaux – went off to the local antique dealers, lock, stock and barrel.

Having always lived in rented places we had nothing of our own that would look right *in situ* in our new house. We would need furniture, we would need tables, chairs and a sideboard, we would need carpets and curtains. In short, we would need everything we had let slip through our fingers. At first we went off to modern furniture shops, the kind where I had worked as a young lad of 16. I had thought the stuff there was reasonable when I was selling it but I now saw that most of it was brash and not very solidly constructed. There was no nice polish to the surface of the tables, no rich colour, no sense of age or history to any of it. We ended up trawling around salesrooms hunting for those very pieces we had been offered originally by Mrs Thornley.

I started to look properly at such things as the patina, which is the polish and wear of ages – the wax polishing, the touching of hands, even the dropping of ink – on the surface of wood. I started to compare original handles and styles with new or fake ones. From then on my casual early interest in antiques really sprang to life. Whenever I had time I would go to salesrooms, local auctions, country house sales and antique shops, starting to accumulate items for our own use and pleasure.

Whenever we were abroad, particularly in historic places, such as the old part of Madrid, we'd be scouring around the old antique shops there, looking. Many things in the Seventies were very affordable – there were none of the high prices of today – and by gum, we bought them. At the time I had a 2+2 hardtop E-type Jaguar sports car that I had bought so we could drive to Lorne's engagements on the Continent and have a car there for our use. We gained a great deal of pleasure driving along the roads through France or Spain and elsewhere, stopping at very nice hotels and restaurants. It was all part of the craic.

Lorne would be working from ten till midnight singing, but beyond that we were free to roam through the old quarters of the cities we were in. In Spain we bought wonderful crystal or perhaps embroidered tablecloths; in Portugal it would be ceramics. Everything, from chandeliers to statues, would be strapped to the roof-rack and we'd drive home over potholed roads, rattling onto the cross-Channel ferry, praying that there would be no breakages.

When Lorne appeared at Tito's in Palma we would drive to the ferry at Barcelona and take the eleven o'clock overnight boat to Majorca. On the crossing we slept in a cabin and arrived at seven the next morning. We always took an apartment for the season so we would have more space and privacy. We had the car for getting around the island and exploring during the day, or to take us to the really lovely, almost empty beaches you could find then, and I would drive Lorne to Tito's in the evening. Tito's was a nice place to work. It had a huge auditorium overlooking the harbour and was always packed with people from all over the world. Lorne's success was assured when she greeted as many holiday-makers as possible in their own language. It was a pleasant existence and, as I sometimes reflected, a million miles away from the difficult period I was getting over when I had first come to the Balearic islands.

On our travels we found looking for antiques to furnish and decorate our home very stimulating. Gradually we were filling it with all manner of lovely things, from rugs to grandfather clocks, dining room chairs to oil paintings, not to mention the collectibles that we smothered every surface with. It became a real passion. At that stage we did it in an amateur way; but without being aware of it, I was starting to develop my eye, that part of you that tells you at a glance whether a piece is good and original or a fake. That glance that quickly sums up its style and value and a whole lot else besides.

During the term the children went to local schools. Catrina went to a local primary school. For a time young Robbie was a boarder at a very nice junior public school in Cheadle Hume that we thought would be the making of a man. It offered a fine education; but boarding school is not for every child. When we saw that Robbie wasn't very happy there we took him out and let him go to the same day school as Catrina. For most of the year we were usually away from home for one or two weeks at a time. In the summer the kids would join us in Spain for a month. They had their own bedrooms in the apartment. A local lady baby-sat in the evenings while Lorne did the shows. The shows didn't finish until 2 a.m. so we slept in late. Lorne would have laid out the children's breakfast of cereals for when they got up and we shared a nice meal in the evening. For the rest of the day we set up an account with a local beach bar to enable the children to order whatever they wanted for lunch, be it roast chicken, pizza or hamburgers and, of course, as many cold drinks and ice cream as their hearts desired. The owner of the beach bar also agreed to keep an eye on the children, who were happy and free the entire summer long, either in the apartment pool or playing on the beach. It was a way of life that had given me such happy memories of a similarly carefree childhood in Brixham – one which I am sure built up my confidence and made me an independent young lad. It was a wonderful childhood I will never forget and I wanted Robbie and Catrina to experience the same.

Even though we did a bit of travelling, often being away for a total of six months each year, we made sure the children never suffered. The most impor-tant part of their well-being was the good housekeepers we found to run our home and to always be there 24 hours a day if required, to see to the needs of the children. These priceless women would make sure they were well fed, well turned out and always went off to school spick and span.

Over the years we employed just three housekeepers, which shows we were all happy with the arrangement. The first time we decided we needed someone was a bit nerve-racking because hiring such a key player was new to Lorne and me. We debated about how we could tell which applicant would fit in, which one would be kind to the kids. We advertised, and got Muriel, a charming and homely widow. She was a lovely, mumsy type who was perfect. She had her own room and privacy and for some years it worked out well. She left amicably when the kids were a little older and we looked around again. A series of people beat a path to our door. None of them proved suitable.

One day I came home and Lorne greeted me looking like the cat who'd got the cream.

'I think I've found just the right person,' she said. 'She's a very plain little Irish girl. Her name is Mary O'Dee. I think you'll like her.'

'Where is she?' I asked.

'I asked her to return at five o'clock for you to inspect her,' Lorne replied.

At five o'clock on the dot there was a knock at the front door. It was Mary O'Dee, standing on the doormat, wet through. She had come early to make sure she would be punctual and had stood under a tree around the corner in the rain. To me, it showed the calibre of the woman. Lorne gave her a towel to dry herself with. When she was at her ease, I asked her the relevant questions. Covertly I was inspecting her nails, her attire and so forth. She was clean and tidy, her nails scrubbed – I won't say I looked to see if her neck was clean, as Nanny used to do with me, but it would have been! She was plain and charming, a single lady. We took references, she passed with flying colours and we took her on, into our hearts and home. I'm glad we did. She was an endearing character, with delightful ways, who looked after us and the children wonderfully well for five years. She had been brought up on a farm in Ireland, staying on when her brothers and sisters had married. She said she'd always been in service, in some great houses. Her cooking skills were second to none, taking me right back to the wonderful meals I'd had in Nanny's kitchen.

I have to smile when I think of Mary O'Dee. She used to answer the phone in her soft Irish brogue with, 'Hello, I'm afraid the sir and the madam aren't in.'

She got used to us so well that when she heard the usual household sounds, such as me showering and shaving and coming downstairs, she had my breakfast off pat. As I hit the kitchen, her smiling face and 'Morning, sir!' would greet me. She would turn from the stove with my breakfast cooked to perfection, ready to be to set down on the table before me. It was a different breakfast each day, poached eggs and a slice of grilled bacon, grilled kidneys and tomatoes, boiled eggs, an omelette, scrambled eggs. I was thoroughly spoilt.

More importantly, she also looked after the children marvellously, seeing to their every need whether we were there or not. When we had dinner parties she had her white bib on, fussing around with her soft voice and gentle ways, producing course after delicious course. She was a real gem. I couldn't stop her working.

Often, I used to say, 'Mary, stop! Go and watch a bit of telly, it's your time off,' to which she would reply, as she did some last-minute tidying up or ironing the children's clothes for the next day, 'I know, sir. But idle hands make mischief.'

Whenever we had the house painted I was not backward in lending the workmen a hand – and neither was Mary.

She'd be up the ladders behind me, 'Is there anything sir wants up there?'

Whatever it was, brushes or rags, turps or tea, there was Mary with it to hand. The children were tickled pink watching her. She never spent any of the money we paid her. Her only vice, if you can call it that, was that she went to Mass in the local RC church two or three times a week and to bingo on one night a week. She didn't smoke, didn't drink – she was perfect. So much so that a pal of ours, a local well-to-do entrepreneur who often used to come to dinner, would say, 'Mary, if you ever want to leave the Dickinsons and come to work for me, no problem. I will build you a church in my garden.'

She'd laugh, 'Oh, sir, you are a one!'

Peter Stringfellow lived just around the corner from us, in Cheadle Hume. I first met him when he put his Corvette up for sale. I popped around to have a look. It was about six months old and in perfect condition and I bought it. Like me, Peter had been born to the sound of wartime bombs, in his case in Sheffield. We hit it off from the start and became good pals, dining regularly at each other's homes. When Peter moved to London we kept in touch. The Corvette replaced the E-types throughout the latter part of the Seventies, when Lorne and I drove back and forth into Europe. Over the years since I have had several Corvette models.

From Tito's, and the apartment in Palma, Lorne and I expanded into the mainland of Spain. In Barcelona it was Don Chufo's club, where famous international stars like Sacha Distel appeared regularly. In Madrid it was at the Florida Parque in the centre of town, where Lorne was spotted by Spanish television, who invited her to appear on different shows. One television favourite of hers was the great Rafael, who was very much the Julio Iglesias of his day in Spain. A little guy with a massive voice, he took to Lorne and they would sing duets together on television.

When she wasn't working we would wander around the old part of town, on the antiques trail. Often we would drive straight to Portugal. Over the years we went through two E-types. The old roof-rack was always brought out for these expeditions in anticipation of our finds. I think that was part of the thrill, never knowing what we would stumble across – and I think it still is. The excitement of antiques-hunting motivates many people to start on the trail and then it becomes a lifelong interest, as it did with me. After every trip we'd load up with many goodies, such as cooking vessels in terracotta or iron. Often it was large quantities of hand-painted Portuguese tiles and pottery. In the small town of Caldas da Rainha – named after a queen who found the local hot mineral springs cured her illness – we were very taken by the local pottery made there, much of it by famous artists who specialize in realistic things like cabbages and lobsters, as well as in humorous figures. It has become enormously collectible. We still have two pieces on the wall of our kitchen today. I was well and truly bitten by the collecting bug and there was no return.

Lorne's circuit became internationally wider. One of the best was a wonderful booking at the five-star Mandarin Hotel in Hong Kong. Arranged by London Management, it was to become a regular venue of hers. We always enjoyed flying out there, seeing Victoria Peak emerge from the clouds, although I have to say it was a hair-raising experience landing at the tiny Kai Tak airport, which, according to the pilots we spoke to, often scared the pants off even them. As the plane decelerated and flew ever lower, until you could almost reach out and touch the rooftops, we would be gripping the arms of our seats hard, convinced that this time we weren't going to make it. The new airport has been built out into the sea, using millions of tons of infill, and the experience of landing there now is far less gruelling on the nerves, thank goodness.

In the Seventies at the Mandarin there were various grill rooms and restaurants offering a wide range of cuisines, from Chinese to Japanese. The Harbour Room, on the top floor, had sensational panoramic views of Hong Kong harbour and this is where the big cabaret shows took place after a special dinner. Most of the stars were English, names like Frankie Vaughan, Derek Nimmo, Dora Bryan and Lorne Lesley.

Being booked into one of the best hotels in the world for a month every year for several years at a cracking good fee made this a plum job that always came with first-class air tickets. And it was first class the rest of the way. A member of the hotel staff would meet us at the airport with a Rolls-Royce, and the general manager, Peter Stafford, was always there to greet us as we rolled up like royalty. He would trip down the steps, as he did for stars and presidents, to welcome us into the foyer, where the heads of departments were lined up for us to meet. The head chef, the housekeeper, everyone from front of house: all would be introduced with military precision. Then Peter would click his fingers for a senior member of staff to escort us to our suite, always the finest in the hotel. One of a bank of private high-speed lifts would shoot us straight to the top to the penthouse floor, where we would rub shoulders with the likes of the Rockefellers and A-list American movie stars.

The suite was unbelievable. A tree – an actual living tree, with spreading branches and healthy leaves – was growing in the centre of the suite, through the floor. Wide windows gave a sparkling view over the harbour. The furniture was oriental lacquer, the furnishings sumptuous.

The first time we walked in, after the member of staff had gone, we sank into adjoining deep sofas and Lorne said, 'This is a bit of all right, isn't it?'

We started to laugh – it was so fantastic it seemed unreal.

During our long stays at the Mandarin down the years we always met many interesting people. On one occasion, while Lorne was rehearsing, Peter Stafford came in with a very charming man; we greeted him but didn't take much notice of him at the time. It was only later that we discovered that this was Stanley Ho, the billionaire who owned a huge part of the waterfront in Hong Kong and most of the casinos in Macao.

People always came forward after the show for a chat and to ask Lorne for autographs. One evening a gentleman presented himself who had known Lorne many years before as a youngster in Cardiff. He had done well in life and was now a stockbroker with a firm of English brokers based in Hong Kong. Lorne was delighted to see him and to discover how well he was doing. He smiled.

'You're not doing too badly yourself,' he commented.

He turned and introduced us to other members of his staff who had shared a table for the evening. One in particular was titled but otherwise appeared very relaxed and low-key. He was the kind of man whose brogues had been repaired 50 times and who probably wore his great-grandfather's tweed suit to go stalking. He was fascinated by Lorne and ended up asking her advice on how to find himself a girlfriend, which was quite touching. As he left he asked if we liked sailing. We said we had done some in Spain.

'Right, I'll arrange for you to go on my small boat,' he said.

Later, Lorne remarked, 'Did he say how big his boat was, David? Do you think he expects us to handle it on our own?'

I said, 'Well, he's bound to have someone there to show us the ropes.'

A couple of days later we were up bright and early. The concierge rang to let us know that someone was downstairs waiting for us. It was a young chap, looking the business in a blue and white Victorian sailor's outfit. Outside, a chauffeur-driven car waited. It was beginning to look like a very grand jaunt indeed. At the quay we were driven up to a huge, custom-built junk, made of teak, gleaming with brass. We were both astounded when we were whistled aboard in the time-honoured way. I have seen this done on films and in documentaries when the admiral inspects the fleet, but never in my wildest dreams did I think it would happen to me. The captain and hands, eight uniformed young boys, stood to attention, saluting. I wasn't sure what the protocol was. Did we salute back, or inspect the troops, or what? In the end, I think we nodded and raised our hands in a little half-wave, or perhaps, like Churchill, we put our hands behind our backs and strolled like pros to the poop deck.

The crew ran about, the sails were raised and caught the wind, and majestically we set off into the China Sea. Just the name resonated with romance and legend. At noon we anchored at a small cove on one of those small green islands that rise like cliffs from the waves, for a picnic consisting of delicious fresh seafood, fruits and wine.

On the return voyage, as we watched some flying fishes dash through the water ahead of us, Lorne said, 'I could easily get used to this.'

As we approached Hong Kong Island we saw the lights of a million tightly crowded buildings climbing up towards Victoria Peak. Below, the lights of Aberdeen Harbour, where all the floating restaurants were, shimmered like fireflies in the dusk. It was a spectacular end to a perfect day.

CHAPTER NINE

•

Throughout all our travels Chris Haworth, my boyhood friend, had remained very much on the scene. We continued to see each other socially. Whenever Lorne and I were at home we would often go to visit Chris and his wife at their house and they would come to ours. Our interest in antiques had overlapped. Chris had also become a private collector. He would join us on trips to the salesrooms and we would compare and discuss our buys. We'd both dipped our toes in the water, had both been buying pieces for a few years, me for our home, he as a collector. But we were novices who had started off buying modest things.

One day we were discussing antiques and dealers when we suddenly said, 'Hey, we could do this.'

In many respects it was like a light bulb switching on mutually in our heads. We grew animated, discussed it further and really believed we could do it. Perhaps the real motivation for me was family pressure, wanting to spend more time at home, and perhaps, too, I had an eye to the future, aiming to build up a business I would enjoy, wanting something to fall back on. Chris and I decided, with our wives' encouragement, to invest about £3,000 apiece in a small shop and some stock. In the early Seventies that was a reasonable sum, enough if we were careful but not so much that we would regret it if we lost the lot.

Chris went out looking for suitable premises and found them on the main A6, going towards Buxton, in the village of Disley. There were a few antique shops in that area already, and using a tried and tested business strategy – if you open a business where there are similar ones established, you can't go too far wrong – we took a lease on our first shop. The next step was to decide what stock we would get and what the shop would look like, and so forth. That initial look and impact was crucial because that would be how the public – and the trade – would perceive us. We knew we were incredibly green, we knew we had a great deal to learn, we knew we needed to formulate our taste, so we decided the only way to gain experience was to get stuck in and learn by looking, touching, handling. In effect, to do a little market research.

From the start we both had eyes bigger than our bellies – me more so than Chris. I wanted our shop to be the best it was possible to make it. The one thing we totally agreed on was that it would be smart and upmarket. None of your Auntie Wainwright junk shops for us! At first we drove around the district, inspecting as many of the local antique shops as possible. We stood outside and looked at the windows, assessing the displays and asking ourselves, 'Would that shop window intrigue us and make us want to step inside?' We tried to work out what it was about that particular window that appealed or, conversely, didn't appeal. We went inside the shops, assessing the stock, getting an impression of the overall look, seeing how the dealers themselves treated us, the customers. One valuable exercise was checking on prices. At this stage we really hadn't much of a clue about valuing different items and we knew that was going to be a hard lesson to learn quickly. We went to salesrooms and noted how much a nice early Victorian dining table might go for. Then we looked at similar tables in antique shops and saw how much they had been marked up at. It was all a valuable learning curve.

During this process Chris and I discovered that we had different tastes, which wasn't a bad thing. It made us a good combination. I was slightly more flamboyant, drawn more towards the more decorative, such as lacquer and oriental works of art, the beautiful veneered woods, the ormolu, the porcelain plaques inset, the magnificence of exhibition pieces, the brass telescope or the terrestrial library globe, while Chris was a plain brown person, more into country furniture. I was the more forward one, whose imagination and aspirations would take flight, while Chris was the quiet one with feet more solidly set on the ground. It was an ideal working relationship. In a way we checked and balanced each other. We had known each other since we were teenagers and had never had an argument. Nor did we after we went into business together, which is always a time when even the best of friends can fall out. I think I had a pretty strong flair for the job. I'm not saying that Chris didn't but I was more instinctive. Chris realized that and so allowed me more scope .

After we had researched the local area I decided that the only way we would really make our mark would be to go to London and see how the big boys operated. Now many people might have said that we were heading in the wrong direction, that we should have stuck to our level and used provincial shops as our model. I'm not saying that there was anything wrong with provincial shops. Far from it. Many of them have a good name and reputation and are very stylish, as, I have to say, with our grand ideas, we intended to be ourselves! But I'm a great believer in saying if you want to learn, go and look at the very best. I tell beginners: go to stately homes, where pieces out of the reach of all but the wealthiest are to be found in abundance. Go to museums, where the best examples in the world are on display. Just because the Duke of Wellington's desk is worth £5 million, that is no reason for you not to look at it. After all, a cat may look at a queen. By looking at the best you will learn what *is* the best, and why. When you buy your more humble pieces you will understand what it is about them that is special, even if they are that much less valuable or important. You will get your eye in and come to recognize quality. Sometimes you might even spot that rare object, the sleeper as it is known in the trade, that has escaped detection – and you might walk away with a find. These are the things that I tell beginners today and they are the same things that I decided would work for me and Chris when we were beginners ourselves.

Like Dick Whittington and others before us, we ventured to London and headed straight for the big salesrooms in the glamorous locations of Mayfair and Belgravia. Like little country mice we sat in on auctions at Christie's and Sotheby's and Bonhams. Yes, some prices did spiral beyond our wildest dreams, but somewhat to our surprise we saw that many items were knocked down at quite reasonable prices. We learned a valuable lesson: that in the provinces when something startling turns up it gets a lot of attention from a lot of people and it will go for a high price, whereas the standard of merchandise going through the London salesrooms is a lot higher so there is more to go around and the competition is not as fierce. I'm not saying that the finest antique wouldn't bring the finest price – it would – but that still left a lot of things that were within our reach. We also learned that if the big dealers turn out in force at the provincial auctions they will not want to lose out to their rivals and go home empty-handed so, for all their experience, they will sometimes get auction fever, that urge to bid that is the plague of the amateur. In London this fever wouldn't be as prevalent since there are many more quality goods to go around.

After going to the auctions in London Chris and I would wander along to the antique shops themselves, where the fruits of the salesrooms were on display.

As we gazed into the nicely lit windows, where just a few pieces were tastefully displayed, I can remember turning to Chris and saying, 'This is how our shop should look. We should have only one or two wonderful pieces on display. This gives a sense of style, which people who are looking to spend good money on antiques want. They don't want to think they are walking into a junk shop because that will imply that they are going to be putting junk into their houses.'

Chris agreed with me at once. That is how our style and the look of our shop was formulated, right there in the heart of St James's. One of our favourite ports of call in London was Arthur Davidson's shop in Jermyn Street. We would stand outside and gaze almost hungrily into the window, like poor kids on a Christmas morning. It was a huge shop, crammed with the most fabulous decorative antiques. There were large telescopes, huge dressers, plank-topped tables, sets of 12 chairs, armada chests – all manner of wonderful things. Arthur's eye for displaying antiques was second to none. The arrangement of the displays and the lighting of them were all exactly right. We weighed everything up and thought: this is it, mate, this is what we want to do.

Still scouting for ideas we wore out our shoe leather walking the length of posh Mount Street in Mayfair, the smart Fulham Road and the little streets of

Knightsbridge and Belgravia. We would seek out the exclusive antique shops to be found there, looking at the way they displayed their wares, the lighting, the styles, the pricing. We saw how in upmarket London shops they would put just one or two pieces in the window, on a well-polished floor, with pinspot lighting to draw attention to some detail like exquisite marquetry or a small vase placed strategically on top of a chest of drawers. We felt that by reproducing this effect we would be sure to stand out against the ten other shops we were competing with in the Disley area. These sold mainly country furniture, much of it in oak – tables, chairs, coffers – plus brassware and candlesticks. Each of the ten shops offered pretty much the same sort of stuff and they would all cram as much of it as they could into their windows. The kitchen sink was there and the bath-tub, too. Chris and I decided not to copy them; we wanted to be different.

We went back to our small shop in Disley, next to the Co-op, and started by stripping everything down to the bare bones. We got rid of the patterned wall-paper, replacing it with grass-weave. We laid plain hessian carpet on the floor and put in discreet spot and pinspot lighting. Everything was designed to make a neutral, tasteful background for our wares. Everyone pitched in. I got Robbie and Catrina earning pocket money by polishing the pieces as we brought them in. Our wives also did their bit while Chris and I went on the road, buying.

Not everybody was looking for country goods; some people wanted pieces that had a bit more flair or were more original in design and style and we decided that our strength would be to cater for them. We would go for quality decorative English and Continental furniture, some giltwood, some lacquer, some oriental. When we brought these things back to our small village and put them in our shop, by Jove, we started to get noticed.

I often had to leave Chris to hold the fort because Lorne was still working all over the world, with engagements coming in thick and fast. Her schedule slotted together very nicely. It would be Majorca, Spain and Portugal in June, July and August, then Australia later in the year when their spring came around in November, through Christmas and into their summer. This meant we enjoyed summer for most of the year, which suited both of us very well, sun people as we are. Her trips to Australia took a great deal of thought and commitment because the tours out there would last for three or four months and this was a long time to be away from the family and to leave Chris to manage things on his own. That we could do both was thanks to our excellent housekeepers, especially Mary O'Dee, who was still with us, and to the calibre of Chris himself.

Lorne had been in Australia in the late Sixties, before we met, and had enjoyed it. I contacted NTL, her agents out there, and rekindled the relation-ship. Her first engagements were through NTL in Sydney. They booked her in to the huge self-built football league clubs known as Australian Rules Clubs. These were very Las Vegas, with floors of slot machines, restaurants, bars and

RIGHT My Grandfather Hrand (Harry)
Gulesserian.
BELOW My Grandmother Marie
Gulesserian.

RIGHT My grandfather was a millionaire at 24 years of age.
BELOW Grandfather's house. My mother on a horse with the nanny surrounded by other staff.

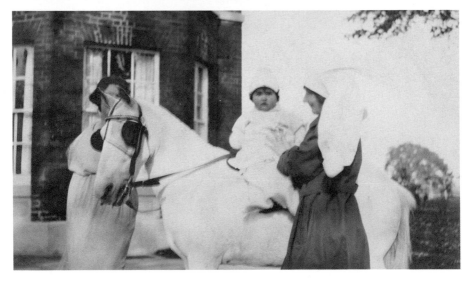

TOP My mother Eugenie Gulesserian (back) with brother Jack and sister Marie.
ABOVE My aunt Marie.
LEFT My mother.

ABOVE My primary school, Cheadle Heath School,
I am 5th from the right on the back row.
RIGHT Nanny with Auntie Ethel and cousin Debbie.

BELOW LEFT Me as a young boy.
BELOW Jim and Joyce Dickinson, my adopted parents.

ABOVE Lorne and I.
TOP RIGHT Our first house, 265 Bramhall Lane South, Cheshire.
RIGHT Myself, Lorne and internationally-renowned star, the great Winifred Atwell in 1969.

ABOVE Working on the restoration of my barn with one of the builders.
RIGHT Me with the Minton peacock in Long Island, USA.

3,000-seater show rooms. We set up contracts with the TV stations Channel 7 and 9, doing variety shows and the *In Town Tonight* shows. Lorne had night-club bookings, too, so there was a lot happening. Most of her appearances were on Thursdays, Fridays and Saturdays, leaving ample time off. On many of her free days we would visit Winifred Atwell, one of Lorne's oldest and dearest friends. Winnie had been a great honky-tonk piano player, one of impresario Val Parnell's biggest stars. In fact, all the way through the Fifties she was never off British television. When I met her she had semi-retired with her husband, Lou Levinsohn, to Australia, a country she loved.

For me there was a lot of nostalgia attached to meeting Winifred Atwell because my beloved Auntie Ethel had been a great fan of hers. I remembered growing up as a lad and watching television, seeing Winifred on *Saturday Night at the London Palladium*. To meet her and become a friend was a very nice experience. She and Lou had a large apartment by the shore where we would stay for the weekends after Lorne had finished work. While Lorne and Winnie caught up on the latest news, Lou and I would go off to a local bar and have a few beers, chew the fat and have a laugh. Lou was a great character, a real old Yiddish boy who loved a bit of horse racing. In the bar he'd put a few bets on and watch the action on the telly. Round about two o'clock the call would come to the phone behind the bar, telling us to go back for lunch, and the barman would grin and pretend to look around.

'Is Lou still here?'

Winnie was warmly thought of in Australia and still played publicly there. We would often go and see her shows. She, and then Lou, died in the late Eighties, but I can still visualize that wonderful smile, the red lipstick she always wore, the white teeth, the bright eyes, playing Scott Joplin-style and boogie-woogie on her honky-tonk piano.

One club that Lorne was booked into was South Sydney Junior. Matt Munro had been booked for the week before. Lorne, Winnie, Lou and I went to Matt's last night. We went to the dressing room before the show, had a drink and chatted. It soon became apparent that it was Winnie who had given Matt his first big break. He had been a bus driver and after he went on one of her television shows he was an instant hit. (In fact, it's said she even influenced John Lennon, Elton John and many more of the younger generation of stars with her boogie-woogie-style piano. Elton has said that every time he sits down to play Winnie is there with her broad smile.)

After a drink, Matt stood up – he was just a smallish fellow – and said, 'Time to go.'

He walked out into the single spotlight, sat quietly on a stool with no other props, and that most memorable voice singing 'Born Free' filled the room.

Christmas was a good time to be in Sydney. Many of the big stars were out there at that time of the year: George Shekiris, one of the stars of *West Side*

Story, José Feliciano, riding high with 'Light My Fire', Liza Minnelli, Tom Jones, they all appeared and we dropped in on them all. It's strange how stars away from home are glad to see old friends and faces. They congregate together and exchange some reminiscences, enjoying the craic. For some reason, the night we went to see Mel Tormé, there was a poor crowd. The few who were there gathered together at the front and made a hell of a row while he put on his show – and believe you me, our table and a couple of others more than made up for the lack of an audience. It's a hard thing to see a great star no longer received with quite the same affection as he was in his heyday.

In Sydney we met an extraordinary woman, Del Aldred. She was in her early sixties and had been married to several entrepreneurs. Obviously she was doing rather well because she lived in stylish Vaucluse Road, the Mayfair of Sydney, where she had a Mediterranean-style villa, complete with a swimming pool surrounded by life-sized marble statues. It was quite spectacular. I always saw her as the Rita Hayworth of Sydney society, with her long red hair and very sharp, trim figure. I have to say that her face was a bit weathered with the sun but that is the case with many Australian women. She wore some astonishing diamond brooches and I still remember Lorne's eyes sticking out on stalks at the sight of the full-length chinchilla coat she would wear with casual aplomb, just like a Hollywood movie star.

Del invited us to the Black and White Ball, which we subsequently attended regularly for years. All Australian society could be found at that gala. Everyone, from Prime Minister Bill McMahon and his wife, Sylvia, to the entire cabinet used to dress up and mime to records in a kind of upmarket karaoke. The first year we went, Del came dressed as Auntie Mame. She mimed to a record of 'Hello Dolly', in front of the 25 male dancers in top hat and tails she had hired, wearing her notorious full-length chinchilla. As a climax to the song she slipped out of her coat and stood there, apparently naked. There was a bit of a gasp then the whole crowd roared, getting to their feet and cheering wildly. In fact, she was in a flesh-coloured body stocking, but it was very effectively done, thanks to the lighting.

Through the agency, NTL, we were booked into an apartment in a huge mansion in Buckhurst Avenue at Point Piper. This was an exclusive area where you needed a key to get onto the private beach from the garden. Many of the high rollers of Sydney lived there and used this beach, from the Rupert Murdochs to the Kerry Packers and the odd retired prime minister. Just along the coast was Double Bay, another very posh area, about which it was said, 'Double Bay – Double Pay.'

I say we rented the apartment but in fact we were 'allowed' to rent it for three months or so at a time by the owner, an eccentric and vastly wealthy woman. I'm sure she wasn't doing it for the money, though I could never quite work out what her reason was. Our apartment was beautifully furnished, with a silver tea service and the finest china and linen, and stuffed full of antiques. She told us that her father used to have this 'bloody smallholding'.

'Oh yes,' I said politely. 'What's a smallholding over here?'

'Bloody 80,000 acres,' she said. 'Bloody small, really.'

They had struck all kinds of minerals on this smallholding and money flowed like water after that. It was astonishing how much wealth there was along that stretch of coast.

Lorne and I continued to move between Sydney and Melbourne, crossing the paths of many performers on Graham Kennedy's *In Town Tonight*, like Lovelace Watkins, as well as meeting Paul Hogan in his own TV show. We had met Paul for the first time at Wrest Point Casino when he was just starting out, long before *Crocodile Dundee* made him an international movie star. He had been a painter on the Sydney Harbour Bridge when he was spotted on a talent show. He was typically Aussie 'g'day mate', with a laconic, laid-back sense of humour that I enjoyed. Wrest Point Casino was in Hobart, Tasmania, a new venue that had just opened. Lorne was booked to appear in the second week. As always, she spent the first week rehearsing, while the previous star finished his run. In this case, it was Jerry Lewis, I think, who had opened the casino. Apparently he hadn't been the great success expected. I think the trouble was that people would come along expecting to see the gangling crazy kid from Martin and Lewis films and instead they got a very sophisticated performance from a multi-talented man in a dinner jacket who sang, played instruments and danced. If anything, it was too slick, too Vegas, and not at all what they wanted. It had not gone down at all well and the management told us that he'd gone backstage afterwards and smashed some stuff. In complete contrast, they loved Lorne and gave her standing ovations night after night. It just goes to show that however big you are, the audience are in control. If they don't like you, they'll let you know in no uncertain terms.

My experience of seeing Marlene Dietrich in action in one of her last performances showed me just how much audiences know what they like. But the star has to recognize this and use a fair bit of psychology to get that rapport going. This is what makes them stars and keeps them up there long past the sell-by dates of their contemporaries. In 1974 Lorne was doing her usual month's stint at Tito's in Majorca when word came from the management that they had secured a coup: the legendary Marlene Dietrich had agreed to appear in the middle of the following week. After many years she had come out of retirement and was back on the international circuit, doing dates in Paris and Berlin before her adoring public – and she was coming to Tito's! Would Lorne mind very much if she had a week off, and would she very kindly vacate her dressing room for the great lady? Naturally, they said, we would see Dietrich's show as their guests.

Years before, when Lorne had recorded in Germany for Deutsche Grammophon, she had met Dietrich at a gala concert and was looking forward to seeing her again. On the afternoon of Dietrich's first day at Tito's we went along to watch rehearsals, hoping to meet her. The word came, 'Not this time.' But she would be delighted to meet us that evening before the show. We watched the rehearsals. Dietrich was in full flow, with the same orchestra that Lorne used, but with her own musical director. For many years she had used Burt Bacharach as her MD, now she had this other man, who also conducted the orchestra. That day she didn't sing but spoke into the microphone to test its values. Apparently she had had a recent operation for cataracts and was still receiving treatment. Today many theatres have electric stage lights but in those days they used carbide lanterns, which emit a very powerful glare. This is dampened down by sliding in various coloured gel frames. Dietrich had brought along her own particularly flattering gel. The lighting box at Tito's had some powerful carbide light cannons that were all too evident as the operator slid out the old frame and slid in the new one – forgetting that he still had the carbide lights on full glare. The bright light hit Dietrich full in the face.

She stopped dead, pointed and shouted like a machine-gun spitting out bullets: 'Stop that!'

This outburst gave the lighting man such a shock that the big round ring of spotlights started to shake furiously, the lights splaying all over the place, as he tried in his nervous haste to insert the proper gel. The poor guy was replaced.

The schedule for that evening was some Spanish dancers first, then Dietrich at nine o'clock prompt. A little beforehand we went to have a drink at the backstage bar.

I spoke to a member of the staff and 30 minutes later Dietrich's personal assistant came up to us and said, 'Miss Dietrich will see you.'

We were walking along to her dressing room – Lorne's room for the season that she had been pleased to give up temporarily – when Dietrich walked out and stood in the corridor. She must have been in her seventies yet she looked amazing. She was already dressed for the stage in that famous gown with netting from wrist right through shoulders and chest. Her waist was well pulled in, her figure waspy, from corseted bosom, to tight waist, to the classic line of her hips and legs. She looked like the Dietrich I remembered from *The Blue Angel*, with those slightly hooded, lazy-looking eyes, those high cheekbones, the smooth blonde Marcel waves clinging close to the skull.

She had that legendary look, her hands on her hips, her head slightly tilted to one side, that brought shivers to my spine. To be looking at that icon in person was indescribable. It was like watching all her movies. She was very pleasant. She knew Lorne was starring there and had vacated the No 1 dressing room, and thanked her. Lorne mentioned that they'd been introduced at the gala for Deutsche Grammophon. Dietrich smiled.

'I remember,' she said. 'I have heard good things about you. They say you have a wonderful voice, Lorne.'

I stood quietly in the background and I'm afraid I stared. When you meet a legend, whether it's a Dietrich or a Sinatra, you do look closely. After she had returned to her dressing room we went back to the backstage bar and waited, along with many others, for her to come out again. I have an idea we were all going to clap her progress as if she were royalty, which, of course, she was in that world. Nine o'clock came and went. She didn't appear. I asked the musicians. They didn't know what was happening. I wondered if she was ill, or not going to show at all. What I didn't realize at the time was that this was just one of her normal ploys to keep people waiting and guessing. The anxiety level always rises. The owner of the club wandered about distractedly, perspiring profusely. The musical director's dinner suit was soaked through. They all knew how temperamental she could be. She was known to change her mind, she wouldn't do this, she wouldn't do that. Tension built, sweat continued to soak the clothes of those with a big stake in this show.

This atmosphere permeated out into the audience, a room packed full of people of all different ages. Many looked to be of her generation but others were quite young. There were elderly Germans, perhaps thinking nostalgically of the war years. But there were also young people who would know the name and the legend but would not allow that to cloud their judgement. They were there to say, 'Come on, let's see what the great Dietrich can do. Let's see if you're any good.' If the show hadn't been to their liking they would have shown their displeasure – as an Australian audience had with Jerry Lewis back in Tasmania.

By now Dietrich was 30 or 45 minutes late. More time passed. Word came that she was almost ready so we left the bar and went and sat in the auditorium. Lorne and I were right at the front, by the wings. Suddenly the lights went down, the MD stood up. The orchestra struck up with the Marlene Dietrich overture, which consisted of combined segments of her great classics. This normally lasted for eight minutes. There was a crescendo, a climax. The MD was still standing at the piano, playing. A spotlight swivelled on him.

'Ladies and gentlemen – Marlene!' he announced.

The spotlight swung quickly to the wings, making a circle of light on the stage. No Marlene.

Immediately the MD struck up with the overture all over again for the full eight minutes. Again the spotlight, again the announcement.

'Ladies and gentlemen – Marlene!'

The MD was like a rabbit frozen in the headlights of a car.

The lights swung to the wings again; everyone held their combined breaths. I could feel the tension. And this time Dietrich came out into the pool of light. Following some previous instruction, the cannon of footlights came up and into the room. Everything was lit. She walked to the front and stopped. There was a deathly hush.

'What the hell now!' I thought, wondering if she was going to announce that she wouldn't perform, she was dissatisfied and was leaving.

She stared at everyone. That stance, head slightly to one side, hands on hips. She stared for a long moment. Suddenly the applause began. It started centre front, then along the rows, then rippled to the back of the large room. She walked very catlike along the edge of the stage, looking out into the auditorium, nodding, smiling slightly. The applause grew louder and louder. It spread throughout every inch of the room, the entire nightclub – you felt it might be spreading throughout the entire island. She had pulled it out of everyone by sheer charisma and strength of will. It was an incredible performance.

Eventually she stopped in the centre of the stage, held out her hand and it was like a Mexican wave from front to back. I've never seen anything like it in my life. We were all hypnotized as we rose to our feet. When our fever was at its height she did that little flick of her hair off her face and walked straight off again, right through the wings.

'Bloody hell,' I thought, 'She's gone!' Moments later, while we collapsed, almost drained, she picked up a microphone, walked back on and started with one of those legendary songs: 'Falling in Love Again'. Her craft and timing were quite remarkable.

Through her repertoire of all the great songs the older members of the audience were shouting, screaming and banging. Even the youngsters were overawed by the legend. Her vocal ability was limited but her presence, her timing – the magic of that great superstar was something I had never seen before, or since. It was a show I will never forget. I've heard people talk of timing, and commanding or manipulating an audience, of having them in the palm of your hand, but I've never seen anyone who could do that with more consummate skill than Marlene Dietrich.

She knew what her audience wanted and she gave it to them. In a way that's where Jerry Lewis, a hero of my childhood, went wrong. He didn't understand that an Australian audience is not a Las Vegas one. The following year, when Lorne was again in Australia, Dietrich was also appearing in Sydney. She slipped off the stage on 29 September 1975 and broke her hip. After that she went into her final retirement and never came out again, so we saw one of the very last performances by this legendary woman.

CHAPTER TEN

Lorne and I had always got on well with the general manager at the Wrest Point Casino in Tasmania but I was still quite surprised when he telephoned me out of the blue one June or July to say that he had been head-hunted. He was now working in Indonesia, as general manager of the Borobudur, a grand hotel in Jakarta.

'David, I hope I've caught you before you have accepted any bookings for Lorne for the New Year,' he said.

I quickly checked the diary, and although some things had been pencilled in nothing was confirmed. He sounded pleased.

'Good. Look, we're having this spectacular New Year's ball for the generals here in Jakarta. There will be a cabaret and we'd like Lorne to be the guest star.'

I was aware that he was talking about Suharto and the ruling junta who were running the country. I wasn't sure how wise it would be to go to suharto at a time of political unrest, but he assured me that all was well in that direction, and since he was a decent chap and we had never been to Indonesia, I said, 'Certainly, we'll consider it.'

He asked our requirements. When I gave him the figure for Lorne's fee he gulped.

Before he had time to recover, I added, 'And two first-class air tickets out to Jakarta; we will expect to be met at the airport, the best accommodation and an 18-piece orchestra.'

I told him the musical configuration Lorne required and checked on the amplification system. You were never sure what hotels had by way of stage equipment and I always covered this ground so they could hire the necessary stuff. We agreed everything, then he asked if we would like to go before the New Year bash as his guests over the Christmas period.

When Lorne and I flew out I had no idea it would be to a shadowy world of espionage, prawns and pineapples. At first it was exactly as we had anticipated. As always we got first-class treatment all the way, from being met at the airport to being ushered into the most magnificent oriental-style suite. The country was beautiful, a lush wonderland of richly perfumed flowering vines, colourful birds and all the smells and sounds of the tropics, with cicadas by day and frogs by night busy filling the air with their buzzing, sawing and croaking. There is something about the tropics that appeals to the senses. Like dark chocolate, it is something rich and smooth, and captivates you. Of course, it's always nice to spend Christmas at home with jingle bells, robins and snow and all the other traditional things that you look forward to but, having already spent so many Christmases in an Australian summer, we were used to experiencing it in a different, perhaps more exotic way.

Over Christmas our friend the hotel manager had laid on many private functions to which we were invited. He introduced us to a wide cross-section of business associates and friends either living or staying in Jakarta itself. Some of these were very interesting people and at first I took them to be just ordinary international businessmen. Gradually I came to see that not all of them were as they seemed. One, an elderly man of perhaps 70, originally a Canadian, was now based in Hong Kong, working for the Hong Kong and Shanghai Bank. He was the only western, non-Asian director of the bank. I learned that he was on a business trip to Jakarta, arranging huge loans for the ruling junta. At these cocktail parties and dinners I also met many Australians who were in construction in a big way. They had some enormous contracts, worth billions, with the military regime to build dams, bridges and roads. It was then that the penny dropped. The banking man was setting up the loans to pay for the construction. This was a very big boys' club indeed. Everyone was so chummy, so open, as only this kind of expatriate can be, that we became very close friends with them.

At one cocktail party I was introduced to an Australian, the head of the Southeast Asia branch of Cathay Pacific, part of Qantas. I also met the American president of an airline charter company. He was a tough-looking individual with a half-inch crew-cut and an impressive scar, the type of man who could chop wood with his bare hands. I believe he was a top CIA man and for the purposes of discretion we'll call him E.D. He was surrounded by quite a few clones, younger guys in T-shirts, with rippling muscles, all very tough, fit men, who looked as if they had seen a lot of action in various hotspots of the world. I know it sounds a bit fanciful, a bit James Bond, but I think many of the men I met at the Borobudur Hotel were involved in the CIA. You read about men like E.D. being last in and out of Vietnam but in his case this actually happened. His was famously the last aircraft out of Da Nang.

My memory was jolted when some time later I saw Reuters' newsreel footage of the rushed withdrawal by the Americans from South Vietnam. E.D. was flying the aircraft when they evacuated Saigon as the Vietcong were pouring into the South. A military chopper pulled the last US civilians and military off the American embassy roof and flew them to waiting planes. The last plane of all had been rushed by a group of South Vietnamese soldiers, desperate to get on before the Vietcong arrived. There was a picture of my new friend standing on the steps, holding back some of the soldiers while he gave the word to take off. They did so, with the runaway steps still in position. As the plane started to taxi, the steps fell away, the door was closed, and off they went, all very touch and go. This was the 'Orphan Flight', when E.D. rescued 57 children, for whom he took personal responsibility. Oddly enough, when he arrived on American soil they tried to fine him $218,000 for violating immigration rules.

What E.D. and the others were doing in Jakarta I do not know. There were a lot of undercover operations going on concerning East Timor at the time and perhaps there still are. The Borobudur Hotel was also the meeting place of quite a few international journalists and it was one of them, perhaps after too many cocktails, who told me that E.D. was a high-ranking CIA officer. It was all very much a new world for me to get involved in, if merely on the fringes looking in, and I have to say I was hooked. It was the kind of thing you read about or see in films. What made it even stranger was that they were all so close and chummy. I don't know whether there was a kind of Christmas spirit in the air and they would all be different afterwards. I don't think so. I think in Jakarta at that time there was a melting pot of spies and espionage, like the mixture seen in the film *The Year of Living Dangerously*. It was very much spy versus spy.

All of this was very eye-opening. One day the hotel manager took us to a barbecue brunch hosted by one of the Australian construction men. He was renting a 'little bungalow' from the junta, about three hours' drive from Jakarta, up in the hills. We set off in a convoy of cars, and after a long climb through some pretty spectacular scenery a sumptuous traditional building emerged through the trees. This 'little bungalow' turned out to be the old summer palace that had once belonged to Sukarno, Indonesia's former president.

As we were welcomed and shown around, I murmured to Lorne, 'I can't imagine what he is paying for this extravaganza.'

I thought the house and grounds must be part and parcel of a deal cut with the military government. Much of the life I saw seemed to operate on fringe benefits that sweetened deals and oiled the wheels.

We saw the Australian construction man and, indeed, most of the others in this fascinating group of expatriates, most days, at the social events we were invited to. He was in his fifties, with a glamorous wife, a kind of Zsa Zsa Gabor complete with the Hungarian accent. It was always 'Darlink, how are you?' I have to say she was charming and fun. The Aussie took a real liking to me and we would talk for many hours. Eventually he was to tell me that he owed the magnificent palace and its contents to a senior general, whose son was losing his sight. The general had approached him at his wit's end. He had most luxuries that life at the top could supply but he couldn't help his son. The doctors needed to replace the corneas to save the boy's eyes but for some reason they were unable to get any in Indonesia. My new chum arranged it all at his own expense. The corneas were sent on ice from Australia on Qantas. They were met by military escort and rushed to the hospital, where an operation was undertaken to restore the young boy's sight. As far as I know, it was a great success. In turn, the general had given the Australian this incredible house to use for the duration of his stay in Indonesia.

We'd often go there for lunch or dinner. The house was so full of oriental antiques and beautiful works of art that each time something different would catch my eye. There was porcelain, lacquer and much else, including a collection of very early Balinese hand puppets of the kind that are used in shadow theatre. There were specimens from different centuries, museum-quality items in fabulous condition all given to the Australian as a mark of thanks by the general whose young son he had helped.

Dinner was usually served on the patio near the swimming pool. At the end of the pool was a huge aviary. There were no birds in it, however; it was occupied by a huge orang-utan. These large hairy orange apes, the closest to humans in intelligence, are now protected. At that time there wasn't today's awareness that having them as pets isn't very kind – although this one seemed to be well looked after and appeared happy enough. It was put in the cage when guests came, so as not to upset it or alarm them, but usually it was allowed to roam free and would wander around the pool happily holding the Australian's hand. Highly intelligent, like the one Clint Eastwood befriended in *Every Which Way But Loose*, the orang-utan would come to the table and sit on a chair next to us, being fed on fruit.

One day, as we talked, the Australian asked almost casually, 'Have you ever considered living out here, David?'

I thought about the question seriously. Lorne and I had been to many beautiful places and sometimes we had wondered what it would have been like, living there permanently. At the end of the day, though, we had always considered England was our home.

I shook my head and replied, 'Not really. Lorne works on an international level, of course, but –'

I broke off, again mentally summing up all the reasons why we didn't want to live there, or anywhere else.

The Australian said, 'My wife and I really like you and Lorne. I have a substantial business here –'

I knew he was talking billions of dollars.

'Why don't you come out here and work for me?' he continued. 'You're an exceptionally bright young man with a good head for business. I'll teach you all I know about the construction business.'

'It's a specialist field,' I countered.

'Yes, perhaps, but the business side is much like any other business.'

I nodded in agreement. That was my opinion exactly. Businesses are very much the same in principle the world over. I knew that the chairmen of massive conglomerates hopped from one type to another with no obvious ill effect. Many of them floated between textiles and banking, from telecommunications to motor cars; all business seemed to be the same at a certain level.

He mused, 'My wife and I have no kids, no one to leave it to. I will retire to Australia in, say, five to eight years' time, and when that happens, all this will cease. I can offer you a very substantial salary and bonuses, with the business itself at the end of the day.'

It was an astonishing offer. I said I would think about it. Lorne and I did seriously discuss it. We considered what it would be like living there with the children. In the end, though, we couldn't think of a good enough reason to accept the offer and I turned it down.

The night of the New Year's Eve ball came around. All the major military figures and bigwigs were there. Suharto himself was not, but he had not been expected. In the interval between dancing we were called to the buffet. I have seen many buffets in many five-star hotels over the years but I have never seen anything quite as lavish as this. The centrepiece was an enormous ice tableau, carved into a fantastical seascape. Laid out in it were hundreds of lobsters and other sea creatures used as decoration. Frozen oysters flown in from Sydney, prawns of all shapes and sizes – blue, red, striped – many with tails as big as lobsters. There was conch meat in scallop shells, fish of all varieties from snapper to swordfish, some baked in salt, some fried in black bean sauce, cooked in every way imaginable.

At another long table there were cooked meats of all descriptions except pork, since this was a Muslim country. Chickens and wildfowl were being roasted over spits by uniformed chefs on the open terrace. The desserts were a glutton's dream, with every sweet indulgence known to man. This table looked like half a mile of Carmen Miranda's headgear, piled high with tropical fruits – pineapples, small sweet bananas, papayas, guavas, lychees, mangoes – plus cakes, pastries, jellies and ices. Such an abundance of food I had never seen before. So often you go to these kinds of event and you will see a cluster of people ransacking the solitary table holding a few lobster tails or prawns or vol-au-vents. The table will be stripped barer than a field of corn hit by locusts before you can get there. But here, men in full military uniform and women in traditional costume or couture evening dresses were going along in an orderly, polite fashion, taking a small portion, then walking away.

We were seated at tables decorated with flowers and at about eleven o'clock the entertainment started with a local band and traditional dancers. Lorne was announced. Away she went. At the end there was a standing ovation and rousing cheers. People took the flowers off their tables and tossed them towards the stage. Lorne ended up ankle-deep in flowers, laughing and holding out her arms. It was a scene I will never forget.

The hotel manager had become so attached to us that he asked us to stay on. A couple of days later we were still there, eating dinner in one of the restaurants, when we were approached by a middle-aged American woman, perhaps in her forties. She sat down next to Lorne and launched somewhat excitedly into a speech about how much she had enjoyed the cabaret. She had a Southern accent, which was a little hard to understand. I was eating and took little notice.

After she had exhausted her congratulations, she asked, 'Do you mind if I join you for a little chat?'

'Not at all,' said Lorne politely.

It seemed to me that the woman had already joined us but I said nothing. After a while I noticed that the chit-chat had changed in tone. It became quite astonishing. The woman was saying that she was an American citizen, that she had been brought here somewhat against her will by the security services. She was being looked after by the CIA. I glanced at Lorne as if to say, 'What the hell is she talking about? She is obviously a crackpot.' However, she wasn't drunk. I started to listen in earnest. She continued, telling us that she had been in the hotel for some time, everything was provided for her, she didn't have to lift a finger – but the only thing she couldn't do was return home.

As I heard this tale developing, it sounded like a work of fiction, though the detail she provided almost artlessly seemed quite convincing. She was, she said, somehow connected to J Edgar Hoover, though I could have got this wrong since I hadn't been listening from the start. According to her, she had been in Hoover's home when she was privy to a most unusual gathering of all types of powerful big shots. She had overheard a conversation between Hoover and some senior political or military figures and major industrialists. She mentioned no names, although she assured us they were heavyweights who were discussing the assassination of Bobby Kennedy.

Something about her story suddenly seemed to have the ring of truth. The hair started to stand up on the back of my neck. I thought, 'Hang on a minute here, Dickie! We shouldn't be getting involved in any of this. If there's a grain of truth in it we could be listening to something extremely dangerous.' I knew that the hotel was full of the CIA; were any of them her minders? My eyes were scanning the room. It was reasonably full. Were there any burly crew-cuts nearby? What about those three Mr Muscles at the table nearby? Maybe she was being looked after by Indonesian security. Hell, we could meet with an accident. This was Jakarta – who would be any the wiser?

Standing up, I said, 'We have to be going.'

Lorne was engrossed in the conversation and I had to drag her away. Common sense told me that this tale was a load of baloney. But strange things can and do happen in the shadowy world of politics. J. Edgar Hoover was the head of the FBI and as such, for a while, was the most powerful man in America. It was said he was more powerful than the president, even. He was also one of the most secretive men in the United States. For such a public figure, little was known about him at that time. Any number of people could have been connected to him as the woman we had met in such strange circumstances in Jakarta claimed to be. Could there be a grain of truth in her story? We will never know.

CHAPTER ELEVEN

Through a British agent who had been established in America for 20 years, I was able to help Lorne achieve that pinnacle of success in the cabaret world: Las Vegas. She would go on to appear many times in the gambling city that had been built from almost nothing out of a small silver-mining town in the Nevada desert by visionary mobster Bugsy Siegel.

The main show rooms of Las Vegas were reserved for superstars like Sinatra, Dean Martin and Elvis Presley. The casino-hotels like the Sands were so huge that in order to accommodate all their customers who might already have seen the main show – or who perhaps hadn't been able to obtain tickets but still sought entertainment – special side rooms were constructed that were designed like theatres. It was in these that Lorne would appear. She always found these bookings very stimulating and exciting. She in turn won admirers who had connections we weren't fully aware of at the time.

Our Las Vegas contact also booked Lorne to appear at El-Casino, a huge purpose-built gambling and entertainment complex on Grand Bahama. It was a particularly magnificent casino-hotel, resembling a Moorish palace. After that first time she would often top the bill there. She wasn't used to the way things worked, though, and this did cause some tension. The casino operators used to time all the rehearsals with military precision. At first Lorne didn't understand why but she quickly found out. The bosses liked to have the shows in their casino, but they never wanted them to overrun the allocated 60 minutes. The first 30 minutes would consist of supporting vaudeville acts, like comedians, dancers and jugglers, who would whip through their repertoires like greyhounds out of traps. Then the star would appear, with a very tight set of 30 minutes precisely. It allowed little scope for Lorne's usual friendly banter and the chatty introductions she incorporated into her act to put the audience at ease and create a rapport.

The casino manager told me that time and motion studies had shown that when 2,500–3,000 people were kept away from the gaming tables it cost the establishment around $20,000 per minute in lost revenue. And it wasn't only a question of the 60 minutes the gamblers spent watching the show; it was also the time it took to get such a large number of people in and out of the theatre – with those vast profits slipping away by the second.

As Lorne and I spent more time in the Bahamas over the years I came to learn more about the background of these lavish casinos. It was rumoured that when the Mob's gambling interests were closed down in Cuba by Castro after Batista was overthrown they looked for other areas for a lucrative offshore gambling haven. The boys in Las Vegas backed Lynden Oscar Pindling, who headed the opposition Progressive Liberal Party, to win the election in the Bahamas, and when the government changed hands in 1967, with Pindling in control, the gaming concession was given to the Bahama Amusements Co., which was controlled by Meyer Lanksy, one of the top financial men behind organized crime in America. The connection was so blatant that even in 1967 the newspapers and magazines were publishing headlines such as 'Gambling in the Bahamas: the Mafia at work' above photos of Lansky together with the Bahamian casino bosses and leading politicians.

P.J., the manager in charge of theatre seating at El-Casino, was quite chatty and would tell us some surprising things. He had previously been the restaurant manager of the Lacayan Beach Hotel, which was the other main casino-hotel on Grand Bahama. This had been built before Pindling's election to power and it had a huge room that didn't seem to have any particular use. As soon as Pindling was voted in, this room was cleared overnight and was instantly equipped with all the paraphernalia of gambling, with roulette wheels, craps tables, bars and so on. It had all been waiting in storage for the green light. P.J. smiled as he came to the end of this story.

'It helped that Lynden Pindling was chairman of the State Hotel Commission,' he said.

All the casino bosses and the big 'families' flew in for the opening night of this casino, which been so magically conjured up – men like Lansky, Lucky Luciano, Frank 'Lefty' Rosenthall – the 'wise guys', as P.J. called them.

'We had a huge number of seatings for dinner,' he told us. 'There were so many guests we had to have three sittings. It was very hard work.'

After dinner, when the crowd was in the casino, one of the 'wise guys' came in and clapped his hands to get everyone's attention.

He ordered a tablecloth to be placed on the floor and said, 'Ladies and gentlemen, your attention please. I want you to show your appreciation of P.J. You know what to do –'

Everyone clapped, then a shower of gambling chips hit the tablecloth. P.J. said they were worth $6,800 – a great deal of money in 1967 and a massive tip for him.

It was openly said that the Mafia owned two Bahamian islands, one of which was used as a US Navy submarine-testing base. It was also alleged that 90 per cent of the cocaine entering the States passed through Norman's Cay. Pindling allowed all this, and much else besides. All of this was very embarrassing to the American government.

It so happened that our contracts were with the Grand Bahama Company but despite P.J.'s chatty information I was too naive to appreciate the link. When we visited we always found it an exciting, razzmatazz place but we were never fully aware of the Godfather connection. To be honest, I don't think I was even aware in the Seventies that the Mob existed as such a huge and powerful entity. Not many people in Europe were. It was quite a secret organization and since it controlled quite a lot of Hollywood through major studios, making films about organized crime was taboo. I can't think of a single film about the Mob until a lot later on, when unsanitized films like *The Godfather*, *The Untouchables* and *Casino* were made. I had seen Lefty Rosenthall in Las Vegas but it wasn't until I saw him portrayed by Robert de Niro in *Casino* that the penny dropped.

Lefty is the man known as 'Chicago-born and casino bred' and that just about sums him up. He's the man who sets the odds for thousands of book-makers from coast to coast in the US. When I saw him he was running four Las Vegas casinos and one hotel simultaneously, including the Stardust.

On one memorable occasion Lorne and I went to Las Vegas to relax, not to work. We had been to Los Angeles to look at some potential television business, intending to fly straight home, when our long-time Vegas pal invited us over as his guests.

'You'll love this,' he said, 'Ginger Rogers is doing a show. I'll get you guys tickets.'

Of course, we couldn't resist seeing the legendary hoofer. We had always been fans of her dancing and sense of humour, and loved all her movies, particularly those with her regular dancing partner, Fred Astaire. She had been retired for some years and had only recently put a cabaret show together. This was a wonderful opportunity not to be missed.

We duly flew in and drove to our hotel on the Strip. All the big casino-hotels had huge billboards which showed who was appearing where. In those years it was Presley, Sinatra and Wayne Newton, with Tom Jones and Engelbert Humperdinck from across the pond. Then we spotted the billboard announcing Ginger Rogers. It was a thrilling moment to catch sight of those famous legs, that strawberry-blonde hair. Our pal had already called us to say that he'd managed to get us tickets for the supper show, which was just drinks.

'It's Ginger's opening night in Vegas,' he explained. 'Everyone's buzzing. The dinner show was sold out in a New York minute.'

After changing our clothes we joined our friend and had something to eat. Later we went down to the hotel where Ginger Rogers was appearing. It was one of the early original hotels there, a solid old-fashioned place from the days of Bugsy Siegel and Meyer Lansky, down at the end of the Strip. The dinner show was not yet turned out so we went to kill time in one of the lounge areas. These were like small theatres, often used for entertainment, the kind of room in which Lorne would sometimes sing when she was herself appearing in Las Vegas.

As we found seats and ordered a drink Lorne looked around and commented, 'It's strange to be at this end of the room for a change.'

We had been there for about 15 minutes when the music started. Suddenly I became aware of four huge men, Italian-looking, olive-skinned, dark-haired, in dark suits and dark glasses, walking around the room and glancing at people. They eyeballed me and I stared back.

I was about to say, 'Excuse me, do you mind – ?' when our host touched my arm and gave me a warning 'Sshh!'

'Cool it, David,' he muttered out of the corner of his mouth.

When they had moved on, he said, 'They were looking to see if there's anyone here they recognize.'

I said, 'What do you mean?'

He smiled slightly and said, 'Wait.'

The men left the room, but briefly. Within moments they returned, completely surrounding two elderly, quite insignificant Italian men and their wives. After another glance at me, they sat at an adjoining table. Soon, celebrities started arriving for the main show. I recognized some elderly Hollywood movie stars. Then Richard Burton came in with an entourage of people. It was amazing to see him in the flesh. He was no longer with Elizabeth Taylor (they were divorced for the second time by then) but was married to Sally Hunt, ex-wife of the racing driver James Hunt. Burton was in his early forties at the time, in his heyday of drinking, not stumbling but you could still tell he was a heavy drinker.

At the front, the show started. A man came on and introduced himself. He was the Sicilian singer Sonny King. Well known as a friend of Sinatra's, he had appeared in cameo roles in such films as *Robin and the Seven Hoods*. He started to sing in Italian in a quite unique way. The *Godfather* films hadn't yet been made, but when they were some of the singing in them, particularly when an old man gets up and sings at a wedding, immediately brought this man in Las Vegas to mind. I didn't understand the words Sonny King was singing but according to our host they were on the dirty side.

'Don't worry, David,' he said. 'You either understand them or you don't. There's lots of Italian speakers don't understand this Sicilian lingo.'

Quite a few people in the room obviously understood and enjoyed every last innuendo. They were rolling around with laughter, particularly the two elderly men and their wives who were sitting nearby.

When Sonny had finished his first few numbers, he said, 'Thank you very much indeed. There are lots of celebrities here this evening. Can I introduce you to some of them – ?'

A small spot moved around the room.

'Donald O'Connor... Richard Burton... '

There was a lot of clapping and Burton went on stage and did a small recitation from Shakespeare. He was quite charismatic. When he had finished and returned to his table, Sonny introduced several of the Vegas bookers, names you would normally recognize from seeing them over the tops of the huge billboards on the Strip. Then he gave a name out in a respectful way and looked straight at the table next to us. One of the elderly men stood up. There was a ripple of applause. I turned to our host.

'What's that all about?' I asked.

Again he hushed me: 'Don't raise your voice, David.'

He gave me their names later. All of them were senior Godfather figures from Chicago and Detroit. Perhaps I shouldn't have been so fascinated to have been in the proximity of such men – but I have to say I was.

For the supper show in the main theatre we were in a good position three or four rows back. The best seats were the front rows of deep-buttoned leather alcove-type seating, reserved for mostly elderly men with big cigars.

Our host leaned close and whispered, 'This is a sight you will very rarely see.'

Old Mafia types had come into town just to see and support their old friend Ginger. I was told that she had been a favourite of the Mob since the days when she had worked for the old-style RKO studios, which had been owned by organized crime.

The show Ginger put on was spectacular, extremely well choreographed, and she herself was amazing. For someone in her sixties she was vibrant. Her athletic young male dancers worked hard, running about the stage, picking her up, passing her from one to another.

Men in the front seats were calling out, 'How ya doin', Ginger?' and she in turn was coming to the front: 'Nice to see ya, Louie – Giovanni, good to see ya.'

In a strange way it was very intimate, very friendly. I felt as if I were looking in on a bit of history that I knew I would never see again.

Not all the hoods were in America. A rather frightening engagement was booked for Lorne through London Management to top the bill in a nightclub in Tehran, Persia, as it was called then – now it's Iran.

On the face of it there should have been no problem. It was a solid Equity contract, the usual deposit was paid and guarantees made and, although it was a new club, a few big stars had been booked as well as Lorne, names like Demis Roussos and Lulu, for whom guarantees and deposits had also been lodged in a London bank. Lorne was to be the first, the others were to follow on.

We agreed the usual fee, first-class air tickets were provided, the best hotel suite booked, all was in order. We arrived in Tehran, were looked after well, and went on to meet one of the owners of the club, Mahmoud Ghorbani. All seemed fine. Mahmoud seemed a nice, personable young man who spoke good

English. I learned that he had recently been divorced from Googoosh, one of Iran's most famous singers, the pop diva who had introduced the miniskirt to the country. From the Middle East to Turkey, and beyond to Russia, she was considered as iconic as Elvis Presley.

Mahmoud Ghorbani's connections seemed impressive but what we didn't know was that he was quite infamous in Persia.

It was customary for foreigners to hand in their passports for inspection when they arrived in the country. Mine was returned but Lorne's had to be kept by the club while a work permit was issued. She was booked for two weeks and the arrangement was that she would be paid at the end of the first week. Normally you would be paid up front, but I wasn't concerned at this stage because a bond had been placed in a London bank for all the stars who were to go to the club, then or in the future, against any problems with their contracts.

There were two major Persian singing stars on the same bill at the club: Darius and also Haidi, a massive and charming woman who must have weighed at least 20 stone. Then Lorne came on and wowed the audience, closing to rapturous applause and her usual standing ovation. The Ghorbanis and their associates were delighted.

After a few days Mahmoud asked if we would like to go on to a disco after the show. He told us the place belonged to one of the Shah's relatives (this was before the Shah was deposed in 1979) and it was very trendy.

'Everyone who is everyone goes there,' he assured us.

We said we would love to go another time, not that night. The next day we got a telephone call to say that Mahmoud had been arrested. That's all we were told. Our hotel was some distance from his nightclub, and it wasn't our habit to go in during the day unless there was some work needed on Lorne's show, so we learned nothing more until we went to the club that evening.

The hotel had put a car at our disposal, with a driver, a nice young man, who took us everywhere, to and from the nightclub as well as sightseeing. Tehran had boomed – its population had grown from 200,000 to six million in the last half-century – but the old city was beautiful. In spite of extensive modern development there were still many old palaces to be seen, and parks that resembled the hanging gardens of Babylon, with a range of spectacular snow-capped mountains in the distance. One feature was the wide gutters along which flowed constant fresh water, more so after it rained. As always, we took long walks during the day for exercise and to explore. Often there were some wonderful antiques to be discovered in the little back streets of the cities we stayed in, and Tehran was no exception. With the shop now up and running in Disley, looking and learning was always at the back of my mind.

We were out sightseeing as usual during that day but when we got to the club that evening I went immediately to see the management.

'What has happened with Mahmoud?' I asked.

They told me that apparently Mahmoud's bodyguard had been involved in an affray and everyone had been clapped in jail.

I said, 'We've been here six days so far. Lorne is due to be paid tomorrow, what will happen about that?'

'Mahmoud's brother will pay you,' the manager assured me.

I accepted this at face value, but I'm a cautious sort of bloke. I decided I would take the opportunity to go along to the office to meet the elder brother, known as Mr Ghorbani, and at the same time give him a little reminder about the pay.

I was shown in, introduced myself and said, 'Mr Ghorbani, I'm very sorry to hear there have been some problems.'

He merely grunted. Unlike his brother Mahmoud there was nothing charming about him. I persisted by gently reminding him that Lorne's fee was due to be paid in dollars the next day.

'It will be no problem,' he said, somewhat tersely.

Accordingly, before the show on the following night, I went straight to the office to collect the money and to sign the contract for the second week. There was no little pile of dollar bills waiting on the desk, no one made a move to open the safe, nothing was forthcoming: the cupboard was bare.

Feeling a bit like Mother Hubbard's dog begging for a bone, I said, 'It's not good enough. I don't know how you do business here but this is not how we do it in Europe.'

'My brother has the money. You will get it,' he said.

I said, 'Very well. Lorne will do her show since she's a pro and is already here tonight. But that's it. Unless she is paid tonight, she won't appear tomorrow.'

He nodded. 'Come and see me after the show.'

The show finished at midnight. Leaving Lorne in the dressing room, I said, 'I'm off to see Mr Ghorbani. Get ready to quit if necessary.'

When I entered the office I was faced by Mr Ghorbani seated at the desk. I stepped forward and the hairs rose up on the back of my neck. You get 180-degree vision at moments like that. I felt eyes piercing into me. I glanced sideways. Behind me were eight very dangerous-looking Arabs. One had a glazed look, which made me feel uneasy.

Mr Ghorbani said in a very threatening tone, 'You be here tomorrow.'

I thought, sod this.

To him I said, 'We'll be at the hotel. When the fee is paid, we'll start the second week of the engagement,' and I walked out of the office.

As I was leaving the club, one of the male dancers called me to one side and told me he had heard I'd had words with Mr Ghorbani.

'Watch out,' he warned me. 'He is a powerful man.'

I thanked him for the tip. Lorne and I got into our waiting car and left.

In the early hours I woke from a deep sleep to hear a loud knocking on the door of our suite. I got out of bed, went to the door and listened. On the other side of the door I heard two voices speaking to each other.

I said, 'Yes? Who is it?'

'Police.'

I asked, 'What is it about?'

They said they wanted to see my ID papers. I knew the door was very thick, not to be broken down in a hurry, so I told them to wait. I went to the phone and called down to the front of house desk and asked for the night manager to come up and check this situation out. He came up in the lift, knocked and introduced himself.

Only then did I open the door. There was no one else there. The two men had scarpered. Obviously they had not been the police. The night manager said if they had been bona fide they would have informed the management of any irregularity and invited him to accompany them up to the suite. I didn't like the feel of this at all. I rang the driver at his home and instructed him to come at 7 a.m. sharp.

'What's the problem?' he asked.

He was a perceptive young man, who had turned out to be very useful.

I said, 'We're not safe here.'

Lorne and I got dressed and packed. When our driver arrived I told him to take Lorne and the luggage out to the car as quickly and as carefully as possible while I went to the desk. Our hotel suite had been arranged by the nightclub, and had been paid in advance before things had started to go wrong, so there was no outstanding account to be settled. I got into the waiting car, locked all the doors and we went to the big American Intercontinental Hotel in the centre of Tehran. After we had checked in, I asked to see the general manager, a European, and I explained the situation.

'I'm not surprised,' he said. 'Mahmoud Ghorbani is notorious.'

'We would leave immediately but they have Lorne's passport,' I said. 'Any ideas how I should sort it out?'

He suggested I should see the chief of police to ask his assistance. Before I had a chance to do that, I was contacted by the local agent who booked acts for the club. Using all manner of inducements he tried to persuade us to return.

'It'll be fine, it's just a misunderstanding – ' and so on and so on.

Quite coldly, I said, 'No, the deal's finished.'

All the time I was aware of the holding bond in London so we were covered.

The agent became more threatening. We couldn't leave the country, the contract had not been fulfilled, we were in breach, they'd sue us, they'd have us arrested. I wouldn't wear it and told him he was wasting my time. I went to the police, where I explained what had happened, starting with Mahmoud Ghorbani's arrest and the incident in our hotel suite.

'We want to leave Tehran but they've got my wife's passport,' I said.

The police chief was sympathetic but said he could not intervene in a contractual matter. It was something I would have to sort out myself.

'Will you look into it?' I asked. 'Surely you must know about Mahmoud Ghorbani?'

'Indeed,' he said smoothly.

Back at the hotel I called the club's agent and told him yet again that we wanted Lorne's passport back.

'The police are investigating,' I assured him.

'Let them,' was his unresponsive reply.

This went on for two or three days. By then we were running low on cash. We had credit cards and a chequebook, but I had taken little cash with me because we had been confident of getting a bundle of dollars from the club. I called into one of the big central banks to transfer some funds from England. The manager turned out to be an Armenian. I told him a little of my background, that my family were Armenian traders, well known in the north of England. He was very interested and we talked for a while. He told me that it would be a long-drawn-out process to get the cash transferred. How much did I need?

I said, 'Oh, about £800.'

He said, 'Write me out a cheque for a thousand. I'll be in London in two months to accompany my mother to the London Clinic. I'll cash it then.'

I thought that was a very nice thing to do, for someone you've never met before. It was the Armenian connection that I had unwittingly tapped. (He did come over to London later, cashed the cheque and all was fine. We have spoken on the telephone several times since.)

We now had enough cash to last but, try as I might, I had met with a brick wall where Lorne's passport was concerned. In the end, inspiration struck. After OK'ing it with the hotel manager, I called the chief of police and told him I was going to call a press conference at the Intercontinental. It was where all the international journalists hung out but, just to make sure, I was going to make it formal. It would be attended by the English newspaper fraternity and Reuters. I was going to ask why two bona fide people such as the international cabaret star Lorne Lesley and I could not leave the country.

'We have been virtually kidnapped,' I said. 'It's a strong story and will make the headlines around the world. The only breach of contract here is that they haven't paid us. Now we find out they are people of ill repute. Your country will not come out of this very well.'

'There is no need for such extreme action. Hold fire on the press conference, let me see what I can do,' he said.

'Very well, I will hold off for 24 hours.'

Within 24 hours, he rang.

'Mr Dickinson, I have your wife's passport.'

We took the next plane out. At times it had been a bit frightening but I had stuck firm, kept my head, got Lorne out of the danger zone and back to London – and, as always, got paid.

CHAPTER TWELVE

Before I met her, Lorne had done a lot of recordings in England and in Europe but had never had that major elusive hit. I knew that while she had built a formidable career as a top cabaret star, much in demand around the world, she needed a hit record to make the big time, to become a Liza Minnelli, a Barbra Streisand, a Shirley Bassey. We talked it over and came to the conclusion that while she undoubtedly had the voice, the song was the thing Lorne needed that great song that she could make her own. Such songs are rare and don't come along every day. The ones that make it and last – songs like 'Yesterday' – are called evergreens, or standards. It became my mission to find Lorne a song and a record deal.

As one does in any business I went to consult an expert. Brian O'Donohue was a friend who had started out as an A & R man, head of Buddha Records for Polydor, where he was behind Melanie's massive hit 'Ruby Tuesday' (a Rolling Stones song). From there he went on to EMI at a time when the Beatles were in and out of Abbey Road Studios. He handled Elton John's early records as well as Slade's. From EMI he had been head-hunted by the Stigwood Organization to be head of Europe at a time when RSO was pretty strong. *Saturday Night Fever* had just broken and the Bee Gees were right at the top. RSO also had Olivia Newton-John, Eric Clapton, Andy Gibb and a host of others signed up to them. I wanted to find some good songs, perhaps some Bee Gees material, for Lorne, and so I approached Brian. He suggested I should also ask Mike D'Abo to write something. Mike had been the replacement for Paul Jones in Manfred Mann and had had several hits with them before going solo. He wrote wonderful music, songs like 'Miss Me in the Morning', 'Annabella Cinderella' and 'Handbags and Glad Rags' as well as scoring the Goldie Hawn/Peter Sellers movie *There's a Girl in My Soup*, among other things.

At the time Mike D'Abo was represented by an unconventional young entrepreneur, Tony DeFries, who was a bit of a mystery. A former legal clerk and solicitor's dogsbody, he seemed to have come from nowhere to form his Main-Man company. In fact, he was associated with quite a well-known accountant, Laurence Myers, who handled the financial affairs of Micky Most, the Stones, the Apple Corp, the Animals, Herman's Hermits, David Bowie – the list is almost endless. DeFries set up offices on the corner of Regent Street and Cavendish Place and started to control a large chunk of the pop industry, including the New York Dolls and Mott the Hoople. He adopted David Bowie when Bowie's career was going nowhere in fits and starts and the press had dismissed him as a one-hit wonder because after 'Space Oddity' nothing much was happening for him. In an aggressive Svengali-like way, Tony DeFries became the driving force behind Bowie's rapid move to superstardom by providing stretch limousines, chauffeurs, bodyguards and press conferences at London's top hotels with caviar, champagne and cigars laid on. Bowie wasn't a massive star before that – but he certainly was one after.

In all innocence, not realizing what a tough businessman he was, I went along to see Tony to get permission to use some of Mike D'Abo's songs. Bowie was sitting waiting in the reception area, holding some tapes. I said hello and we got chatting. I mentioned Lorne, who had known him when they had both been working in Germany and Scandinavia, Lorne as a star and he as a humble session musician. He remembered her name.

Suddenly he said, 'Do you want to listen to my tapes?'

I nodded and he put on 'Hunky Dory', which he was waiting to play to Tony. It was magnificent.

'What do you think?'

I said, 'Bloody hell, it's great!'

We talked about it a bit. Not realizing that he was quite possessive with his material, I asked him if he would be interested in writing something for Lorne, but he was non-committal. Bowie even had to be persuaded by DeFries to give Mott the Hoople the song 'All the Young Dudes', which became a No. 1 smash. 'Hunky Dory' did well, but not as well as I thought it might have done. 'The Rise and Fall of Ziggy Stardust' and 'The Spiders from Mars' then burst onto an unsuspecting public. I wish he could have written something for Lorne but our paths didn't cross again and it wasn't to be.

I later learned that Bowie and DeFries parted company very acrimoniously. DeFries went on to manage others, including John Couger Mellencamp, and lived like John Lennon in great style in New York.

As for the search for a song (which sounds like a title for a TV show), the big one never came along at the right time. It eluded us. The one song that we really wanted was the one that got away. Barry Gibb wrote it and when we heard it we thought it would be great for Lorne. But Barry had promised it to a young Australian singer, Samantha Sang, who was also represented by Stigwood. This was 'Emotions', which soared to the top of the charts and became a No. 1 for Samantha in both the UK and the US. It was to be her only hit in the UK, however, because her visa expired and she returned home – a curious example of a promising career foundering on the rocks of the British Immigration Office.

By the mid-Seventies there was a dearth of big songs to cover because after the Sixties the singer/songwriter was invented big time. If you wrote good songs you didn't give them away, you sang them yourself or formed a band as a vehicle for them. Songwriting and song publishing is very big business indeed. Hopefully you could sing your own songs, like David Gates of the band Bread, who wrote 'If'. The writer of a song would usually get the first bite of the cherry then others would cover it. Take 'MacArthur Park', covered by Richard Harris, or 'Windmills of Your Mind', the theme song from the original *Thomas Crown Affair* movie, which was covered by half the world. Paul McCartney played 'Yesterday' for Alma Cogan to listen to. She thought he was offering it to her and was devastated when she realized that he wasn't. She knew it was going to be a massive hit and begged him for it; but she didn't get it.

Lorne and I were optimistic for a long time that I'd find the perfect song and with it a record deal, but that big song or a movie theme just didn't come along at the right time.

I had often been in London before I met Lorne, when I used to come down from Manchester to sell my suit lengths. In the early days I would drop in to the various 'in' clubs, like the Speakeasy where Jimi Hendrix, Thin Lizzie and Deep Purple played and hung out, the Scotch of St James's next to the Apple offices, the Bag O' Nails just off Carnaby Street and, most frequently, the Ad Lib, which was above a cinema just off Leicester Square. I remember bumping into Paul McCartney and various Beatles at the Ad Lib. It was an exciting time to be around London. Then the Marquee and Ronnie Scott's took over and later, when I was with Lorne, we would go to more sophisticated clubs when we were down from the North.

When we were in Hong Kong once some good news came from London Management. Lorne was to star at the Talk of the Town in London, the most acclaimed venue of the day for international cabaret artistes. It was a milestone that Lorne looked forward to. At the time, Danny La Rue was packing them in at the Prince of Wales. He came across to see us during rehearsals, for a chinwag. I had never met him before but he and Lorne already knew each other well. He came to her opening night, which was a fantastic success. We threw a very crowded party afterwards in Lorne's dressing room. I remember looking around at all the stars who had dropped by to congratulate her, thinking what a close community this world was, and how they all looked out for each other. All of us knew how easy it was to slip from this pinnacle of success.

I thought of Judy Garland, who had used this same dressing room in her three-week engagement at the Talk. She was going through a very difficult time and was unable to cope. Her first night, as all the reviews testified, was sensational. All her friends turned up to wish her well – Ginger Rogers, Johnny Ray, Danny La Rue. But she couldn't sustain it. She started to turn up later and later, sometimes in the early hours when the place was being closed. Sometimes she would get confused while she was dressing and this star, the woman who used to shimmer in the most sensational clothes and had always looked like a million dollars, would appear with smudged lipstick, a false eyelash missing and, once, in her carpet slippers. She got catcalls instead of standing ovations. She slipped right off the rainbow to the dark side of the moon. Lonnie Donegan was drafted in to fill in for her most days. One June night she went home to her rented flat in Mayfair and never woke up.

'You're only as good as the day before,' Lorne would say to me. She was always highly professional. She was never much of a drinker anyway, and she would never have a drop of alcohol, not even a glass of wine, before working. She had seen too many artistes the worse for wear on stage. This has remained with me as a lesson in life. I get up, do the job and never have a drink during the day. In the evenings I might have a couple of glasses of red wine with dinner. Only when I get home, looking forward to a few days off, will I put my feet up, with a glass of Scotch and ice on the table beside me.

In the latter part of the Seventies I got Lorne a booking at a new casino in Ibiza. Gaming had just been given the green light in Spain. The various regions invited tenders from bona fide syndicates. It sounded a simple matter but there is a lot more involved in opening a casino than just setting up a few tables and opening the doors. It took a lot of experience to install the equipment and security, and to find the right staff. It was the kind of expertise that was lacking in Spain at the time and the big boys flocked in from across the Atlantic. Instead of being sent packing – as people like George Raft had been when he arrived hotfoot in London when casinos there were given the go-ahead, albeit a cautious one – the Spaniards turned a blind eye to the Vegas boys. There seemed to be a two-way traffic, with Spanish personnel being sent to Vegas to train there. Apparently, the legendary bandleader Xavier Cugat, whose band was to provide Lorne's music for the season, was the man who had initiated this.

Everything was so new when we arrived in Ibiza that the paint was barely dry on the walls. We already knew that the great Xavier Cugat orchestra would be playing at the casino. We weren't expecting Xavier himself to do the opening show because he'd had a stroke and one arm was quite badly impaired. When he did step forward, he was really just going through the motions and a pianist conducted on his behalf. Usually, he'd sit the shows out; it was enough that he was there, fronting it.

We were staying at a five-star hotel nearby and went to the casino for a rehearsal. When we arrived the huge 24-piece orchestra was waiting for Lorne – and there was the small legendary man himself. I instantly thought of his Coconut Grove orchestra and his old flame, Carmen Miranda, with whom he had starred in all the old Busby Berkeley type of movies, with titles like *Flying Down to Rio*. Carmen Miranda seemed to wink at you from out of her posters, wearing her enormous headdresses piled high with more and more fruit.

She seemed to be saying, 'I know it's silly and outrageous, but ain't it fun!'

'Call me Cugie,' said Xavier.

He had a long-stemmed briar pipe clenched in his teeth. He had never smoked a pipe in his entire life but, like his narrow moustache and the small chihuahua that went everywhere with him, it was a trademark. He was one of the most colourful characters I have ever met. For some reason, we immediately bonded. He was a lady's man and, as he told me, he always would be. He still had a gorgeous woman in tow when he was 90.

His eyes used to roll whenever he saw Lorne and he'd say, 'Oh David, I'd like to come out and conduct for Lorne.'

'It's OK, Cugie,' I'd say. 'We've got the pianist.'

Cugie's arrangements for his brass line up were like none other before or since. They created a unique sound, one that people simply can't afford today. The more I got to know him, the more interesting he became. He was a wonderful old boy, a bit of a rogue, but with a fascinating insight into the early life of old Las Vegas. He had his old-style S1 Rolls-Royce with him, a two-tone gold and sand colour, with the original plates: CUGAT–NEVADA. We would go off to the dining room together and chew the fat. Mostly, I listened. He told me about his women and wives: Carmen Miranda from Brazil, who died young; American singer Abbe Lane; Dolores Del Rio at the time of the first musicals; Latin-American Charo Baeza; and Mexican Yvonne Martinez, who met him when he was 78 and living in the Ritz Hotel in Barcelona.

'Ah, David,' he would say mournfully, 'if I'd had a woman like Lorne I would have stayed with her. If you two weren't married I'd make her Wife Number Four.'

I noticed an unusual crucifix around his neck and told him I had never seen anything like it.

'Cugie, where did you get it?' I asked.

'My friend Salvador Dali made it for me,' he said.

Already having my toe in the art world, I thought, 'Blimey, that must be worth a few bob!' When he told me that he had three very large canvases, about four feet by three, by Salvador Dali, my eyes widened.

'You know, Cugie, they're worth millions of dollars.'

'Well, David, if I ever want to part with them one day, I'll let you handle it.'

My eyes were sparkling but some time later, when I mentioned this to Cugie's business manager, he smiled and said, 'Well, he did have them. But he sold them about 20 years ago to settle his alimony payments.'

At other times Cugie would tell me about the old days. His life story was certainly something. He had been born on the first day of the first month of the new century – 1 January 1900. He was a Catalan, from Gerona, and would never forget either the region's music or its tongue. When he was four years old his family fled to Cuba because his father was in trouble for his trade union opinions. As a child, he was sent to work in Havana at a workshop where they made and repaired stringed musical instruments.

'I would pick them up and play them when no one was looking,' Cugie told me. 'My father gave me a violin when I was six. I was in ecstasy.'

It seems he was a child prodigy. By the age of 12 he was playing with the symphony orchestra at the National Theatre of Havana. The opera singer Caruso heard him there.

'Come and stay with me in New York. I'll introduce you to Pablo Casals, he's a cello player, but maybe he can teach you,' Caruso offered, handing the boy a slip of paper with his address on it.

'Did you go?' I asked.

The great Caruso – the very name had a resonance, and here was someone who had met him in the flesh.

'The First World War happened. I had to wait until it was over,' Cugie said. 'As soon as I could, I went to New York and looked Caruso up. He wasn't there. He was in Italy, with Puccini.'

I sat up straight. Could this all be true? (It was.)

'I was lost in New York, with no money, just my violin. I ate bread from bins, I drank water from street hydrants. I slept in parks. Then I bumped into August Borgunyo. He was a piano player, older than me. We played in bars, then in theatres. We saved up money and headed for California. Movies were just starting, silent pictures. We were made for silent pictures.'

'Come on, Cugie,' I said. '*Silent* pictures?'

'Certainly. We played in the pit at the Pasadena. I married a piano player. Her name was Rita Montaner, a classical musician like myself.'

This relationship led to a tour of the concert halls of Europe. By the time they returned to California the movies had soundtracks. Cugie divorced himself from Rita and classical music at the same time. He couldn't get work and started a job as cartoonist for the *LA Times*. The deadlines were too rushed so he resigned.

'I was down and out, thinking about busking on the sidewalk, when I had an inspiration. I invented Afro-Cubana! It was sensational, like nothing ever heard before,' he said.'Or since,' he added after a thoughtful pause.

The aptly named band Cugat and the Gigolos was born, forerunner of his trademark Coconut Grove Orchestra. It was 1920, Hollywood was booming. Cugie knew all the greats as personal friends: Garbo, Rudolph Valentino, Mary Pickford, Douglas Fairbanks, Buster Keaton, Charlie Chaplin, Harold Lloyd.

'Ya know what my ambition is, David?' Cugie asked me.

'No. What?'

He grew animated. 'I wanna start a radio station beaming out around the world, just like Radio Liberty –'

He was talking of the CIA-funded station that beamed music and news to the countries behind the Iron Curtain from the hills behind Marbella.

'But mine would be the Coconut Grove Station. Cococabana... rumba, salsa, boogie-woogie. I'm telling you, David, it will be great. I'm gonna put the transmitter on the roof of the casino. Then I'm gonna get back into movies.'

'On the roof of *this* casino?'

'Sure. They'll be happy to oblige.'

I listened avidly to him talking about the old Las Vegas days. He knew all the stories about the Mob and what went on, at first hand. He had first met Bugsy Siegel in Cuba, when they were both connected with the big casino-hotels there run by organized crime. Charlie 'Lucky' Luciano had built the Tropicana in Cuba, with a hundred showgirls on stage.

'Charlie put the groups together,' Cugie said. 'He was just a kid. He did this overnight sweep, wiped the opposition out and they took over. Hell, they were all kids, but hungry, know what I mean?'

The notorious bosses of New York, Chicago, Detroit and Las Vegas would meet regularly in Havana to discuss policy and smooth out any problems. Cugie was on close personal terms with Lucky Luciano, Albert Anastasia, Meyer Lansky (the financial brain of the Mob) and all the other infamous figures.

'David, I remember they used to say, "We only kill each other."' he told me.

'Was it true?' I said.

'Yeah, I guess so.'

In Cugie's book, Lucky Luciano was quite a guy. He said that from prison Luciano had negotiated the Allied landings in Sicily, helping to pave the way with local connections. According to certain rumours Luciano actually led the invasion but I thought this was unlikely. What is true is that his jail sentence was reduced in recognition of some undefined assistance to the government and he was shipped home to Italy after the war.

Cugie told me about Bugsy Siegel, whom he knew very well, in some detail, Siegel was a man with great foresight. Originally from Hell's Kitchen in New York, he was sent to Hollywood by the Mob to make sure they had a toe in the door of the new movie business. Driving into the desert on one of his days off, he came across the abandoned silver-mining town of Las Vegas and instantly saw the potential importance of its location in Nevada, where the laws on gaming were non-existent. Using money borrowed from the Teamsters Union, he built the first casino-hotel, the Flamingo. He was murdered because, it was said, he couldn't keep his hands out of the till.

'What was he like?' I asked Cugie.

'Bugsy? Pretty realistic, I'd say. He'd asked everyone, all the big movie stars, to the opening night of the Flamingo. There were storms on the West Coast and all the planes were grounded. The bosses flew in from the East Coast. Then there was a bomb scare – the rumour was planted, it was enemy action – so very few people came. Of course, the bosses weren't happy. They could see their millions of dollars going down the toilet. Top of the bill that night was Jimmy "Schnozzle" Durante, then Carmen Miranda and the Xavier Cugat orchestra. Durante had a wicked sense of fun, sent everyone up. There was a little girl, came from the Colony Club, doing eight minutes as an opening act. Now, what was her name – ?' Cugie pretended to think. 'Oh yeah, I got it. Lena Horne.' He laughed aloud. 'Little Lena Horne, what a doll.'

George Raft, who inhabited a shadowy world between the Mob, the movies and the casinos, appointed himself Bugsy's driver. Like Bugsy, he had come from Hell's Kitchen. Cugie said he was a wise guy. I couldn't figure out in what sense – as in clever, or too smart for his own good? Years later, after Bugsy was assassinated, Raft went to work for various casinos.

I asked Cugie what the great days of Vegas were like. Because of his connections with the Nevada operators he had worked there for at least 30 years, possibly more, after his film career had slowed down.

'When my fame as a headliner dropped away the word went out, "Cugie works,"' he told me. 'I worked the small lounges for several years. That's when I got to know Elvis real well.'

Albert Anastasia was the man behind this, the man who said that Cugie always had to be looked after.

Cugie told me in confidence that when the Spanish casino licences were issued he was approached; and he, in turn, set up a meeting between the principal shareholders of the casino and Vegas operators to negotiate the 'loan' of key Vegas personnel to train croupiers and security teams in Spain – this was when the big boys took it as an open door policy and moved in. In return, Cugie was given an eight-year contract to play for three months each season in Ibiza at a handsome salary. But when he drove off the ferry with his classic Roller and arrived at the casino to work, the Spaniards were all stunned. Here was this very elderly man who'd had several strokes, who was unable to do little more than front an orchestra.

'If they effing think they'll get me outta here, they ain't,' he whispered, 'unless they pay me the whole eight years. That's the only kiss-off I'll take or they can kiss my ass.'

One night at dinner, over the spaghetti, he said, 'You know, David, they don't make spaghetti like Big Al's mom used to make it.'

'Who?'

'Ya know – Capone. Al Capone. We used to go there after a night out and eat supper. She was a nice woman.'

When Lorne's show finished we would go back to the hotel for a nightcap. After a while Cugie would look at his watch. 'Time for bed, I'm tired,' he'd say, hiding a yawn. He would then disappear towards the foyer. The first time this happened, his manager grinned.

'Watch the doorway,' he said.

Sure enough, a few moments later we'd see Cugie tiptoeing past to slip off to the nightclubs of Ibiza. He'd be out until four or five in the morning. How a man that age had the constitution, I don't know. At the time *Hola!* was prominent in Spain and Cugie featured in it regularly. You'd open it and see pictures of him in the fashionable nightspots with a bevy of young girls around him. His attire was straight out of the Forties: an ivory-coloured suit, basket-weave leather shoes, a pull-down hat like a fedora, a large handkerchief hanging out of the top pocket, and a malacca cane with a silver top.

He was stronger than he looked, a tough old bird. I walked in on his dressing room once and he was frenziedly beating his manager about the head and back with that malacca cane as if he meant business. Yet the manager remained with him. Without a doubt, there were many mysteries about Cugie. He always had two strapping young local lads with him at all times, one to drive his Rolls and the other just hanging out as some kind of bodyguard. When he complained that they were always there, I told him to get rid of them. He rolled his eyes and shrugged.

'Well, you know, David, the people in America called the people in Spain and told them to look after me. So, they're looking after me.'

He lived an extreme and luxurious life, one of those amazing characters you never forget. After we left, he would often ring me to chew the fat. He spent most of the rest of his life at the Ritz Hotel in Barcelona until his death in 1990.

When I heard he had died I remembered how he had once told me that his proudest moment was having a street in Gerona, his Catalan birthplace, named after him: Boulevard Xavier Cugat. I thought this was perfect casting. Cugie was the world's most accomplished boulevardier.

CHAPTER THIRTEEN

The entertainment world as we knew it was changing. Gradually, the night-clubs and the venues that Lorne had shone in withered away. The Talk of the Town closed, Tito's became a disco and the wonderful Harbour Room at the Mandarin in Hong Kong was converted into a health club. Over the 10 or 12 years that Lorne had appeared at Tito's she had become a legend. When the news went out at the start of each season that she was back, people would turn out to see her and throw flowers from the balcony. But the rich patrons who'd regularly park their yachts in the Mediterranean had gone the way of the dinosaur. It became mass package tours, where people just wanted the free drink. The management used to tell me that trying to get them to buy another one was like pulling teeth.

During these years Chris had held the fort at the Old Bellows, our shop in Disley, although it was not always easy for him to go out to buy new stock and keep the shop open at the same time. I did my bit when I was at home between trips and we'd stock up as much as possible. Eventually there came a point, with the closing of the big international venues, where we decided it would be better for Lorne to go into semi-retirement and for me to focus on my antiques and fine arts work.

Chris and I had worked very hard down the years to achieve success. That we did succeed was, I believe, due to the fact that we were ambitious and had open minds. Yes, we were in the provinces, but our attitude was not a provincial one. We'd done our homework, investigated the established antique shops in London and decided to emulate them. There was no question that those shops catered to an international clientele. They had a flair, a 'look', that special *je ne sais quoi* that we aspired to and, I think, achieved. Part of our success was that we never thought, 'It can't be done.'

Neither Chris nor I were brought up in homes filled with antiques – perhaps a few of Nanny's knicky-knackies in my case, and maybe a few nice pieces and a couple of oil paintings in Chris's, but nothing of any real value. But I had travelled and had seen the big shops in Madrid, Barcelona, Paris, Hong Kong and Beverly Hills and I had recognized how different they were from the provincial and country-style outlets in Britain. I had used my eyes and never stopped learning. I liked that particular high-class look of the Mayfairs, the Champs Elysées or the Rodeo Drives and I concentrated on acquiring it.

Starting from scratch, as we had, showed me that anyone could aspire to what we had achieved, which is why I will say to anyone, 'You can do it, too.' We had nothing special to assist us, no magic bullet, no vast financial resources, only hard work, an acquired skill and a desire to formulate our own style.

When we first started, the old-fashioned antique dealers we met and got to know well had been in the business for many years and were happy to pass on their knowledge. For our part, Chris and I were like sponges, absorbing everything. Often, while waiting in various salesrooms for lots to come up, we would take a wander to the little wagon outside that served tea and snacks and get into conversation with the old-timers. We'd hear their opinions on what was coming up and their anecdotes and memories, perhaps about those very same pieces going back many years.

They'd say things like, 'We can remember when grandfather clocks were as cheap as chips. You could snap them up at £5 a time and now they're going for £1,000.' Someone else would cut in and say they remembered when they couldn't give them away. 'We'd have so many, they'd be lining the walls of our shop hallways.'

To start with, Chris and I used to look at the old guys, as young men do, and think, 'Silly old geezers, they're slowing down.' But, gradually, the penny did drop. 'By gum, these men know what they're talking about!' I even catch myself at it today, when a piece I once saw for sale in the Seventies for, say, £500 comes up again 30 years on for £15,000 and I'll say, 'Blimey – that's a lot of money!' And I'll catch eager and upcoming younger dealers turning around and looking at me with – dare I say it – pity in their eyes. I can see them thinking, 'Silly old codger!'

A few of these legendary old dealers were treated with awe when they swanned into view. God-like figures like Maurice 'Dick' Turpin. He is a larger than life man with a walrus moustache and a huge booming voice and there's no mistaking it when he's around. His fruity opinions can be heard a mile away from the back of many a salesroom. A world authority on eighteenth-century English furniture, he has been in the business almost since the Stone Age – perhaps 50 or even 60 years – and what he doesn't know about it isn't worth knowing.

Antiques will often circulate. We say, 'What goes around, comes around.' They might have appeared 20 or 30 years ago in a small provincial sale, been bought, and then years later put in a sale again. I was once viewing a major sale of walnut furniture and happened to bump into Dick Turpin inspecting the 20 or 30 bachelor's chests. In his usual style, Dick strolled past them, giving them all a good coat of looking at, recognizing each and every one.

'No effing good, no effing good, no effing good – that's all right – no effing good. I remember that one in the Forties, it was no effing good then and it's no effing good now!' he announced loudly.

Dick was so spot on because he knew the chests' histories – he even knew who had restored them and when.

On another occasion, at a very posh sale of important English furniture in London, a naive young auctioneer announced, 'Ladies and gentlemen, Lot No. 56 – a pair of exceptionally fine eighteenth-century console tables.'

Sure enough, riding in from the rear with an undoubtedly expert opinion, came this booming voice: 'They're no effing good and they never were any effing good!'

That's the kind of knowledge I aspired to when, as a young man I stood huddled around the refreshment trolley on a cold and blustery day at some small salesroom in Derbyshire or Devon, avidly listening to the old-timers, taking in every word, every joke. It was hard spotting a find, let alone snapping it up against such long-in-the-tooth experts like them, and often I would find I was only being allowed in to clutch at the crumbs they didn't want. But I persevered. I listened, watched and learned, and eventually there came a point when I was allowed to stand amongst their number as an equal.

Like any young man starting out, I made mistakes and, the same old thing – my eyes were sometimes too big for my belly. One of my earliest forays into the world of the salesroom was at an out-of-the-way sale in Carmarthen in West Wales. I had followed the rule book by going the day before to inspect the goods, noting the pieces I would bid for and writing down my limit against each piece. So far, so good. The next day, I was at the salesroom bright-eyed and bushy-tailed, ready to make my mark.

Suddenly, out of nowhere, I heard the auctioneer say, 'Ladies and gentlemen, who'll start me at £1,000 for this wonderful Victorian seven-piece salon suite?'

Not a flicker of movement, not a blink from anyone. This suite was not on my list of needs so I had scarcely given it a glance when I had viewed the previous day. Now I tried to check it out from the back of the room. I craned my neck and caught a glimpse of some velvet and some walnut or mahogany.

By then, the auctioneer was appealing to the crowd, 'Who will give me £200 for this fantastic suite? Ladies and gentlemen, it's a steal! Will nobody bid?'

Well, up shot my arm and down went the hammer. *Sold!* Sold to the greenhorn at the back of the room! When I came to finally inspect my amazing bargain I found that it was riddled with worm. Some of it was as spongy as an Aero bar and not worth taking home with me. How the older dealers must have been grinning up their sleeves at young Dickie Dickinson on one of his first outings putting his toe into the water. Well, you live and learn. It was worth it for the lesson, because, believe you me, I never bid sight unseen again.

One of the ways Chris and I learned was by reading all the trade papers and magazines. We had bought these publications, including the very high-class, glossy *Art and Antiques Weekly*, right from our earliest days, and would study them avidly. That was when we got the idea of putting our goods on the prestigious back page. It was enormously expensive but paid dividends in spades. I think almost everything we advertised on the back page sold in record time.

I started to build an extensive library of books, adding to it year on year until I had many hundreds. These books may have cost from £10 to £100 but they have been part of my stock-in-trade. They have become part of my life – and part of my fortune. I will always tell a newcomer to the business, 'Buy your books – and read them!' I would go home in the evening and, no matter how tired I was, I would pour myself a nightcap, put my feet up and turn the pages of a book, absorbing the contents. Without you even being aware of it, things will stick in your memory.

Peter Petro, a good friend whom I have known for many years, has a story of how a book helped him to identify something and make a great deal of money. One day, on his tour of the salesrooms which he takes in every week, he spotted a small gilt bronze figure of Hercules. It was listed in the catalogue as a nineteenth-century bronze, and the estimate was low. But Peter's gut instinct told him that it was seventeenth-century Renaissance, possibly brought back to England by some rich young man doing the grand tour of the Continent to finish off his education, as was customary amongst the aristocracy .

Peter got stuck in on the day of the sale but his heart sank into his boots when across the room he spotted another well-known art dealer who had a reputation for being very adventurous and speculative. 'Oh-oh,' thought Peter to himself, 'he's on to it, too.'

He knew that this could go one of two ways: he could be right about the piece or he could be wrong. Even in the eighteenth century, when young men did the grand tour, there were rogues and sharp-footed people ready to gull them. They might have been walking around Rome or Naples when a little man would appear round the corner.

'Psst! Your Lordship, have I gotta deal for you!'

Even back then there were fakes, replicas of great pieces – and this bronze in the sale could be one of those fakes, from a most impeccable source: a stately home.

Taking a deep breath and keeping his nerve, Peter bid for the figure and it was knocked down to him at £30,000, a huge amount for a potential pig in a poke. He took it back to his shop, the Coach House in London's Westbourne Grove, and with fingers crossed started to do some research. He took it to a few academics, who were unsure. They thought the little figure was too good, too crisp. That gave Peter the clue he needed. He went to the British Library and researched Renaissance goldsmiths, and in one book he found a reference to this particular piece. Now he could get it properly identified and attributed by an expert. It was sold on for £80,000. It's amazing what you can learn in a book.

There is a postscript to this story. Peter told me that in the course of his research at the British Library he had found a letter from the master goldsmith to his patron, referring to the little Hercules that he had made to go on a casket the patron had commissioned.

'I am also enclosing some small terracotta figures by my dear friend Michelangelo,' the letter said. 'Some day, these may be valuable.'

I was thinking how charming and amusing the story was when suddenly I thought – 'Blimey, they're still out there.' And I'm still looking for them.

I think one of the things I remember with much fondness, as well as a great deal of sadness, are the house sales we used to go to in the Seventies. These were amazing for the sheer wealth of the pieces on display, the wonderfully rare things that had been in the same family, perhaps for 300 years; and they were incredibly poignant because the era of the grand historic house was coming to an end. It was all being sold off, lock, stock and barrel. Suddenly, things that had been collected over the centuries by these dynasties, and then hidden away behind private walls, were coming into the public domain. This caused a great deal of excitement: historians were likely to come across unpublished collections of letters and journals; dealers would find valuable pieces that had never been sold on the open market before. They were like sharks scenting blood, moving in for a feeding frenzy.

Art dealers were particularly avid because in those days it was perfectly possible to find a forgotten Titian or Leonardo tucked away in some remote castle. Most of these one-family properties have now gone. There are still a few grand houses left with their original contents from cellars to attics but it is a rare occurrence today to see entire collections of furniture, paintings, ceramics, bronzes, books, marbles and rugs put together in the seventeenth and eighteenth centuries by a recently ennobled peer to furnish his newly built house; or to see the finds brought home by a younger son on his grand tour of the Continent. When you do come across such sales, it's as fascinating to soak up the atmosphere and pine for the history about to be dispersed to the four winds as it is to try to outbid your rival for something you have set your eyes and your heart on.

Many members of these old families were military men, diplomats, soldiers, sailors, travellers, explorers – men who would have circled the globe generation after generation and brought home the most amazing pieces.

One of the first house sales I attended was at a historic house at Par in Cornwall. I sent for the catalogue, and grew excited when I studied it and saw the masses of stuff listed. Surely, there would be something unusual within our price range, I thought, as Chris and I ventured forth with our hopes high. We went down the night before the sale to inspect. Following the directions, we turned off the B-road and drove through some iron gates into a long drive lined with ancient trees under which deer grazed. Fifteen minutes later, we were still driving. Eventually, we approached a perfect gem of a Georgian house, seemingly lost in time, where the same family had lived since Elizabethan days. They'd extended the original house, as many wealthy people did, by cladding it in Georgian stone and adding wings. But the original sixteenth-century rooms would have been found beneath the central portion.

The story here was quite tragic in its way. The ancient family had died out. There was no one left to inherit any of the treasures. The last of the ancient line, a very elderly spinster, had left the house to the local council to be used as an old folks' home. Everything was to go. We walked through magnificent rooms, where all the items were ticketed and ready for the sale the next day, and saw things that went back down through the years, tracing the history of successive generations of this once great family. On the staircase, from top to bottom, were family portraits, many of them of soldiers and sailors, men who had gone out when England ruled the waves and half the world was coloured pink on a map. In the dining room was an enormous oil painting of the Battle of the Nile showing Admiral Gravesaul, one of the men whose portrait was hanging on the staircase. He was number two to Nelson at the battle. And there was the bosun's whistle, presented to him as a trophy by Nelson. Although I was there to buy what I could, part of me was very regretful that all this history, which had not been seen by the general public before and would not have been seen if the family had not died out, was being dispersed so ruthlessly.

Another early country house sale I attended was at Brabham Old Hall, in Yorkshire. There was a wide range of items on sale, but also a lot of canny dealers. I knew that I couldn't compete with the big boys so I had a scout around for something within my range. I picked out a pair of decanters estimated in the catalogue at £200–£300. I didn't know a great deal about glass but these seemed to wink quality at me. I sensed they were special but, being quite green, I didn't know why. However, I was game for a bid. Suddenly it was up to £500 and then £600 and I dropped out. Those decanters went for £3,000, a great deal of money 20 years ago. You may well ask why, as I did. More experienced dealers had spotted they were by a famous glassmaker and, furthermore, they had been given by the Prince of Wales to a member of the Brabham Old Hall family. Moreover, there were only four in existence and the Queen had the other two. They had *provenance*. That made all the difference between £300 and £3,000. Another lesson well learned. In future I would know to ask, 'And have they any provenance?' and bid accordingly.

Mentmore Towers, a vast and romantic pile, had been built by Baron de Rothschild in 1855 in the Elizabethan style with huge mullioned windows and a turreted roof. Rothschild stuffed it full of the most wonderful antiques and objects, as befitted a man of his great wealth and station. The property passed to his son-in-law, Lord Roseberry, who commissioned even more works of art.

Then the house and contents were put up for sale – to huge public outcry. I wept alongside the rest of them but I was there to look, to inspect and to learn – and buy what I could, which in 1970 was very little indeed. I couldn't even afford the collection of milk pails. But then, these were no ordinary milk pails. They were made by Sèvres and were exquisitely decorated with sprigs of flowers and gilded banding, and had once been owned by Marie Antoinette and used in the little farmhouse at the palace of Versailles where she dressed up and played milkmaid.

There was furniture made by the great ebonists, wonderful tapestries, Georgian silver, automatons of the finest quality, and clocks such as I have rarely seen since, including a silver one with a real stuffed swan which would strike time with its wings as the clock chimed. Such items were made for kings and palaces. Many times in that house, and in others, I saw fabulous eggs and *bijouterie* made by Fabergé, crown jeweller to the Tsar and Tsarina of Russia. I remember in particular a Fabergé rock crystal bear with ruby eyes. All this and more went under the hammer at Mentmore and fetched £6 million – a fabulous sum for 1970 – but I doubt you could buy even one of the paintings for that amount today. (Another footnote: the house was bought by Beatle George Harrison for the Maharishi Mahesh Yogi and his yogic fliers.)

Some time in the late Seventies or early Eighties I attended a sale at North Nims Park, outside London, a grand house that had belonged to John Pierpoint Morgan, the American financier and railway man. It was filled with the most exotic of exotica, much of it purchased in the Thirties during the Depression when American tycoons escaped the doom and gloom of home to travel through Europe, buying from important aristocratic families. In France, Italy and Germany they acquired the contents – sometimes the entire contents – of great houses, castles and châteaux. William Randolph Hearst bought huge quantities which he shipped back to his legendary palace in the States, Hearst Castle – called Xanadu in *Citizen Kane*, the film based on his bizarre life.

North Nims Park was filled with the most amazing pieces, many by artists and craftsmen to the French court, men like Riesener, Boulle and Oeben. On the walls hung scenes of Venice painted by Canaletto, and in the main salon was a suite of 12 seventeenth-century Gobelin tapestries. These were bought by Francis of Mayfair (who is still in business today, dealing in textiles and oriental carpets) and I think he got them for £70,000 or £80,000. Today they'd be priceless.

Most of these items were quite beyond the reach of two young guys from Disley in Cheshire, but we did manage to buy a few pieces, costing a couple of thousand in all, and excitedly took them back to the Old Bellows.

Even when the shop was doing well, we didn't necessarily find anything we could afford at these country house sales. I remember going to a sale at Dalhousie Castle, home of Lord Dalhousie, on the Scottish borders. In many respects this sale was a very sad one because much of the contents was to be sold prior to the conversion of the castle from a private home to a hotel, albeit one controlled by the family. This truly magnificent castle, with its battlements, towers and turrets, has been in the possession of one family, the de Ramsays, longer than any other castle in Scotland and has, over the years, played host to kings and queens, warriors, politicians and authors. It is steeped in history and some degree of horror, reflecting its turbulent past. There is a terrible bottle dungeon, for example, a small windowless chamber into which prisoners were lowered by a rope; if they were left there it was tantamount to being buried alive. An earlier Lord Dalhousie had been the youngest viceroy of India at the age of 33 and many of the amazing objects on display – guns and cannons, Indian works of art, pieces of ivory and so on – reflected his stay in the subcontinent.

I'd gone along to try and buy a table veneered in ivory with elephants' heads around the base, but it proved too expensive for me, even though I stuck with the bidding right to the end. I knew I was up against a representative of Mallet's in Bond Street and was banging my head against a brick wall. I told myself, 'You're not going to get this, Dickie' – and I was right. I didn't. I was the underbidder. I believe the table went for about £36,000. I should have bought it. It was sold on for about £80,000. Another marvellous item I admired, but didn't go for, was a copy of Tipu's throne. He was the great Mogul warrior who unified India. The piece had been a gift to the viceroy when his tour of duty ended, and it was made of wood and gilded all over with gold. (The original throne was solid gold!) It was sad to see 800 years of a family's history come under the hammer.

Talking of Tipu, I was at a private sale in Leicester once where I saw what is believed to be his beheading sword, the very one he had apparently surrendered to the British in the eighteenth century. I wondered how many heads it had lopped off and did not buy it. There are some items that you see and buy that seem to be haunted, but you don't always know it at the time. I'm jumping ahead here, but when Chris and I had our second shop at Wilmslow we used to drop into a wonderful emporium in Stratford run by the Wiggington family – they are still in business today. Mr Wiggington specialized in antique arms and was so fascinated by the objects he bought and sold that he set up a small museum to display those special items he couldn't bear to let go. On one occasion Chris and I were looking for unusual and different things, as usual, and my eyes were taken by a very ornate gilded bronze temple – or so it appeared to me. It was presented as a fountain that had a modern electric pump installed to allow water to come out of a series of nozzles. It was crested and the document with it showed that it had belonged to the Maharaja of Baroda. Mr Wiggington often went on trips to India, where he would go from one maharaja's estate to another, buying up surplus goods . He concentrated on his speciality of arms and armour but could pick up anything, from classic motor cars to this 'fountain'. What it had started life as I do not know, but some time between 1900 and 1920 it had been converted to a fountain, not for water, but for champagne. It was highly exotic and I could imagine it as a centrepiece in the palm house of some grand mansion or in a marble hotel foyer so I bought it for about £8,000.

I took it back home to Wilmslow with glee and had it restored. But it was very unlucky, it just wouldn't sell. I sent it out on sale or return to another dealer. On the way, his driver was involved in an accident and the fountain was smashed up. We restored it and sent it off again. It didn't sell and came winging home to us – or I should say 'lumbered', since it was massively heavy. We decided to put it on our stand at the fine arts and antiques fair at Olympia, the grand annual event where top dealers display their finest goods for sale to a wide international audience, usually (but not always) the richest of the rich. The fountain was strapped to long pieces of wood and six men carried it out of the shop and up a ramp into the back of a lorry. It fell, and was smashed again. We had it restored. Don't even ask what the restorer said as he was faced with the same object for the third time.

'There is something evil about it,' I said to Chris, 'Maybe we should throw the bloody thing away!'

But no, we persevered and took it to Olympia again the following year. To our delight – and relief – we sold it at cost to a very wealthy man, who bought it for his home in some grand square in Belgravia.

'Don't overfill it or it will overflow,' I warned him. 'The reservoir takes only about three-quarters of a pint of water – or champagne, of course!'

About a month later the man was on the phone to me at my home one evening. He was furious, yelling that the fountain had overflowed and ruined his priceless oriental carpets.

I said, 'I'm very sorry. How much liquid did you put into it?'

'Only five or six pints,' he bellowed.

'Then it's your fault,' I said. 'I did warn you.'

But when I put down the phone, I thought, 'No, it's not really his fault. The bloody thing is cursed.' I was sure then that it had started life as some kind of Hindu shrine and should still be in the temple where it belonged, not tarted up to shower champagne over guests in a Mogul palace, or anywhere else.

Another tale springs to mind of a haunted piece that brought nothing but bad luck. I was at Olympia, preparing for the grand opening day, when a friend arrived and set out his wares on a stand not far from mine. All our goods were gleaming, buffed and polished to perfection, and vetted by the committee to ensure only the best authenticated items would be on sale. Our hopes as always high, we stood by and waited for the first viewers to arrive as soon as the doors were opened. It's always an exciting and nerve-racking time. You wonder, 'Have I selected the right items? Will people want them? Will I sell anything, or will I return home, tail between my legs?' I have to say that this latter scenario is very unusual and has never happened to me, fortunately.

Anyway, there we all were, waiting with eager hopes and anticipation. I did reasonably well, and I sold several items, but my friend had a spectacular day: he sold 20 pieces of furniture, virtually all of it to one client. Every time I saw him, his face was absolutely beaming. We all used to keep goods in reserve to fill the gaps on our stands but when things went well, with visions of even more success to come, we would sometimes take a wander around and haggle with a competitor to buy something from their stand to sell on, hopefully making the profit ourselves. My fortunate friend was doing just that. Rubbing his hands with glee, he drifted onto my stand and inspected my pieces.

'David, I've had a marvellous day, marvellous!' he chortled. 'Have you managed to sell anything?'

I knew he was ribbing, in the way we all did to each other.

'Oh, one or two small bits and pieces,' I replied, mentally counting the five or six large pieces I had actually sold.

My friend didn't buy anything from me but he saw this fantastic-looking bronze on a neighbour's stand. It was from the great Ming period, about 500 years old, on sale for £12,000. He offered to buy it. The dealer refused. He said that he had a good client who was a renowned collector coming in later. My friend countered with the comment that if the collector didn't come in, the dealer might not sell the piece at all. He offered £8,000 for it. They haggled a bit and eventually split the difference. The deal was struck at £10,500 and they agreed that if the client did turn up, then the dealer would take him across to my friend's stand to view the piece. They shook hands (cheques are normally exchanged at the end of the fair between dealers; it's all done by established word of honour) and my friend walked triumphantly back to his stand with the bronze.

The next morning he came past my stand a bit late, an ashen look on his face.

'What's the matter?' I asked.

'The engine blew up on my new Volvo. I had to call the AA and get a taxi in,' he said. 'It's a brand-new car, I've just taken delivery of it.'

Later that morning, the collector did show up. As promised, the dealer brought him over to my friend's stand. As they approached, the collector stopped and stared at the bronze in horror.

'Oh! You must be joking!' he gasped. 'That's Kow-Lin! That's the bringer of bad fortune. I wouldn't touch him with a bargepole.'

He turned around and quickly walked away – presumably before he was contaminated.

My friend overheard this and his mouth dropped open as he saw his profit walking away as well. But things grew worse. The buyer of the 20 pieces of furniture he had sold on the first day called him on the phone and cancelled the sale. Can some things bring bad luck? Well, I'll leave it up to you to make your own mind up. I know what I think.

As I got more involved with our first shop in Disley I discovered that a large part of my enjoyment of the job was the craic, the thrill of the acquisition, the chase – would it end up a wild goose chase or would I have found the goose that lays the golden egg? Each time I set forth to a sale, be it in a grand country house or inspecting the goods in the home of a little old lady who had telephoned me, it was like a treasure hunt. I always enjoyed the adrenalin rush when I was on to something, or spotted an object that I was convinced was more than it seemed. All dealers feel the same way. It compensates for the occasional bad decision. I have to say here that if the find is in the home of an old lady, any reputable dealer worth his salt would be frank with her. He would say, 'Madam, I'm not sure what this is. It could be worth a great deal of money, or it could be worth nothing. Let's get in a second or even a third opinion. Let's have it expertly examined and researched.'

I don't want to take the moral high ground here, but I would never go to an old lady's house and take advantage of her vulnerability by giving her bad advice or a poor price. It's not fair and it's not right. And what's more, it's bad luck. I believe that what goes around, comes around. I know this goes back to my granny, but I'm more likely to overvalue, and give a poorly off, elderly person an upbeat price, than undervalue. This doesn't mean that if I went to the home of a wealthy businessman or entrepreneur I wouldn't try to get the keenest deal. Anyone who is strong enough and powerful enough can stand up for himself!

Equally, if the potential find is in a salesroom, then it's fair game – you're the one who is taking the risk if you're wrong. To do this job properly, they say you should allow the head to rule the heart. I find that all the great dealers I know use intuition. Their eyes tell them that they are looking at something very special. They go out into the fray and battle against each other. It's a very personal thing. They buy the piece. There is a great rush of excitement, winning on the day, claiming the item and take it back to your base and researching it. Yes! It's a great lot and it's been underestimated or wrongly identified. Then restoring it and bringing it out into an open forum and winning the day with a great return. That's the craic. Of course, everyone wants to earn a living – but they'd rather have the golden egg.

Some dealers do have the most spectacular good luck. Take Steve Bedford. He is a professional runner, well known in the trade. Runners work for themselves, almost in a freelance way. These guys buy on their own instinct and knowledge. They will go from sale to sale the length and breadth of the country, travelling thousands of miles in a week, using their huge amount of stored expertise to find something unusual or something that has slipped through the net. Sometimes they will buy an item that is in the wrong sale, and thus goes for a lower price, then recycle it, either in a more suitable specialist sale where the price will be higher or directly to a specialist dealer, say in porcelain, or armour or eighteenth-century English furniture. Whatever the object is, a runner will know exactly where to take it.

You could say that Steve is like a bloodhound, always on the trail of the unusual, as was the case at a salesroom in the Midlands where he spotted a very small object in a glass case with a catalogue estimate of £80–£100. Instantly, the hairs stood up on the back of his neck and he knew. He didn't even touch the object. He walked away.

He returned when the bidding started and bought the object for £500. A short while later he put it up for sale at Christie's and it made £750,000. What was this small object? It was a single chess piece, a king from a ninth- to eleventh-century chess set, one of the earliest chess pieces ever recorded. Steve knew that another piece from a similar set had turned up a few years before and had made £130,000 at Sotheby's. With his good memory and that specialized knowledge he was able to back his judgement when he spotted another. It had come into the salesroom in a mixed box of bits and pieces and the auctioneer hadn't recognized its value. Steve did. That goes to tell you that there are still some wonderful items to be found, but you need to have the knowledge, do the research and then demonstrate the courage of your convictions.

One dealer I know of went to Sweden as a very young man in his twenties and recognized a graceful marble as being the work of the Renaissance master, Giambologna. He snapped it up and in turn sold it to the Getty Museum for a huge sum. It turned out to be the lost *figura serpentinata*, of a beautiful nude woman shown bathing, and it was all the more valuable because marble works by Giambologna are very rare. A Franco-Flemish sculptor, he moved to Italy in 1550 and quickly established himself as the chief sculptor to the Medicis in Florence, mostly making wonderful bronzes.

Another dealer I know went out and bought a pair of vases purely on intuition. They had been taken into a major London salesroom for a valuation and opinion. The person in the department had dismissed them, saying, 'No, they're not of a good enough quality for here. They are nineteenth century. Take them to one of our provincial salesrooms.'

They were duly entered and my friend recognized them for what they were, but nobody else did. He got them for just a couple of thousand. They turned out to be Imperial Ming and were eventually resold for a few *hundred* thousand pounds.

Another friend of mine, who came into the business through his father, a very clever and wise antiques dealer, inherited his father's substantial stock and business. Among the items was a small bronze that his father had kept back, out of the general stock. The older man had said to his son: 'I believe this is something very special. It's rare, treasure it.' My friend told me his father always believed that this small bronze figure of a knight on horseback dated from the period of the Crusades.

He took the bronze to all the major specialists in the field – at the V & A, the Ashmolean and many other museums and academic institutes.

'This is a nineteenth-century fake,' declared the experts without exception.

They didn't care what my friend's father had said, he had got it wrong. Apparently, something about the knight's armour or apparel didn't seem quite right. Another pal of mine, a leading specialist in Renaissance bronzes, looked at the figure. He wasn't sure, it wasn't really his period, but that old gut feeling kicked in.

'Tell you what,' he said to my friend. 'I'll give you 25 grand for it, on spec.'

This is what we call a 'speckie', or a speculative offer. I don't think he really knew, but his eye and knowledge were telling him that here was something interesting, something exciting. My friend appreciated the gesture but declined.

'Thank you very much,' he said. 'It's a brave offer, no one has ever come up with a price like that, but my father told me it was special, and I know it must be.'

In good faith, he kept the bronze for many years. Then just four or five years ago he entered it in a Sotheby's specialist fine arts sale, where it fetched close to three-quarters of a million pounds.

What this shows me is that no matter how experienced academics may be, their current knowledge is based on research – and new information comes along all the time. At the end of the day it's down to an individual to make judgements, for better or worse. I don't want to give the idea that all the judgements we make are the right ones. Some are probably wrong – but even if something doesn't work out exactly the way you dreamed or hoped, you'll still learn from the experience. I was certainly learning all the time.

This is what was always driving me and Chris right from the start: that hope that you will find the next exciting piece. With a dealer it's all about making money, which you must have to pay the rent on your premises, to cover the wages and buy new stock. But that is only part of it. I quickly learned that once I had started I was hooked. I woke each day looking forward to what that day would bring – and no one can ask more than that.

CHAPTER FOURTEEN

Our stock at the Old Bellows in Disley continued to increase because we ploughed a lot of our profits back into buying more goods. In those days there was an initiative scheme called 'stock relief', where you could roll over and reinvest your profits over a few years without paying tax. Accordingly, Chris and I each took only a small salary out of the business so, when we had cleared our overheads, we had the freedom to buy lots more stock, always going for the best quality we could afford.

As we went down the pecking order at the various sales we attended, there was always something to fit our needs and our price range and we would often come back with some fabulous items. Gradually, as the early years passed and our knowledge and stock increased, we found that we were no longer the poor boys on the fringes of the big salesrooms, or at country house sales, but were starting to take our place next to the big boys and compete with them.

We were doing so well that eventually we were able to buy our shop for £10,000 instead of paying rent. It was a watershed moment and we felt like princes. We truly were lords of all we surveyed as we stood outside in the street and looked at our premises with the very stylish window filled with some lovely pieces. By now the Old Bellows was getting some serious attention within the business. The odd runner would drop in and see that we had some spectacular piece or other, he would pass the information on to a big London dealer and we would then make a sale. It was the nature of our business that we had to give quite favourable discounts within the trade but we were also happy to do a little bargaining with our everyday customers who lived locally. There were several other antique shops in Disley and in order to compete we had to have an edge. We achieved this by making sure the shop looked attractive, inside and out, by displaying the best type and quality of goods and by being willing to negotiate on price. What we didn't ever expect was to sell out our entire stock – not once but three times.

One of our regular clients who lived locally was a Swedish lawyer, an affable fellow. We would chat about this and that and got on well. He said we had some nice things and that he would mention it to his contacts in Sweden. We thought he was just being polite and we didn't pay much attention. After all, why would a Swede want to come all the way to Disley in the north of England to buy something from us? But one day our lawyer friend did turn up at our shop with a tiny man in tow. He was an amazing sight. After all, it's not every day you see a five-foot Swede come walking through your door dressed like a cowboy, from the heeled western boots to the Levis, the plaid shirt, the leather waistcoat, the bolo with bootlace tie and the stetson.

During the introductions we learned that he was so obsessed with the American West that he went each year to the famous Tucson Roundup in Arizona. He looked around our shop, inspected each and every piece, nodded approvingly a few times, then, speaking through the lawyer since his English was limited, he said he was very impressed. Well, we were impressed with the way he looked and the time he had taken.

'Good, I'm glad you like it,' I said.

'Yes, it is just what he wants,' the lawyer said. 'How much is it?'

'How much is what?' I said. 'What piece has taken his fancy?'

'All of it!' the lawyer replied. 'He will buy everything.'

Chris and I were too amazed to speak.

Finally, I said, 'Am I to understand he wants to buy our entire stock?'

'Of course,' said the lawyer, as if this were an everyday occurrence. 'He will take it all to Sweden. And we would like your best price.'

'We'll see what we can do,' I said, my head reeling.

It takes a lot to knock me off my perch but this had almost achieved it. Chris and I asked for a moment or two to discuss the discount we could offer and disappeared into our office. In the end we decided it would be easiest and fairest to simply open our stock books, show them what each item had cost us and add on a straight 17.5 per cent profit on top. They thought this was very fair and reasonable and the deal was struck.

Some of the pieces had been a mistake and some had been overpriced, and we had bought them because of our inexperience. My eyes were sparkling because I was thinking, 'Wow! This is a total clear-out of all the good, bad and indifferent blunders that we have not been able to sell.' It was a golden opportunity to turn all our stock into cash in one fell swoop, then to go out on the road again and go shopping with the hindsight of experience.

Meanwhile, in the mysterious way that news travels, the word had gone around the other antique shops in Disley that Dickie and Chris had caught themselves a millionaire from Texas. Everyone came to get an eyeful of this rare bird but he didn't buy from anyone else. Everything was carefully packed, an international shipping company came with a huge pantechnicon – and off our entire shop went to Sweden.

Before he left, our new cowboy chum invited us to visit him in Malmö. His name was Bent Erlanson and he was known to his friends as 'Little Bent'. He said he had some kind of a holiday camp, called the Ponderosa. That figured!

In due course Chris and I did go over there and this remarkable little man surprised us all over again. He turned out to be one of the wealthiest men in Sweden, a billionaire entrepreneur with many commercial interests. His 'holiday camp' in Malmö was a lavish Disneyland-type theme park built exactly like the Wild West, with replica clapboard buildings, wooden sidewalks, shoot-outs in the street and Wild West shows. Along Main Street were saloons, a jail, a feed store, a livery stable or two and several replica stores selling souvenirs.

At the end of an entertaining day, we had to ask the question: 'Where are the goods you bought from us?'

Little Bent took us along to a warehouse and there it all was, stacked high. He already had the souvenir stores and now he was going to open an antique shop in Main Street.

Word obviously went around that we were two young men with good taste, who you could deal with, and our little cowboy returned to Disley to clean us out twice more, bringing with him, in due course, three compatriots: one was the marzipan king of Sweden; one was the frozen food king of Sweden; and the other held the Swedish franchise for Burger King.

Little Bent was an art-lover and I thought of him when a dealer I knew told me that he had access, through a client, to a Modigliani, the much sought-after Italian artist who painted in flat, sludgy colours, mostly nudes of women with apricot-skin, almond eyes and long giraffe-like necks. All his paintings are immensely valuable, so my ears pricked up. My new Swedish contacts were always asking me about Continental artists, in particular Edvard Munch, the Norwegian painter best known for *The Scream*, a frightening and iconic picture. Not surprisingly, Munch ended up in a lunatic asylum. I mentioned the Modigliani to the Swedish lawyer and Little Bent hotfooted it over to Disley to see it. By then I had got it on sale or return and it was ready to be viewed.

It was a small picture, measuring 22 x 10 inches. What was unusual was that it had been drawn in chalk or black crayon – perhaps pastels – on a plank of wood. All the knots and grain running through it had been cleverly incorporated into the drawing. It was of a reclining nude and on the breasts the nipples were exactly where the knots fell. It was beautifully done. When I first saw it, I thought, 'There is only one piece of wood like this. It's so spot on, a forger could never find another identical piece like it to draw this nude in this way.' It was signed by the artist and there was a lot of documentation which referred to an exhibition at the Museum of Utrecht some eight or nine years earlier – this was in the early Seventies. This documentation included a signed certificate from the director of the museum, saying that the picture had been on display there, and there was even a letter from the model herself, who had been one of Modigliani's mistresses. All seemed above board and in good order. The price I had it for was £36,000 so, not being too greedy, I said we would sell it on for £46,000. (Those were the days! In recent years large, important Modiglianis have made millions.)

The deal was agreed with Little Bent but, naturally, he wanted me to double-check the authentication for the picture all over again. Yes, I had all the right documentation – but was it bona fide? Accordingly, I made an appointment with the director of the museum, packed the painting up carefully and flew off to Utrecht. At the Dutch customs I explained that I was bringing it in for the day only and, with high hopes and anticipation, strode into the museum with the small picture firmly tucked beneath my arm.

'Was this picture in the exhibition?' I asked the director.

He nodded his head somewhat mournfully.

'Yes, it was. But I'm sorry to tell you that, out of the 30 pictures that were here on loan from various institutions and private owners around the world, nine of them have since turned out to be fakes – and this is one of them.'

Well, this was a body blow. My heart fell into my boots.

'Are you sure?' I asked.

I was so certain that no faker could have come up with a second piece of wood with all the right grain and knots in precisely the right position. This had seemed so hunky-dory.

'Yes, we are sure,' said the director. 'There is no doubt that this is a fake.'

He went on to tell me that the fakes were so good because, they now knew, they were by Elmyr de Hory, the greatest forger of modern times, who had lived in Ibiza – where he was briefly imprisoned and where he eventually committed suicide, in 1976. Elmyr was able reproduce almost any style but favoured artists of the late nineteenth and early twentieth centuries, such as Van Gogh, Monet, Chagall, Picasso – and, of course, Modigliani. By his own admission he had forged at least 2,000 pictures. He could knock them off so easily, with such style and perfection, that even today many of his pictures are still to be found around the world in major museums, galleries and private homes, passed off as original masterpieces. His fakes are so valuable that fakes of his fakes are often forged. Orson Welles made a film about him, *F for Fake*, based on a book written by Clifford Irving. And Clifford Irving was the man who would go on to fake an autobiography of Howard Hughes – based on diaries and letters faked by that great master-faker: Elmyr de Hory. Irving also ended up in prison. It's a funny old world.

As I flew home from Utrecht, carrying my discredited picture, I reflected on the astonishing story told to me by the director of the museum. I had acquired the picture on sale or return and, as always, I thanked my lucky stars for my caution.

Our business was prospering; we were getting stronger and had about £100,000 worth of stock. Chris and I set our sights on a new gallery. After scouting around and weighing up all the various pros and cons, we settled on Wilmslow in Cheshire, a very fashionable area. They say there are more millionaires in the villages of Wilmslow, Prestbury and Alderley Edge grouped together than in all the rest of the north of England combined. I don't know if this is true but certainly Wilmslow has long been one of the most fashionable suburbs of Manchester. Then as now, the houses were huge (the homes of top executives) and, if it's any criterion, all the smart car dealerships could be found there, selling Mercedes, Rolls-Royces, Bentleys and Porsches. You would often see the ladies who lunch driving around in their drophead Mercedes, their hair immaculately coiffed. The place had the best fashion shops, the best shoe shops – you name it, if it had a designer label, it would be there. It was the Mayfair of the northwest and we were ready to make our mark.

However, there was a cautionary note: I was told that though this was an area where people appeared to be very wealthy, and a lot of them undoubtedly were, much of their income was tied up in huge mortgages, children's education, Continental holidays and keeping up with the Joneses at the country club. It was said of Wilmslow that it was 'all frock and no knickers'. But Chris and I had our sights set on having a fashionable gallery in a top spot and ignored all the warnings. We put our premises in Disley on the market and got £32,000, a good return on our investment.

Shortly before we sold up and moved out to Wilmslow, a strange thing happened. Just behind the shop in Disley there were some small terraced cottages, most of them occupied by elderly people. One of these neighbours, a very charming and friendly woman of about 80, would often come and knock on our back door. She would come in, and if business was slack we would have a chat.

One day she said to me, 'You know, David, you remind me of somebody I used to work for when I was a young girl in service.'

'Who is that?' I asked.

'A former employer of mine,' she replied. 'A Mr Gulessarian. He was an Armenian gentleman. His wife was French.'

Immediately, my ears pricked up. This was an unbelievable coincidence. She went on to say that as a young woman she used to work in a very large house in Chorlton, in those days a prosperous suburb of Manchester where merchants and businessmen lived.

'They had another house as well, further in the country,' she added. 'The house in Chorlton was close enough to Manchester that Mr Gulessarian could go into work each day to his job as a silk merchant. I remember that there were two children in the family, Jenny and Jack.'

I knew about Jack, of course, though I had made no attempt to contact him since the phone call made by my solicitor. The old woman went on to tell me about the wonderful house, the servants, the quite exotic furniture, the paintings, the silver and crystal, the luxury open-topped cars, and the gardeners to tend the large grounds. But what made my eyes widen was when she told me about a woven carpet that my grandfather prized. What made it special and spectacular was the real gold and silver thread woven into it.

'It made the carpet very heavy,' she said.

As a dealer that immediately attracted my attention. Such a carpet would be rare and very valuable. I thought to myself that if I ever came across it I would buy it at any price and never sell it. After that remarkable conversation we went on to have many more talks about my family. I mentioned this to my mother the next time I telephoned her but she didn't recall the woman.

'I would have been only a very young child if it was just Jack and me,' she said. 'My sister came along later.'

I had to be satisfied with that. My mother never would expand that much on her family.

By this time Lorne wasn't taking so many bookings, but there were still one or two enquiries coming in and if the offer was good enough we would accept. Just before the move to Wilmslow a call came from one of Lorne's regular venues in Barcelona and we flew out. We would often go on a walkabout during the day for exercise, looking at the shops. One day we came across a very elegant antique shop that I hadn't seen before. Right in the centre of the window was the most magnificent vase, which I knew immediately was from the French Sèvres factory. It was huge – and I'm talking huge – of great girth and over six feet tall. It was a wonderful deep blue, hand-painted with eighteenth-century courtiers dancing, perhaps men and women from the French court. It had cast-bronze ormolu handles and an onyx top and and stood upon a pedestal that was a further three feet tall. So the thing in its entirety was well over nine feet.

By then I had been in business a while and only once before had I seen a similar pair of vases, but without the pedestals – which went for £25,000. I felt a wave of excitement.

I said to Lorne, 'If that's the real McCoy we could be lucky.'

Nonchalantly, I entered the shop. The owner came forward.

'Can I help you, señor?' he asked.

'Tell me about that vase in the window,' I said. 'It's a pity you don't have a pair.'

'But señor, it *is* a pair,' the man said and invited me out to the back.

Tucked in a dusty corner was a matching vase, complete with pedestal. I felt a mixture of awe coupled with a flicker of doubt. This seemed too good to be true. Were they authentic? Would I find another six stacked up around the corner? The only way to tell would be to check the provenance very carefully and to give each vase a good going-over. The dealer told me that he had bought the vases privately from an old family. This was a good point in their favour, since everyone hopes to get unspoilt goods, something that has come fresh onto the marketplace and hasn't been the rounds. But the real clincher was when he produced the original invoice from when the family had first acquired them.

'What's your best price for the pair?' I asked.

He wrote down a figure in pesetas with a long row of noughts. I converted it in my head and was stunned when I calculated he was asking £130,000.

'This can't be right!' I said.

He took another look and smiled.

'No, señor, there are too many zeros,' he said.

The amended figure was £13,000. It was a wonderful price – if the vases were authentic.

I crawled all over them, noting that the decorator had signed them, a sure indication of quality. I looked for signs of age – not easy to find in porcelain, which does not acquire a patina as a piece of furniture does. The patina is that unique surface that a piece of old wooden furniture accumulates over years of handling and polishing – a kind of visible 'skin'. It gives us an indication of a piece's history and age because it acquires a depth, a glow, a richness that new wood just doesn't have. Old bronze and marble also acquire a type of patination that comes from the atmosphere, from oxidization, from dust and nicotine, which is different from that acquired by wood. Porcelain is another matter. To maintain its highest value it should remain pristine, with no chips or other signs of wear, and the colour should be as bright and as fresh as the day it left the factory. The decoration and gilt on smaller pieces will wear if they are washed or handled too frequently and they will often acquire that kind of 'crazy paving' or crackle known as craquelure.

But in the case of this pair of massive Sèvres vases, which would probably have sat in the same place on the floor of some grand house or palace for a century or so, the only wear they would have got would have been the flick of a rag or a feather duster wielded by a servant. Finding a piece that is authentic, that looks new but is old, is a fine balance and takes an expert eye. Fortunately, dirt gets trapped in ormolu fittings and a little oxidization occurs, and I concentrated on this area in my inspection of the vases. Now you might think that dirt can be faked – and it often is. However, experience soon tells you the difference between any old dirt that has been slapped on any-old-how and the genuine dirt of ages that has gradually accumulated. To my eye, the dirt under the ormolu of these particular vases was genuine. Their fittings hadn't been taken off or replaced in a hundred years. The clincher was finding old cobwebs in the bottom when I turned the vases over. These are impossible to fake. But even so, I needed to do a little more research. I wrote down the signature and factory marks and went back to our hotel suite and telephoned Chris, giving him all the details. In turn he checked these out, even to the extent of telephoning a few museums and auction houses for advice. He discovered that the decorator had worked in the Sèvres factory in the 1880s.

'I think we should buy them,' I said. 'They will make a marvellous statement in the window of our new shop.'

Chris agreed with me and I returned to the dealer. A period of hard bargaining ensued and I won the vases for £10,000. It was almost a steal – but not quite. I still had to ship them home and pay for the insurance. In due course the vases arrived, in perfect condition. We were so taken with them that, although we had planned on putting them in our new as yet to be found gallery in Wilmslow, we couldn't resist displaying them in the window of our Disley shop straight away, even though we had no intention of selling them.

The vases attracted a great deal of attention but we told everyone who enquired that they were not for sale. Three or four days later I got a telephone call from an Iranian based in London who was one of the biggest dealers in nineteenth-century art.

'David, about your vases,' he said with no preamble.

'Blimey,' I thought, 'that was quick!' I realized that a runner must have spotted them and sent a report back to the Iranian.

'They're not for sale,' I said.

He ignored this.

'How much do you want for them?'

'I told you, we are not selling them. We are keeping them as showpieces for our new shop,' I replied.

He obviously thought this was just a ploy to raise the ante. This man dealt with sheikhs and kings and was a millionaire in his own right, with wonderful homes around Europe and the Middle East, and he didn't get there by taking no for an answer.

'Come on David, you must want to sell them,' he pressed. 'Everything has a price.'

'Well, these two vases don't have a price,' I retorted.

We haggled back and forth a bit until, losing patience somewhat, I said, 'I'm not selling them, but if I were, I would want £30,000.'

'Ridiculous!' he said.

'That's my price.'

'See you this evening,' he said, and hung up.

I didn't think he meant it but he was there that same evening, with his brother, having come up on the train from London. When they walked into the shop they completely ignored the vases.

'Well, where are they?' they said.

I grinned to myself. It was all a game and this was their way of saying, 'These vases are so insignificant we have not even noticed them –' Hard to do when they were nine feet tall and in a brightly lit window.

'You have just walked past them,' I said.

'Oh dear, they're dark blue! We wanted pale blue,' they said.

'Since they're not for sale it doesn't much matter what colour they are,' I said.

This kind of banter with an edge went on long into the night. We went off for dinner and they still haggled. I held firm. In truth, although the dealer in me wanted to take the £30,000, the showman in me wanted to keep those magnificent vases as showpieces. Having something someone wants that you don't want to sell is a very strong position to be in.

Midnight came and still I hadn't budged. Eventually, I drove the Iranians to catch the milk train out of Stockport station. It was a bitterly cold night. Several tramps were bedded down in the waiting room as we walked back and forth, still negotiating.

As the train drew in, the first brother said, 'Oh, very well, we'll have them! What's your lowest price?'

'You know it,' I said.

You should have seen those how those tramps' heads swivelled as the sum was mentioned out loud. But I had kept my own head and won the day. And although 300 per cent isn't a bad profit to make, a bit of me was still sorry not to have hung on to that pair of Sèvres vases.

It was shortly after this that Chris and I found our new premises in Wilmslow. Nothing was available for sale in the centre (and we couldn't have afforded it even if there had been) but we found a good property to rent on a prominent site next to the Rex cinema. We papered the window so no one could see what was going on, then we sent decorators in, who again covered the walls in a grass-weave type of paper, giving a slightly oriental look. Tasteful plain beige carpets were laid, our stock was shipped in and we arranged it to its best advantage. Inside the shop we had all manner of exotic and lavish things: French *bureaux plats* (writing tables), commodes (chests of drawers), Chinese lacquered screens, porcelain, bronze and marble. Our large windows displayed a couple of pairs of blackamoor torchères, two library globes on stands (real apparatus used by Georgian and Victorian scholars but now kept mainly for decoration) and two or three large telescopes with six- and eight-foot barrels. These were all ideas copied from our old friend Arthur Davidson, who often had a couple of spectacular items aimed at gentlemen in his Jermyn Street windows – toys for the boys, you might say. We knew that there were many businessmen and top executives in the area around Wilmslow who had wood-panelled libraries and studies so we hoped these pieces would appeal to them.

I will always remember the very first piece I ever bought from Arthur Davidson. It was the carved and painted little wooden figure of an admiral that had originally stood over the doorway of Frodsham's, famous nautical and technical equipment suppliers in London, where men such as Nelson used to buy their telescopes and sextants. One night, some nineteenth-century, high-spirited young naval cadets – perhaps even young Nelson himself – stole the Little Admiral and took him back to Portsmouth with them. It's said they thought he was missing the sea and was not happy with the constant hurly-burly of horses and carriages clip-clopping over the cobbles of London town. Then they thought he would enjoy a taste of the ocean waves so he went to sea with them, sailing around the world. He was mysteriously returned to Frodsham's a year later, being sold on to wind up, eventually, in Arthur Davidson's emporium. That story fired my imagination. I was smitten. I returned time and time again, as a young dealer, to gaze in at the window of the Jermyn Street shop before eventually getting up the courage to set foot inside.

Mr Davidson was a big man who dressed in cashmere sweaters and always had a Zeppelin-sized cigar in his hand. Face to face with him I quailed, but managed to pull myself together.

'Excuse me, Mr Davidson, how much is the Little Admiral?' I asked.

He looked me up and down as if saying, 'Who is this upstart from the provinces?' And in his deep voice, he rumbled, '£3,800.'

Very politely, as if walking on eggs, I said, 'Mr Davidson, I have seen it in your window for some considerable time. It's not been sold yet so will you take an offer from me?'

He looked me up and down again over the smoke curling from his big cigar and he said, 'Well, if you're not too silly about it.'

'I'll give you £2,500 now,' I said.

He puffed again, looked at me with deliberation, and said, 'Make it £2,800 and you've bought it.'

I was so astonished at being taken seriously by the great man that I said, 'Right!' fast, we slapped hands and it was done.

I advertised the Little Admiral in the back pages of the glossy trade magazine *Art and Antiques Weekly*, and after sitting in that grand London shop for a year or more, it was snapped up within three days from our little shop in Disley for £3,800. The buyer was a collector from the North and he still owns the carving. (And I've spent 30 years trying to buy it back – but that's another story.)

Now, here I was, some ten years on from the spirited novice I had been, looking at the wonderful display in the Arthur Davidson-inspired window of our new gallery in Wilmslow and at all the quality goods laid out tastefully on the new beige carpet, ready for our grand opening. I felt as if I had come a long way – and I had.

CHAPTER FIFTEEN

•

We took down the brown paper from the window and opened our second gallery with a flourish, bright and early one Saturday morning, just before the Christmas of 1980. I can remember standing on the opposite pavement in the heart of Wilmslow and staring at our new premises before the traffic built up. It looked splendid, a perfect copy of a West End gallery. Chris and I turned to each other and shook hands.

'Are we ready for this?' we said.

The answer was a resounding yes! We had done our homework, placed advertisements in the right papers and magazines, done interviews in the local newspapers and sent out embossed invitations. People started flocking in. There were lots of local prominent businessmen and their wives, old friends, and dealers we knew who dropped in looking to see what Dickie and Chris were up to. We had something for everyone, with items priced from £100 to £20,000. Our total stock at that time was worth about £120,000, so obviously there were only one or two items at the top of the price range. The best piece, as always, was in the window where people could get an eyeful and be drawn in like bees to honey. On the first day two or three people who came in gave us quite big orders. That night, when we closed, we were tired but confidently ebullient that we would do as well if not better than we had done in Disley.

My energy was boundless. We didn't just sit back and wait for customers to come to us. I also went out looking to fulfil requests, searching out those special deals that are a combination of research, intuition and hard work – and when I say hard work, I mean bloody hard work. Take the story of the peacock I went in pursuit of. Now, I'm proud of the peacock I found and when I tell you the nitty-gritty of how I worked on this case, you will understand why.

One of my contacts was an American collector of Minton majolica, those wonderfully decorated, often brightly coloured pieces made by the Minton factory at Stoke-on-Trent. Theye range from the practical, such as tureens and vases, to the exotically ornamental. Some are large, some are small, but without exception items in perfect condition are getting increasingly rarer and consequently more valuable. I had already found a few truly sumptuous antique Minton pieces for this collector, including a pair of handsome, large, dark blue vases, decorated with leering horned heads of Bacchus and swags of flowers and grapes; and I had also advised him on the purchase of a pair of blackamoors that went for the then enormous sum of £36,000, so I knew he wasn't short of a bob or two to indulge his passion. (I felt that I gave him excellent advice because Sotheby's recently sold a pair of identical blackamoors for close to £200,000.)

'David, have you ever seen a Minton peacock?' the American asked me. 'Ya know, one of those that are larger than life-size, about four or five feet tall? Now, I'd give my right arm for one of those.'

Well, that was a challenge, and as anyone will tell you, I never turn a challenge down. I love the thrill of the chase, following the leads, and the research involved in pursuit of that special quarry. I knew exactly what my collector wanted. Those exotic peacocks were among the most fabulous items ever produced by the Minton factory. They were modelled by a famous sculptor, Paul Comolera, in about 1873. With their crest of feathers and sumptuous long tails, the pieces had been very hard to make and were very fragile. It was thought that there were only about 12 left, and one of those was in the Minton museum. None had ever turned up for auction.

I knew the task was a daunting one, so you could have knocked me down with a peacock feather when I opened my mouth and said to the American, 'I'm sure I can find one, leave it to me.'

I did some research at the Minton museum with the help of a dear friend, Joan Jones, who is the curator. I thought that was a good starting place. The first bird I discovered was in a Derbyshire hotel, the Peacock View, I think it was called, appropriately enough. I jumped in my car and drove off to the Peak District. As I walked into the hotel lobby I saw the peacock at once, but to my surprise it was not complete. When perfect, the piece is a free-standing, larger than life model of a peacock with a wonderful long train of feathers, sitting atop a pile of ivy-clad grey rocks. In this case, however, the bottom half – the rocks and half the bird's tail – were missing and the remaining top half had been cemented into a wall. It was a sad sight. Disappointed, I got back into my car and drove home. As far as I know, the poor bird is still there, stuck to the wall.

The second peacock I located was also in a hotel, this one on the Isle of Wight. Again I rushed in where angels fear to tread, without making an appointment or even checking that the piece was still there. When I walked into the hotel lobby my heart stood still: there it was, a magnificent, full-size bird in all its original plumage, standing in a corner. I could hardly believe my luck as I carefully inspected it for damage. Not a crack – it was perfect. The peacock, with its crest and long tail, was intact, as was the base on which it perched. Now to persuade the owner to sell. I made my pitch and he instantly refused. I tried a little persuasion, but he told me he had inherited the piece from his mother and was not willing even to consider an offer. In the end, he walked off into his office, firmly shutting the door in my face.

I did some more research and located a third peacock through some correspondence I'd come across. This one was in Australia. Even for someone who had gone to Derbyshire and the Isle of Wight without appointments, flying to Australia without first checking things out was a little too hasty. From the address on the correspondence I managed to find a telephone number through international directory enquiries. I called and spoke to the owner in Sydney.

'Yes, I have a peacock,' she confirmed, and described it. It sounded perfect. She then added enthusiastically, 'There's another one in the museum in Melbourne. It's insured for a million dollars.'

'That's a great deal of money. They're not worth that much,' I said, wanting to nip in the bud any aspirations she might have towards riches.

'Well, that's a shame,' she said. 'I thought I was in with a chance.'

'No chance,' I said, 'but I'll make you a fair dinkum offer.'

She laughed, and went on to tell me the story of how an Australian museum came to own a Minton peacock. Apparently, it was on its way to the 1880 International Exhibition in Melbourne when the ship carrying it, the *Loch Ard*, broke up and foundered some 14 miles off the coast. The peacock was washed ashore, still in its original crate. The Melbourne museum acquired it and today it is known as the 'Loch Ard peacock'.

A long period of telephone negotiating ensued. Eventually, the woman in Sydney agreed to sell me her peacock for £13,000. I called my collector in Long Island and told him the good news – I had a bird in perfect condition for him. We agreed a price of £25,000, which would cover my expenses, including shipping and insurance costs, and my margin of profit. Carrying a certified banker's draft in my pocket, I bought a round-the-world ticket and flew to Australia. *Yes! Bingo!* The peacock stared me proudly in the eye from a corner of its owner's modern living room. I patted it on the back and posed for a snapshot – me and the bird, side by side. (And I've still got the picture – my, we do look a pair of bobby dazzlers!)

The woman told me a remarkable story, which again explains why I love this business, which has so much unusual and interesting history behind every piece. Her husband had agreed to sell the peacock to an Indian maharaja and it was duly packed up and sent off. But World War II intervened and the bird remained crated up at the docks in India for the duration. For some reason it was never delivered to the buyer after the war but was shipped back to Australia. By then, her husband had died.

'He really loved this peacock,' she said, gazing at it somewhat misty-eyed.

I was so sure that she was about to change her mind, I asked the waiting shippers to carry it out at once and crate it up in the van instead of in the house.

With the bird finally in my hand, so to speak, I telephoned the American collector and told him I would be sending it to New York by sea and it would be with him in a few weeks. But he was so red-hot to see the piece that he asked me to fly it over myself and blow the expense. This I did. When he was told that it had arrived and had already been unpacked at his Long Island home he was so excited that he abandoned a multi-million-dollar property deal mid-discussion in Manhattan and hared back to his house. He loved it, of course – what collector wouldn't? For my part, I was in awe as I looked at his large and lavish collection of some of the most wonderful pieces of Minton in the world. And I have to say that in my opinion the peacock beat the socks off all of them for sheer size and colour, with the exception, perhaps, of the pair of blackamoors I had recommended before.

I thought everything had gone remarkably well and I was feeling pretty pleased with myself when he took the wind right out of my sails: he tried to renegotiate the asking price. With the peacock unpacked and already placed within his collection, he thought he had me over a barrel. He even went to the extreme length of tracking down the air freighter and checking the bill of lading to see how much I had originally paid for the piece in Australia. He completely ignored the three months of hard work I had put into tracking it down, the expense and time involved in flying around the world, the insurance, the freight costs. That man wanted his cake and he wanted to eat it, too. I explained that my margin of profit was about £7,000 and said that he probably made far more profit on his property deals. I wouldn't budge on my price and in the end he gave in. He finally handed over the banker's draft that had been in his pocket all along – it was already made out for the sum that we had previously agreed.

He then did something that showed me why he was a millionaire and I wasn't. When the time came for me to leave his house he told his wife to go and fetch his railway season ticket. This monthly pass allowed him to travel back and forth between his home in Long Island and Penn Station in Manhattan, where his office was, as many times as he wished. As it happened, it was the last day of August and the ticket would expire at midnight.

'Here, David,' he said, pressing it into my hands. 'This'll save you a dollar fifty!'

I was amazed. This wretched man had just argued himself blue in the face over £25,000, yet here he was, actually chortling with glee at the idea of saving me a measly $1.50. I took the ticket but when I got to the station I threw it away and paid the full price for my train trip to Manhattan.

I can't leave this tale without saying that in 1995 an identical Minton peacock was sold at Christie's for £95,000. Today, the price would be far higher. This tough and over-cautious American had got a real bargain.

Furniture, ceramics and works of art are not the only antiques worth considering. One of the areas most avidly studied and collected is weaponry – guns, swords, bows and arrows, suits of armour and so forth – and the dealers and collectors who specialize in this field are usually real aficionados. The actor Robert Hardy is an acknowledged world authority on the English longbow;

and Hugh Kennedy, an extraordinary, charismatic dealer who lives in a wonderful Queen Anne house near Shrewsbury full of formidable works of art and
a superb collection of arms, is a leading expert on the trebuchet. As far as I
know, he built the first trebuchet to be produced in England since the Middle
Ages. You may have seen him on television demonstrating it.

I can hear you saying – a *what*?

The trebuchet is a medieval siege weapon, a kind of large slingshot, made of
tree trunks – entire tree trunks. It has a very long throwing arm with a leather
bucket or sling – usually an entire ox hide – at one end that can hold a huge
rock. The arm is wound down with a kind of twisted rope traction mechanism.
This is released suddenly and the rock is hurled hundreds of yards at a castle
wall, with the intention of battering it down. Although the most common way
of taking a castle was through the siege, when starvation and thirst would drive
those under attack to surrender, medieval people also designed weapons or
other ways to threaten the 15-foot walls surrounding fortresses and towns.
Ladders, battering rams and tunnelling were the favoured methods of getting
at the enemy within. But, given the hail of arrows and hot oil or pitch
raining down from the ramparts, medieval craftsmen needed to invent ways of
breaching walls that would keep the attacking soldiers at a distance. And so the
trebuchet was devised; capable of throwing rocks weighing hundreds of pounds,
it was one of the most fearsome developments of the thirteenth century. The
missiles were like bombs, breaking down walls and crushing soldiers on the
ramparts. Even splinters of rock hurled in this way could maim and kill.

By the fourteenth century the trebuchet was so effective it was both praised
as a technological marvel and condemned as a demoniacal weapon. Yet two or
three hundred years later, superseded by gunpowder and cannon, it was obso-
lete and the technology was forgotten. Modern historians believed that these
cumbersome wooden scaffolds on wheels had never been all that powerful.
True, there were drawings and paintings in museums showing them in action,
but there were always arguments about how effective they had really been.
Bearing in mind that a castle wall can be 12–15 feet thick and maybe twice as
high, it seemed reasonable to question just how much damage a large lump of
rock hurled by a bent tree trunk could do.

Hugh Kennedy, one of the most interesting individuals I have ever met, was
of the mind that old records don't lie. He believed that if you bombarded a
castle wall with these huge rocks you could knock a hole in it with the impact
of a massive mortar, and then your forces could charge through, exactly as
shown in old pictures he had seen. Over the years he had produced a few
models and was seen on television expounding his theory, so I'm sure he won't
mind me telling this story. By following the designs he had found in medieval
illustrations he made a full-scale replica of a trebuchet. When it was ready for
testing, he and his mates brought it out onto the fields within his property.

It was a massive beast of a thing, about as big as a dinosaur. A huge hunk of cast iron weighing a hundredweight was used in place of a rock. The trunk of a full-grown green oak tree was pulled back on ratchets and ship's rope as far as it would go without cracking. When it was suddenly released, the hurling arm straightened itself with all the power of Zeus chucking rocks from Mount Olympus. The lump of iron hurtled through the air – and on and on it flew like a meteor before disappearing over the horizon.

Mouths open wide, eyes popping in disbelief, Hugh and the others stared into the misty distance, listening for the sound of a crash or some other indication of where the great hunk of old iron had gone. Silence. Nothing but the caw of rooks in the elms and the contented munching of a herd of cows chewing buttercups.

The doughty medievalists leapt into a four-wheel-drive vehicle and careered around the countryside, trying to locate their missing missile. Unsuccessful, they eventually returned to the house. A few days later, Hugh heard a rumour that a low-flying aircraft had gone over the nearby village and a part had fallen off and gone through a farmhouse roof. It could have been worse. A group of Americans recently made a similar trebuchet, using several old upright pianos, the kind that had solid cast-iron frames. These were hurled in sequence at an area of ground which was miked up for sound and had a camera strategically placed; it was reported that the pianos made a massive crater as deep as a bomb dropped from a World War II bomber. All I can say is, no wonder those medieval peasants called the trebuchet a demoniacal weapon.

Still in the field of arms and weapons, I remember when I called in at Wiggington's once, where I saw and fell in love with a matched pair of cannon. God knows where I would have put them. They were about 20 feet long. The barrels were of bronze and had exotic ends, like dragons' heads. They still had the original panniers attached to carry all the shells. Mr Wiggington told me they had been given as a gift to some viceroy by a Mogul warrior.

I took one look and said, 'How much?'

'Oh, a snip,' said Mr Wiggington rather drily. 'Fifty thousand.'

It was a whacking great sum and too big an outlay when I had no one in mind to sell them on to. I will splash out if I can be sure that such an investment won't sit around for ever but this was too rich for me – even though he did offer to split the pair and let me have one for £25,000. I often regretted not buying them. As I told Chris, they would have looked cracking in our window – if we'd had a window large enough. Years later I heard the pair had gone for at least four times Mr Wiggington's asking price.

Chris and I had been in business in Wilmslow for some time when many changes occurred. The first was to do with a general slowing down of the economy. In turn, our business slowed. We had a reasonable financial cushion but I can't deny that we did feel the pinch. Overheads like rent and wages, heating

LEFT Me with my half-brother, Ken Moss.
BELOW Dear Auntie Ethel.
BOTTOM My mother, 1960.

ABOVE Lorne and myself.
RIGHT Myself, Michael Aspel and my
half-brother, Ken, on *This is Your Life*.

ABOVE Meeting
Princess Margaret at
the Olympia Fair.
RIGHT Winning the
National Television
Awards in 2002.
BELOW Me with
Chris Moyles.

FAR LEFT My stand at Olympia in 1997.
LEFT Frank Skinner impersonating me on the *Frank Skinner Show*.
BELOW The photoshoot for *Radio Times*.

LEFT Lorne and I at home in the barn.
BELOW At home with my treasures.
OVERLEAF Hunting for those bargains!

and lighting and so on don't go away. We hadn't yet reached the stage where we had even considered that we might have to close, when Chris sprang the news that he was leaving. That was a big blow. We had been partners and friends for so many years without a disagreement – perhaps the odd difference of opinion that came from our slightly different tastes in the pieces we decided to buy; but Chris had generally allowed me to have my head in purchasing and I had let him get on with running the shop and doing the paperwork. We were like a pair of old shoes, one left and one right, that fitted perfectly, that you could wear without even noticing.

By then Chris was divorced from his first wife, Sandra, a very nice woman whom I had known for many years, and he had now met a new lady. She decided that her future with him lay elsewhere and she looked around for other opportunities. When she spotted one in a large department store in Florida, where there was an opening for a smart gallery selling antiques – a kind of boutique within a shop – she discussed it with Chris and he was persuaded. Of course, it was a blow and a sadness, as it always is when you come to the end of an era and the parting of the ways with an old friend. But we all have to grow and develop in the way we think is right for us and I put a cheerful face on it, glad for Chris. We agreed that we would split the stock right down the middle, with Chris taking his half to help get the new boutique started. We did this amicably and remained friends. He went on his way to Florida and I looked around for new opportunities for myself.

Sadly, things didn't work out for Chris. Without going into too much unhappy detail, I can say that he returned to England and died of cancer in 1995. His passing was a great grief in my life and I will always miss him. He was a good friend and colleague and we shared some wonderful times – as carefree school-boys in Manchester, then as adventurous young men in Paris and the south of France, and through all the occasionally hair-raising and entertaining years that we shared when we were starting out in the antiques business as young greenhorns.

When Chris went to America I knew I would have to reduce my overheads. Wilmslow had not proved quite the honey trap we had hoped. Perhaps it was an approaching recession, or perhaps it was really true what people said about it being 'all frock and no knickers', but, after an upbeat start, business had not lived up to expectations. I started looking for new premises and thought that the heart of Manchester, where I had started my business life as a young commission agent in men's suiting fabric, would be a good commercial bet.

Chris and I had a good client, Imad Al-Midani, a young Saudi gentleman from an extremely privileged background. Imad and his brother had attended college in Cheshire and had continued to live there afterwards. Their father, Mufti Al-Midani, a man of great standing, was an international mover and shaker in the construction business, dealing in a mega way with governments, mostly on behalf of the Saudi royal family, responsible for building Saudi Arabian roads, bridges, hospitals and so forth. He was a 50 per cent partner in Fairclough-Midani, one of the world's biggest construction companies and was, so I was told, considered to be one of the richest men in the world at the time, worth a conservative £4 billion.

Imad had come into the Wilmslow shop on many occasions to buy pieces for his home, a magnificent period hall in the area, and became not only a client but a friend. Lorne and I got to know him on a social level and found him to be a charming and perfect gentleman, not at all spoilt despite all the advantages wealth and position showered on him. He had been educated at the American School in Beirut and finished his education in England. He and his wife, Jane, an English girl he had met and married locally, would often come to dinner. Always, he would arrive laden down like Santa with the most fabulous and exotic gifts, such as pieces of Baccarat crystal, porcelain, robes or luxurious towels.

Many a time, I would say, 'Imad stop it! We're only having egg and chips tonight, there's no need to stand on ceremony.'

This was an 'in' joke, since we would be having some nice three-course meal, but Imad would smile and present Lorne with some wonderful item, murmuring, 'It's nothing, just a small token.'

That was the nature of him, to be very warm and friendly. Everything about him was modest, diffident and natural. His father was a major shareholder in the Dorchester Hotel in London's Park Lane (as well as owning the Beverly Hills Hotel, the Marbella Club and Hotel and various other hotels in prime locations) and it had just been refurbished at a cost, I believe, of £15 million. (This was way before the Sultan of Brunei bought it.) When Imad invited us to stay at the Dorchester as his guests one weekend he never once threw his weight about. If the dining room was full, even though the maître d' rushed forward Imad quietly told him to attend to the other guests, we'd wait our turn.

We got on well, he was always affable and had many business interests, so I asked him if he would like to be a sleeping partner in a new gallery in Manchester. He readily agreed. He was the perfect partner in every way, allowing me to get on with the work I knew, and offering support or advice only when asked. As I had with Chris, we split the profits equally down the middle. I took a salary because I was doing all the work and Imad, of course, got returns on his financial investment. Whatever was left got ploughed back into stock. Just as an example of the kind of man Imad was: when he bought something he liked from the gallery for his home, he would always insist on paying a margin of profit. Other men might have taken it at cost – but he never would. I think he thought that by doing that he would deprive me of my share of the profit, and that was the measure of the man.

One of the high spots of my relationship with Imad was the trip he took

Lorne and me on to introduce us to his father in Cannes, in one of the many homes he owned around the world. No question, it was like flying on a magic carpet into another dimension. Never in my entire life, before or since, have I experienced such luxury and I doubt I will again, even if I win the multi million Spanish lottery, *El Gordo* – the Fat One.

Imad's family was amazingly wealthy. You don't realize how rich these people are until you see how they live. His father owned many private jets, amongst them a Lear – on which we were to travel. A chauffeur-driven car took us to Manchester, where the waiting Lear jet, piloted by two retired BA captains who worked for Mr Al-Midani, picked us up, and we were whisked off to the south of France. Just before we arrived I asked Imad if I could go into the cockpit for the landing. One of the captains put me into the co-pilot's seat. It was a great thrill to arrive in Nice as the sun went down, seeing the entire panorama of lights twinkling along the Riviera. We taxied to a stop in an area of the airport reserved for private planes. Waiting for us there were two Mercedes Pullman limousines – one for Imad, his wife, their daughter's nanny and his secretary, and the other one for Lorne and me. A small airport van with a flashing light on top led the way and before I knew it we were out on the highway.

I looked round and said to Lorne, 'Where the hell were the customs?'

We had completely bypassed it all.

Our destination was Mufti Al-Midani's 'guest' villa, the Château Treize, a pink fairy-tale castle with little turrets situated on a hill overlooking Cannes in a select area known as Super-Cannes. It was like a Jacqueline Bisset mini-series, with the staff lined up on the curving flight of steps leading up to the massive front doors, the men in striped vests, the women with frilly white aprons and little caps. When we got out of the vehicles they bowed or curtsied, and it felt as though we had arrived on a set in Hollywood.

From here on in, if I spelt it out, there would be an adjective in front of every word, from A-Z, so take it as read. In fact, words failed me, and that's saying something! I kept saying to Lorne, 'I have never seen anything like it' – and it just got more and more amazing. Our luggage was taken to one of the turrets, which was to be exclusively ours. One surprising feature of our turret was that the bathroom, which was on the floor above the bedroom suite, had large windows and no curtains. It seemed a bit too public until one considered that we were perched on top of the hill, like one of those fantastical castles on the Rhine, and it was virtually impossible for anyone to spy on our most private moments, even with binoculars.

We were to spend a week in Cannes. Because of the amount of business that Imad's father conducted, we waited for an appointment to see him. It was remarkable to be back here on the Riviera in such luxurious circumstances. I had been back many times since my impoverished days as a youth, and had even stayed in the hallowed Carlton Hotel, once as a young man prior to getting married to Lorne and many times with her afterwards. Now here we were again, one of those people I had looked at with such envy all those years ago, reclining on those same banquettes, being served cold drinks and looking rather haughtily, I'm sorry to say, at the hoi polloi on the crowded public beach.

After three days Imad told us that his father had invited us to dinner that evening at Château Bagatelle, his own magical villa, which was perched on the mountain high above us. I asked him what I should wear.

He said, 'Wear something casual, David.'

'Casual?' I said. 'Blimey, Imad, I've brought the full monty here! I've got the kitchen sink in my luggage.'

I did have some casual clothes but I also had two dinner suits (one white, one black), lounge suits and blazers.

Imad smiled. 'My father will be very relaxed and would appreciate it if you came in something casual.'

In the end he and I both chose to wear slacks with a shirt and cardigan.

Imad's father might have been relaxed but the strict security surrounding him was not. A car was sent down to get the four of us: Imad and his wife, Lorne and me. We took the mountain road higher up into *super* Super-Cannes, where there was an observatory on the summit. At the top we reached the small road that encircled the Château Bagatelle. I was reliably told it was one of the most fabulous villas in the south of France. We arrived at huge ornate metal gates. A handsome, rather tough man in a leather jacket and jeans came out to speak to the chauffeur. His eyes took us in. He asked for the boot to be opened and he inspected it. He spoke into a walkie-talkie and only then did the electric gates swing open.

The car drove slowly through. On the other side, another five of these tough-looking French guys were waiting. What surprised me was that as the car purred along the drive towards the entrance of the magnificent house, these men were at a trot each side with walkie-talkies, almost like a presidential motorcade.

'Who are these men?' I asked Imad.

Quietly, he said, 'Deuxième Bureau.'

The French Special Branch. I wondered about this but didn't ask any more questions at that time.

The car stopped about ten yards from the house and the secret servicemen slowed down. Another man appeared at the door. He wasn't very tall but he had presence. This was Mufti Al-Midani, Imad's father. We got out of the car and approached him, as if towards royalty. Only when he had come down the steps to greet us in person did the bodyguards back away.

If I had any lingering thoughts that we were going to walk into one of those so-called traditional Arab homes with silk cushions and hubble-bubble pipes I couldn't have been more wrong. An Italian designer, one of the best in the world, had created a breathtaking interior in this superb villa. We entered a large open hallway and walked across a marble floor inlaid with mosaic tiling, marvelling at the Roman statues in the alcoves, carved from Carrara marble. We were led into a reception room and seated while Imad's father excused himself to attend to some business. Every soft drink known to man was brought in on a trolley by a team of young Frenchwomen dressed in uniform. Alcohol was not served, though it would be, on request, with the meal if we wished. Lorne and I sat on Louis XV tapestry chairs before a huge Shibiama-decorated Japanese low table that was covered with an assortment of the most exquisite objects: Fabergé, jade, lapis lazuli. The walls were decorated with fine seventeenth- and eighteenth-century French and Italian oil paintings. It was perfect. Nothing was too bold or over the top.

We then moved on through the house to the dining room. Again, my breath was taken away. It was like entering the hall of mirrors at Versailles. The walls and ceilings were covered in large pieces of plate mirror. Eighteenth-century chandeliers hung from the ceiling, reflected a million times, throwing back scintillating points of light. Along the walls was a series of two large gilt-wood console tables, with a pier mirror with a gilt-wood surround hung above each one. It was mirror on mirror. It sounds a little OTT but the interior decorator had made a splendid and tasteful job of it. In the centre of the room was the most fabulous 20-foot Italian marble and glass table, on massive glass legs. Around the table was a set of eighteenth-century Venetian lacquered high-backed dining chairs. On the table, which was already set, was a huge service of silver, with an enormous silver-gilt centrepiece stretching the full length down the middle. To one end of the room was a pair of seventeenth-century Italian cabinets inlaid with assorted *pietra dura* marble specimens. I've seen some splendid examples in my time but these were absolute bobby dazzlers. On either side of these were two gilded Italian eighteenth-century figures.

Imad must have seen my eyes on stalks but he didn't say anything. We walked through this lavish room to the marble-floored balcony, where we were to dine al fresco. This again was remarkable. If I thought that the dining room was spectacular, I had never seen anything like the terrace. We were seated on modern brass Italian chairs at a huge circular glass table, which was beautifully laid with fine Limoges porcelain and crystal, serviettes and cutlery. At a word from Mufti Al-Midani, a member of staff pressed a button and the convex window on the balcony folded back in sections and vanished into the wall, leaving us in the open air behind a low marble balustrade. Before us lay the whole of Cannes, lights twinkling along the Croisette. And the lights of all the yachts riding in the harbour were reflected in the calm sea and beyond, all the way to Nice.

Ten courses of food came from the kitchens, cooked by Mufti Al-Midani's own chefs, far too much for us to eat. We each scraped tiny portions off the side of giant platters and the balance was returned to the kitchens. 'I could very easily get into this,' I thought, as I gazed at the view from that luxurious eyrie.

After dinner, we walked in the garden, accompanied by the gentlemen of the Deuxième Bureau. Imad's father and I had little in common but he was courteous, a gracious host. I don't think I'm being indiscreet when I mention that he was a close friend of Ronald Reagan and many other heads of state. I was told that a number of French ministers had stayed at Bagatelle while he was negotiating with France on behalf of the Saudi government.

Next day I asked Imad more about the bodyguards. He said they were assigned to look after his father whenever he was in France because it could cause great embarrassment if anything happened to him. He added that his father was given dispensation at the customs in France and in Spain. When we returned to England, still in the private jet, we had to wait to clear customs. It just shows you – and what would a man who had £4 billion want to smuggle anyway?

The following morning, after the memorable dinner at Château Bagatelle, Imad's wife, Jane, said to Lorne at breakfast, 'Let's nip out to have our hair done at the Carlton.'

It sounded so everyday. I laughed inwardly, reflecting on how easy it was to act like the rich live, as I fished in my pocket for a couple of hundred pounds in francs, thinking that Lorne would get little change from that. Off both ladies went in their chauffeur-driven limousine to spend an enjoyable few hours having their hair done. On her return Lorne gave me all my money back. Everything had been paid for. She told me that after visiting the hairdresser they had gone shopping along the Croisette, followed at a discreet distance by the chauffeur, who was carrying all the parcels. I don't think she bought anything herself, though she did see something in a shop window that took her fancy: a small gold-plated gadget used for keeping the bubbles in a bottle of champagne after it has been opened.

At the end of the week we reversed our journey in the Lear jet back to Manchester. On Lorne's seat in the plane was a gift-wrapped parcel.

'Don't open it until you get home,' Imad said.

Lorne did as he requested and waited. When she did finally open the little parcel she found the champagne thingamajig that she had quite casually admired while shopping. That was the kind of man Imad was – generous to a fault. I knew that I had made the right decision by bringing him in as a partner.

CHAPTER SIXTEEN

·

Before Imad and I opened the new gallery in Manchester, while I was still in the throes of reletting the shop in Wilmslow, somebody told me about the Body Shop, so I hung on to the premises a little longer just in case there was an opening for me in the beauty products franchise business. At that time the company had only two outlets, the original shop in the Lanes in Brighton and one that had opened more recently in London, in Covent Garden. I was curious and so the next time I was in the area I popped along to Covent Garden to have a look. This was some time after the old fruit and vegetable market had closed down and moved elsewhere. The beautiful colonnades and cobbles of the historic old market, which went back to the Georgian era and shades of Eliza Doolittle in the Victorian period, had been converted into a trendy place filled with little boutiques and cafes.

The Body Shop was painted a smart shade of fir green, with gold lettering, and the original floorboards inside had been nicely restored. Everything was very simply arranged, all very hessian and wood. The beauty care products on sale were made from natural organic materials with no animal fats, so they did not harm the environment, and I liked the idea of that. Anita Roddick, who was later to become a red-hot businesswoman, was quite laid back and hippie when she started the company. She was so laid back, in fact, that she was selling franchises for a reasonable £8,650. She had not sold many so far and whole areas were still available.

I thought, 'This is all right. I like the product, I like the look of it, in its plain, unfussy packaging, and I like the look of the shop itself. And, most important, it's affordable.'

I packed up a load of samples and took them home with me. I showed them to Lorne and passed them around our circle of friends. Everyone was enthusiastic, except for one particular area: the perfumes. These were oil-based and quite musky, like patchouli. Lorne and her lady friends were unanimous.

'We love it all, but the perfumes are too hippie trail,' they said. 'They'll never sell, especially not in Wilmslow.'

I decided the premises in Wilmslow would be ideal for the Body Shop and I discussed this with Imad. He also had interests in a shopping complex in

Manchester and I suggested that we could open a second franchise there. He agreed that it would be a good idea to buy two franchises so I contacted the Body Shop office straight away.

'I'll go ahead,' I said, 'but I don't want the perfume. I don't think it works.'

The perfumes would initially have cost some £700-£800, not a great deal of money, perhaps, when set against the value of the entire stock, but to me it would have been money wasted if the goods stayed on the shelf. Body Shop said no, I would have to take their entire range of products. In the end I decided not to go ahead. It was a bad decision. There were only two Body Shops trading at the time. I had the possibility of serious financial backing from Imad and I'm sure we could have expanded at a rapid rate all over the northwest, then the rest of the UK and possibly into Europe and North America. The sky was the limit and I turned it down for the sake of £800 worth of perfume. Many millions could have been made and within a really short space of time.

It so happened that these franchises in the northwest, the ones that I was going to take but had allowed someone else to pick up, were later bought back by the Body Shop for about £5 million apiece. But that's how it goes in life. You make the decision to turn right instead of left and travel along that road. I've never regretted it. I will never cry over spilt milk because who knows how things will turn out? You never know what's around the corner, and whatever you decide on at any particular time, years down the line can lead to something else, perhaps something even better or more interesting.

In a lesser way, I often think of the antiques I wish I'd bought, or the ones I should have kept but sold on instead. The Little Admiral was one, and then there was the flag of the Empress of China. This was something I spotted at a country house sale, one of those homes where hundreds of years of collected history were under the hammer. I'm a sucker for the romance of the past and for things that are no more, so when I saw this silk flag in a glass case on the wall, and heard its history, I was lost. It was a unique object, dating from the time of turmoil in China at the turn of the twentieth century, and a wonderful history lesson.

Throughout the nineteenth century China's Ch'ing emperors had watched as Western powers encroached further and further upon their land, forcing them to make humiliating concessions. Foreign regiments, armed with modern weapons, defeated entire imperial armies. Then the Americans arrived. Wanting a slice of the pie, John Hay, US Secretary of State, suggested an open-door policy in China, which would allow free and equal access to trade to everyone in the West. Naturally, the powers already there, such as the English, the Germans, the Dutch and the Russians, objected.

Tsu Hsi, Dowager Empress of the Ch'ing Dynasty, searched for a way to rid her empire of these foreigners. She wanted to close the doors of China to the world. She issued an imperial message to all the Chinese provinces, calling on them to unite and fight. In northern Shandong province a devastating drought was pushing people to the edge of starvation. A secret society, known as the Fists of Righteous Harmony, attracted thousands of followers who believed that they had a magical power, and that foreign bullets could not harm them. They said that millions of 'spirit soldiers' would rise from the dead and join their cause – which was to overthrow the foreigners and also their own government. The Europeans called members of this society 'Boxers' because they practised martial arts.

The crafty Dowager Empress, however, saw a way to use the Boxers. She would let them rebel and attack the foreigners – who would attack them with their superior power. When the Boxers and the foreigners had destroyed each other, the Dowager Empress would unleash her imperial troops and mop up what was left. Soon a new slogan – 'Support the Ch'ing; destroy the foreigner!' – appeared upon the Boxers' banners. In the early months of 1900 thousands of Boxers roamed the countryside, attacking Christian missions and slaughtering everyone. Then they moved towards the cities. Inside the Forbidden City, the Dowager Empress did nothing. She told her frantic ministers that her troops would soon crush the 'rebellion'.

Foreign diplomats, their families and staff, who lived in a compound just outside the Forbidden City's walls in the heart of Peking, hastily threw up defences and faced the Boxer onslaught. An American described the scene in 1900 as 20,000 Boxers charged: 'They advanced in a solid mass and carried standards of red and white cloth. Their yells were deafening, while the roar of gongs, drums and horns sounded like thunder. They waved their swords and stamped on the ground with their feet. They wore red turbans, sashes, and garters over blue cloth. When they were only twenty yards from our gate, three volleys from the rifles of our sailors left more than fifty dead upon the ground.'

The Boxers fell back but soon returned. The foreigners were under siege for almost two months and were out of food, ammunition and medicines before they were relieved by an international force. After the Boxers were defeated the Western troops sacked the Forbidden City. The Dowager Empress escaped to the Summer Palace in an ox cart, disguised as a peasant, but was forced to flee again when the troops advanced. She made her last stand at the summer Palace, before she and her flag were captured.

At the auction the flag I was looking at – the colours of the Dowager Empress – had come from the Summer Palace itself. It made the hair stand up on the back of my neck just to think of all that history.

The estimate guideline was £300–£500. I took it up to £600, then heaven knows why, I dropped out. I was the underbidder on that occasion and could have won if I'd persevered. This is why I always say to people, 'Try to go home the bride and not the bridesmaid – don't lose it for a bid.' Well, I lost the Empress's flag and even after all these years I could still kick myself.

I found a location for a new gallery in the centre of Manchester, in John Doulton Street. The interior was huge, with marble floors, and the display windows were a generous size. Some of the walls were plastered and some were panelled in hardwood. We got the decorators in and had the plain walls painted beige and the wood panelling polished. The floor was cleaned and polished, too, and new spotlight racks were fitted. There was no doubt that it was a glamorous gallery. I hired an assistant, Jackie Mann, a charming woman who ended up as the lifetime companion of my old dealer friend, the amazing Maurice 'Dick' Turpin, and most of the time I was out buying stock.

When I was in business with Chris I had often bought antiques that were more suitable for the international market than a provincial gallery, even a smart one like ours in Wilmslow. I would keep these pieces back until I had accumulated enough (I liked to have around 14 or 15) to make a decent display at the big international fairs in London, where I knew I would reach a wider clientele. I maintained this practice after I opened the Manchester gallery and I continued to take exhibition space at Olympia from time to time to show the finest, most exotic wares I had acquired.

People came to my stand at Olympia from all over the world; there were many Arabs, but also movie stars, musicians and businessmen and women. There were times when things were a little slack and I then had the opportunity to stroll around the fair and chat with my fellow dealers. Ladies tended to come in during the week. They might buy something, or perhaps they would do a recce, depending on what they were looking for, then often return with their husbands at the weekend or on a Friday afternoon.

There were some clients I would welcome with open arms, others I would run a mile from. Sounding a bit like Edward Lear with his limericks, there was a young lady from Qatar who came with another client of mine. She immediately gave me the impression that she wanted to kick me in the balls. We haggled quite ferociously but in the end, when the deal was struck, she was all smiles.

Sometimes the unexpected happened. In the early days, a very working-class lady came by wearing a woolly hat, her Marks and Spencer bag filled with shopping. I was reminded instantly of my granny.

'Is it all right if I look around?' she asked me hesitantly.

'Of course it is, my love,' I said.

'I can't afford anything on here, you know,' she said.

'Don't be silly,' I replied. 'You're most welcome. Look around as much as you wish.'

She stayed a good half hour or 40 minutes. We had a good chat and she asked some questions which showed her lack of knowledge, but a genuine desire to know more. I answered politely as I've always been a great believer in the old saying, 'You can't read a book by its covers.' It's not *who* you are, I always think, but *what* you are.

Eventually she told me she was a cleaning lady and had just finished her regular round of offices. Nevertheless, she seemed a very nice woman. She bid me farewell and asked if she could take a business card. About three days later, a man came on to the stand. He was very pleasant and jovial, in a pinstriped suit. We got into conversation. He said he was a broker and we discussed that a little. He looked at several things and settled on a desk. The final purchase price was about £7,000. He signed the documentation and gave me a cheque.

Just as he was leaving, he turned back and said, 'By the way, you met my mother. She was here a few days ago.'

I looked a little puzzled. He smiled.

'She does office cleaning,' he explained. 'She doesn't need to, but she won't retire. All her friends are cleaners and she enjoys doing it. She mentioned to me that she went to the fair at Olympia and met this charming young bloke who spent all his time with her, despite the fact that he knew she couldn't afford anything. I just wanted to thank you.'

As I say, you never know what is around the next corner. And as I found out at the same fair from a friend who had a glamorous *bijouterie* stand nearby, the super-rich aren't always as arrogant as is often made out. He was telling me as we stood chatting during a quiet period that a very nice gentleman had just come to his stand. He spent about a couple of thousand pounds and gave him a cheque. The invoice was made out to a company, which didn't give away any clues.

'Look, I know you haven't done business with me before,' the client said, 'so when this cheque has cleared I'll send my driver later in the week to collect my purchase.'

'Who was it?' I asked my friend.

He showed me the cheque, which he had not yet banked. It was signed by the Aga Khan – reputedly the wealthiest man in the world. I thought that stood out, that a man as well known and as hugely rich as the Aga Khan would not presume to say, 'Oh, by the way, do you know who I am?' to which, in the script, dealers would respond, 'Oh, my goodness! Your Highness, please take your goods with you! Don't worry about the cheque.'

Imad and I had a very successful period with the Manchester gallery from about 1984 to the early Nineties. Then recession bit. It was a difficult time for luxury goods. Everyone wants nice furniture but in times of recession they tend to tighten their belts and make do with what they have. Chippendale tables, exotic blackamoor torchères and Louis Quatorze commodes are not high on their list of priorities. We stuck it out for a while but it was not to be. This antiques business is not all go, go, go. Things can get very tough. The recession, coupled with the tripling of my rent, made me decide that we should dissolve the partnership and close the shop. I decided I would concentrate on the international fairs, which I had already been doing successfully for many years.

I would make them the main source of my dealings and income. It was the end of another wonderful and fascinating era.

But fate had not yet done with me as far as the ends of eras were concerned, and something else was to come to an end in a very sad way – but, as they say, as one door closes, another one opens. I am talking of my mother and the family I had not yet met.

Over the years my mother and I had kept in regular contact with my usual phone calls, and then, after a while, she said it would be all right for me to write to her, although she still never suggested that we met. Her answer whenever I broached the subject was always the same: I would be disappointed. During my long absences from home with Lorne's career, I would write from wherever we were. In 1989, some 20 years after I had first made contact with my mother, a letter came back marked 'not known'. I thought it was a bit strange. My first thought was that it had fallen into the hands of her husband and he was being a silly bugger. So I wrote back again, thinking she had not received it. This time the husband wrote back to me. It was quite an offhand letter; he said he knew who I was, had always known. Then came a terrific shock. He said my mother had passed away, sadly, and he felt it was his duty to point out that her sister, Marie, lived in the Manchester area. He gave her address. Ironically, it was only 10 or 12 miles from where we lived in Bramhall.

My shock was extreme. Many thoughts went through my mind. Perhaps I relived my life a little, wondering what might have been. I sat there, reading and rereading the letter. I wondered why – *why* – had I not just gone over to Jersey to meet my mother face to face? Of course, I was respecting her feelings, her sense of dignity and her fears as well as her privacy. But it was a blow. At the back of my mind there was always that thought that some day we would finally meet, but it was now never to be.

I contacted Marie on the telephone. She was absolutely thrilled. She said she had been aware of this adoption, she knew I existed. She invited me to call on her. I duly went to meet her and her husband and we spent the day together. She was a charming lady who made me warmly welcome.

When I first walked through the door she stared, then said, 'I'd have known you anywhere.'

She showed me photographs of my mother as a young woman, and I did see a close resemblance, the more so in photographs as we both grew older.

The burning question, of course, was why had I been left at Dr Barnardo's? I understood that as a young nurse with no husband, and with the uncertainties of wartime, it would have been very difficult for my mother to have kept me with her, but as Marie filled in some of the background I came to understand that there had already been much turmoil in their family. Their father, an Armenian, came from a traditional Middle Eastern culture and their home was quite orthodox. More so after his young French wife, their mother, had run off.

Perhaps there was more to it than that, but I don't know. At any rate, he became very strict with his children, so when my mother found she was expecting me, and her sweetheart was dead, she knew that there would there be no help from him; and, not only that, she knew she could never tell him.

Then Marie said, 'You know you have a brother, don't you? His name is Ken Moss.'

'Yes, my mother told me,' I said, 'but he doesn't know about me because I asked her.'

I think that was another reason why she was reluctant to meet me. She didn't want to rock the boat with her other son, to show herself up to him in a certain light. At times I think she would anguish over all this, wondering if she had done the right thing, feeling guilty about how she had treated me – then, when I reassured her that she had nothing to reproach herself about where I was concerned, she would worry about how it would appear to Ken.

Marie immediately said, 'Well, David, you've got to meet your brother.'

'Go easy,' I said. 'I've known about him for many years, since 1970.'

When I left, Marie called Ken and he got back to me within an hour. We spoke at length. He seemed very level-headed even though this revelation had come out of the blue.

'I had no idea you existed,' he said.

He suggested that we meet and I agreed, saying that I would fly to Jersey the following week. When I had made the arrangements, I called him back with the details. Marie had shown me photographs of him in the family album so I knew what he looked like but he had never seen a picture of me. I told him that though we were not exactly dead spits, I thought we shared enough of a family resemblance via our mother and we would have no difficulty recognizing one another.

•

When I came out of the customs area in Jersey I saw a group of people around the barrier and separated out a chap. There was no mistaking him.

I went across and said, 'Ken – David.'

He looked at me and greeted me warmly. It was quite an emotional meeting.

Then he said, 'Would you excuse me, I need to go and get the car.'

He was gone for about 20 minutes. I sat for a while, then walked up and down. I thought, 'Bloody hell, what's going on here? He's escaped! He doesn't want to know.' Many bizarre thoughts chased through my mind. I was wondering whether I should stay in the hotel since it was booked, and then leave, or if I should just check the return flights and go at once, when he came back. His eyes were pretty red, as if he had been crying.

'Is there a problem?' I asked.

'No. Marie had given me a description, but I didn't realize how much you look like our mum. When I first saw you, I was stunned. In fact, I have to say, it's like a reincarnation. You look like our mum in pants.'

It had been very painful because he was instantly reminded of her and I think it brought back the pain of losing her. I was very moved by all that and by his immediate acceptance of me. There was no question of me being an interloper, but rather, I was someone he wanted to know.

We went off to the hotel where I was booked and into the bar, where we had a few drinks. Rather more than a few, if truth be known. We were both very emotional and needed to unwind. It was early afternoon and we sat in the bar until tea time. He said he was going home to get changed and get his wife and we would all go out to dinner. That evening we went to a restaurant. I met his wife, Sue, and took to her. She is a very pleasant, attractive and bright woman, a flight attendant. She was as shaken as Ken when she first saw me because she was particularly close to our mother. When I showed them the first letter Jenny had written to me 20 years earlier, I have to say we were all quite moved.

I spent two days in Jersey. Ken, Sue and I spent the next day together, then went out the following night, and I left. Since then, we speak on the phone all the time, and last year I was over there filming. Ken comes over once a year to see Marie and me and over the past 12 or 13 years we have built up a very nice warm relationship. We have never lived together as brothers, and we never will have that experience, but we do share the same mother and that is a bond.

I see Marie quite often since she does live very close by. She has taken me all the way through the family history and together we have poured over the photograph albums. There are pictures of when my grandfather was establishing himself as a silk merchant. I have gleaned more about his story. He came to Manchester in 1910 and joined his uncle, eventually taking over the family silk business. By the time he was 24 years old he was a millionaire. The photographs show a country house and servants and large luxury cars, with the members of my family: my grandfather and grandmother, my mother, Eugénie, her brother, Jack, and her sister, Marie, who was the youngest.

Marie said it was expected that Jack would go into the family textiles business but he went off to sea and joined the merchant navy instead, becoming a senior captain. His last command was the *Atlantic Conveyer*, which was a supply ship for the Royal Navy. It was later sunk in the Falklands War but Jack had retired by then. Over the years I have come across people working on cruise ships who knew him, and according to them he was a stickler for discipline, just like his father.

I studied the photographs of my grandmother, the flighty young Frenchwoman. She had been tripping the light fantastic with the local doctor, going off dancing and so forth, and eventually she ran off with him, abandoning her own children when they were quite young. Marie said she thought my mother was seven or eight, Jack about six and she herself was four or five. My grandfather must have been quite heartbroken because he became even more strict with the children in case they turned out like their mother. There were years of arguments and the atmosphere was very difficult. When Marie told me this I instantly saw why my mother couldn't go home when she was pregnant out of wedlock.

My mother was working away from home as a wartime nurse in 1941 and so that was how she was able to conceal her condition from the family. Like a lot of women in those circumstances she never forgave herself for giving up her own flesh and blood. It made it worse that her own home was rather difficult with that traditional Middle Eastern morality and her father's macho personality. It didn't help that her mother was a bit of a flibbertigibbet and had run off, abandoning her own children at a very young age. I also learned that my grandfather lost his fortune during the prewar crash of the 1930s and the family had to move to less luxurious accommodation and a simpler way of life.

Looking back, it hasn't left me with a gaping hole. Some people will turn around and say, 'He's a bit of a cold fish' but it was the security I knew in a warm and loving home that filled the gap and set me on the right road. Of course, I did have a yearning to meet my real mother, as all men must have. If I'd been determined enough I would have taken the bull by the horns and flown across to Jersey while she was still alive, and banged on the door. But I was always aware that to do that could have been a disturbing and upsetting experience for her and possibly her husband and son. It would have been all right for me. 'Hello – Oh, your husband's not happy about it? Well, sod him!' I could have been all – 'I want, I want' but that would have been too selfish and could have broken down any fragile peace of mind she had. I could have put her in a position where for the remaining years with her husband things could have been difficult. I'm not saying this would have happened, but he could have treated her harshly. When I first found out about my background, it was 1970. To have gone to Jersey and staked my claim on her might have disrupted a lot of things in their lives over the next 20 years.

Ken has often said, 'Oh, mum was so silly. She should have gone ahead and met you, she should have told me. We would have worked it out, it would have been fine.'

He is probably right. She was so afraid it might rock her marriage, or upset Ken. Or, like a lot of women, she could not face up to meeting the child she had abandoned. She was always pleased and happy to hear from me. I would tell her about what Lorne and I were doing, about our travels, our business, my antique shops with Chris, then Imad – everything. She was very happy to hear it all and I'm sure, very proud.

Ken has also often said, 'Mum would have been very proud of you if you two had met,' and I hope that's so.

But the actual meeting never took place. I have no regrets. It allowed her to carry on with the life she chose without me interfering in it. I'm pleased about that, glad that I could do something for her.

The one thing that has come out of all of this is that I have come to realize there's something genetic that has been passed on. It's quite uncanny. I don't think I appreciated how strong genes could be until I started to meet members of my own blood family and saw not only how alike we all were but also how I had, unwittingly, trodden in my grandfather's footsteps and inherited his taste for the exotic.

CHAPTER SEVENTEEN

•

I have always believed that faint heart never won fair lady. And as it is in love so it is in business. When Chris and I first started out in antiques in 1979 we plunged in at the deep end with a glamorous shop and big advertisements on the expensive back pages of the glossy trade magazines. We also had regular stands at Olympia, one of London's fine arts and antiques fairs, and after he left I continued to exhibit on my own.

These fairs are the *crème de la crème* of the antiques business. One is held at Grosvenor House – that's the really grand hotel in Park Lane – and the other one is based at Olympia, which is further west, way past Harrods and the chic little shops of Knightsbridge. Olympia is a pretty grand venue, too, but in many respects it seems to me to be more open and friendly than Grosvenor House and I always enjoyed it. There are three Olympia fairs, in March, June and November, and many dealers go to them all. It's a good way of meeting up with others in the same line, seeing what the competition has to offer, of swapping yarns and getting your eye in. Olympia is also known as the barometer of the antiques business, the place where people can really get a sense of what is happening in that world.

But international fairs can be a risky business if you don't know what you are doing. I could make a good living by buying carefully and doing two or three fairs a year as I had no staff or overheads, but I should warn those who are thinking that this might be for them, that the stands are very expensive – as much as £10,000 a time or more, which, even though it might not be as much as the rent of a shop in a nice area, is still a tidy sum to risk. Remember, you only have a week in which to earn that money back, plus overheads and profit. And I should also say that the vetting process at the grandest fairs is exceptionally strict so you do need a lot of experience when buying. I liked doing business at the fairs because I was not tied to a shop and so had time to hunt out the most unusual and truly original decorative pieces; it also allowed me freedom to pursue other options.

Many people have told me that whenever they came to the fairs they could always tell which stand was mine, even when they hadn't seen the name on it, because over the years I had developed a distinctive style. I always exercised my own taste when I was buying, and always looked for something that was just that little bit different or exotic because I'd got 400 competitors there. I found that if I bought what I believed in, and only chose what I really liked, I could talk to potential customers with genuine honesty and passion. It actually made life easier for me because when I liked something and was excited about it I could transfer that enthusiasm to my clients as it was from the heart.

Dealers don't spend their lives selling. They also buy, and I was always happy to buy back goods because these were pieces that I truly believed in and genuinely liked. Sometimes, even years later, a client might come back to me and offer a piece I'd sold them. Perhaps they wanted something different, or were moving to a smaller home. I was happy to buy back – and to give them a handsome profit. But if they returned the goods quite quickly, within a few weeks, though I was always pleased to return their money they sometimes found it hard to appreciate that I needed a margin of profit myself and so would offer them a lower price than the one they had bought the piece for.

I have a feeling that people 'sus' you out very quickly when you talk in half-muted tones about something you don't have a genuine regard for. If you don't like a piece why should they? I like all kinds of people from all walks of life and I'll talk to everybody in exactly the same way. You learn a lot, too, and often make lifetime friends. This was the case with Blanche Blackwell.

I was exhibiting at Olympia one year when a very charming lady in her mid- seventies came onto my stand with a friend and admired a beautiful mid-eighteenth-century Chinese Chippendale-style black lacquer bureau-bookcase, a real gem of a piece, lavishly decorated with gold bamboo, flowers and birds. She asked all sorts of questions, which I was pleased to answer. She said she was interested in this small delicate piece because she had recently bought some hand-painted wallpaper in Hong Kong. Men had come over from Hong Kong itself to hang it for her. Now that's a bloody long way to travel to do a little home decorating, and they obviously hadn't come over in a sampan. It made me sit up and pay attention because I saw at once that she wasn't talking about a roll of paper from B & Q, but the real thing. This was obviously a woman of fine taste and discrimination.

'I need to see this piece in my flat,' she said. 'I can't consider buying it without first trying it in the position I would like it for.'

I readily agreed. Many people do like to take things on approval so they can live with them for a while. She lived in Lowndes Street, Belgravia, a wonderful address, and I said I would take it round there and put it in place. I duly did this and admired her Chinese wallpaper and quite a few other beautiful objects, and eventually she did buy that exquisite little bookcase which, I have to say, looked exactly right for that room.

Over the next few years I often saw her at fairs and we became friendly on a personal level. It was a great treat meeting her. She was a wonderful lady who had led a fascinating and privileged life growing up in Jamaica in an old, aristo-cratic plantation family. I introduced Lorne to her and we all got on well. She often asked if we would like to visit her in her other home in Nassau. During our many conversations over lunch I learned that the family had gone out to the West Indies from England in the seventeenth century and had been respon-sible for building vast banana and sugar plantations. Her son, whom I have never met, is Chris Blackwell, a hugely successful entrepreneur who established Island Records. Among his many stars was the original reggae artist Bob Marley, who also came from Jamaica.

A lot of people issue invitations to visit them but they don't always mean it. It's a courtesy. 'You must come,' they say, but since they never set a date, you never get to go. In her case, Mrs Blackwell did mean it. She sent us a formal invitation and a couple of years ago Lorne and I flew out to the Bahamas to spend Christmas and the New Year in her beautiful home close to the exclusive gated community of Lyford Cay where Sean Connery has a house. This is quite appropriate, since the actor played James Bond and, as everyone knows, Bond was created by Ian Fleming, who bought 30 acres of land in Jamaica, where he built his home, Goldeneye. The land was sold to him in 1946 by celebrated beauty and socialite Blanche Blackwell. Talk about connections and wheels within wheels.

As in all interesting stories, there are more connections. Blanche had once owned such a large estate in Jamaica she was able to carve off another small chunk without missing it, and this is where Noel Coward built his retreat, Fire-fly. So on one side Ian Fleming was penning his escapist novels and on the other side Noël Coward was writing his plays, like *Blithe Spirit* and *Private Lives*.

Mrs Blackwell treated us wonderfully well in Nassau and the days flew by in the sun. We swam amongst coral reefs, walked on empty beaches filled with conch shells and strolled through forests where tall bamboo palms, tamarind trees and wild orchids grew. Many colourful birds and butterflies flew through lush stands of ferns and red ginger flowers along shaded paths. New Year's Eve was fast approaching. In the afternoon various people came round to offer their seasonal greetings to Mrs Blackwell and to give out invitations to various func-tions and parties. A business associate of her son Chris dropped by to invite her to a function at a private home in Lyford Cay. He mentioned that many interest-ing people would be there, including Sean Connery and a scattering of American stars. Lorne and I listened to this exchange with eyes growing wider by the moment. To be in the same gathering as Sean Connery, someone I had always wanted to meet, would have been fascinating.

Mrs Blackwell said, 'No, we have our own plans. We know what we're doing this evening.'

She had already booked a table for dinner at Compass Point, one of Chris's hotels, which was famous for having a recording studio attached where rock stars like the Stones and U2 used to record their albums. Then we were going on to see in the New Year at the famous Junkanoo carnival, with music, fireworks and fun. We were very happy to fall in with Mrs Blackwell's thoughtful plans and had a magnificent dinner, and, later, as we strolled along Bay Street through the midnight hour, thoroughly enjoyed the noisy, brash and bright parade, which is very like the Rio one. But I do have to confess to a lingering wistfulness over not having met 'James Bond'.

Early in January Mrs Blackwell suggested that we should fly to Miami, just a hop away, to stay for a few days at the Tides, which is recognized as one of the most fashionable art deco hotels in the South Beach area, and caters to the film and music industry. This was another one of her son's hotels. He also owned a chain of small and rather exotic and beautiful hotels throughout the Caribbean which featured brightly painted cottages.

The three of us duly arrived in Miami and were met by a car at the airport. When we drew up at the Tides we saw huge hoardings all around it and many vans. The hotel was being used as a movie location. I think our driver made a call from the car phone because a member of the staff came out, a woman, who knew Mrs Blackwell. She asked if we could bear with them and wait a few minutes.

'They'll finish the shot, then I can check you in,' she said. 'They're almost done.'

We waited in the car for a while and then the woman came back.

'They're doing another shot, but you can come on in,' she said.

'Who's the star?' Blanche asked.

'Harrison Ford,' was the reply.

'Oh, I know Harrison. He's a friend of my son's,' said Blanche.

Again I sat up. To meet Harrison Ford would be something to remember. We walked into the foyer and there he was, filming with other actors and actresses. We were asked to wait again until the shot was finished. Just then, Mr Ford's assistant came over and greeted Mrs Blackwell warmly.

'Hello, Blanche. Nice to see you again. Look, if you can wait a moment until this is through, Harrison will be delighted to say hello and pay his respects. Maybe a bite of lunch if you have time.'

'Jolly good,' I thought, 'this is more like it.' I was already polishing up my conversational opening gambit for when I would be introduced to this mega Hollywood star.

Already in my mind I could hear him saying, 'Hello Duchess, hello Dook –'

But very politely and quite firmly, Blanche said, 'Oh no, there's no need. Please give my best regards to Harrison but we've got to go shopping and time's getting on.'

I'm thinking, 'Here's my chance to meet Harrison Ford going down the tubes.' Of course, I wouldn't be so rude as to say that. Off we went and did some shopping and continued to spend a memorable few days in Miami touring around and going to restaurants, including a stylish brasserie owned by Michael Caine. But the place that really intrigued me was Joe's Stone Crab Restaurant, known all over the world for its speciality of the claws of giant stone crabs, which are collected by fishermen in the Gulf of Mexico. We were served half a dozen apiece, with a special secret-recipe sauce. At this joint, no matter who you are, no matter how big a big shot, no reservations are taken at lunchtime. You go along and check in with the maître d', then have a drink on one of the terraces and wait your turn

During our stay in Miami I tried to return Blanche's very generous hospitality, though it was hard with a lady who was such a wonderful and determined hostess. But whatever small thing I was able to do, it was quite impossible to repay the hospitality of staying at that beautiful and rather grand house in Nassau, right on the sea. There were maids who had been with Blanche for many years, who looked after us wonderfully well and served delicious meals three times a day – some of them quite formal. I think we must have put on 20 pounds. Over the period we stayed there, Blanche gave us a fascinating insight into the amazing way of life at Wentworth, her Jamaican estate, during its heyday when she was a fabulously beautiful young woman. To one side was Ian Fleming at Goldeneye and on the other there was Noel Coward at Firefly. She described the legendary dinner parties that she hosted at Wentworth and the ones she went to at the homes of the dazzling artistic community that congregated on the island – luminaries such as the Duke and Duchess of Windsor, Richard Burton, Elizabeth Taylor and even our dear old late Queen Mum.

I don't think I'm being indiscreet here when I mention that since then I have come across Blanche's name in a series of articles about Noel Coward published in the *Sunday Times*. Apparently Errol Flynn had once pursued her and asked for her hand in marriage. I must say I was a bit in awe of the long list of people she had known. It's a chunk of history and it must have been quite remarkable to have known them all as personal friends. In this one woman's head there were so many stories and recollections of the most amusing and dazzling conversations which I knew would probably never be told.

Next time I saw her I said, 'Blanche, you didn't mention you knew Errol Flynn.'

She laughed and said, 'You never asked.'

The nature of the clients who came to the international fairs brought me into a much more decorative and flamboyant style of antiques: lacquered cabinets on giltwood stands, gilt-wood consul tables, ivory-decorated pieces, used not just as furnishings but as decoration. I started collecting and specializing in blackamoors, tall decorative figures made of wood and gesso that were used as torchères to hold candles or flowers, or perhaps a cornucopia holding bowls of fruit. Blackamoors started out being made and decorated in Venice in the latter part of the seventeenth century – from about 1680 – and were generally known as Moors of Venice or Nubians. They would have been used at the foot of a flight of a sweeping staircase, or between the double doors of a grand room. Watching their prices rise to dizzying heights in recent years has shown me that my early instinct about these pieces was right.

The first pair of blackamoors I bought was with Chris at Sotheby's. They had encrusted jewelled turbans, all done with polychrome paintwork applied on gesso, and wore exotic gold and black apparel. They also had outstretched hands but were holding nothing. I thought perhaps they would have held some kind of a cornucopia or dish for exotic fruits like bananas or pineapples. When we were in Mr Wiggington's museum I spotted a wonderful pair of eighteenth-century Indian lances.

'Hang on a minute,' I said, 'those would look absolutely superb in the blackamoors' hands.'

Seeing a good bit of business, Mr Wiggington sold me the lances. In turn I sold them to Madame Brandycourt, a French dealer. She sold them to a client in France, then bought them back. I bought them back from her and – well, it's all swings and roundabouts in this business.

By the time Imad Al-Midani came along I had three pairs of wonderful blackamoors that I didn't particularly want to sell because we used them for decoration in our Wilmslow shop. When Imad saw them he asked if I could put a hold on them; he was considering buying one pair but wasn't sure which one. A week later he returned and said he would have all three pairs. What I didn't know at the time was that his father owned the Dorchester Hotel. When Lorne and I went to stay there as Imad's guests those blackamoors were the very first thing I spotted as we walked in.

Some time in the late Seventies I was visiting the Grosvenor House Fair as a guest when I spotted two pairs of enormous Venetian blackamoors, about nine feet tall and made of very dark carved fruitwood, all swagged flowers and bunches of fruit. The figures themselves, of bold Nubians each carrying a massive bowl on their shoulders, were on loan from the Queen Mother. Now it so happened that a while later I acquired a similar single figure out of the blue, so I rather cheekily wrote to Her Majesty asking where she had got hers from and if there was any history. To my astonishment, within three or four days I got a very nice letter from her comptroller telling me that she had acquired them from Christie's years before and had sold them to someone in Barbados. You don't normally think of people like the Queen Mother buying and selling goods but she was known as a great collector and, like anybody else, she often had to make room for more finds.

A year later, I exhibited my blackamoor at Olympia.

Art dealer Robin Hirlstone saw it on my stand and said, 'I know where there are four of those.'

'I think I know the figures you're referring to,' I said, 'and I know where they came from.'

He told me that he had seen the four blackamoors while staying at a house party on Barbados with his then girlfriend, Joan Collins. How they were acquired, I do not know, but bearing in mind what Her Majesty's comptroller had told me, that hers had gone to Barbados, it was more than likely that the ones Robin remembered were the very same figures that I had seen at Grosvenor House.

Many decorative people, as well as objects, floated onto my stand over the years, film stars like Dustin Hoffman, George Hamilton, Ali McGraw and Stefanie Powers, who had starred in the hit series *Hart to Hart*; rock stars like Elton John and Freddie Mercury from Queen; and personalities like Ivana Trump and Oprah Winfrey – so many, I can't recall them all. Then there was Princess Margaret. There was no missing her – there never was.

I first met the princess on the gala evening of the opening day of the fair. The doors had been closed to the public after the daytime session and the show had then been opened again an hour later for the benefit of private, invited guests. On this particular occasion, because we knew royalty would be coming, all the exhibitors were togged up in evening dress. The rush of the previous few weeks was over, the vetting had been done, and our stands were as perfect as we could make them, with every piece polished and looking wonderful. I had made some good sales during that first day and I was relaxing on my stand with a glass of whisky and water.

Amongst my star pieces was an absolutely stunning life-sized figure of a female mandarin. Her body was made of clay and straw, shaped around a wooden frame, and her arms and head were of finely painted terracotta. The head was balanced with small lead weights on two little pegs in the neck, so when it was lightly touched it would move slightly and her eyes would follow you round in a most eerie way. She was beautifully dressed in an original Chinese costume made of a peachy coloured silk, and her small, traditionally bound feet, clad in silk slippers, peeped out from beneath the hem of her robe. I had bought this figure at a fair in Dublin from an Irish dealer, who in turn had bought it at a sale of the contents of one of the big Irish country houses.

The mandarin figure's history was a little obscure. Some people believed she might have been made for display in an eighteenth-century teashop but I thought she was far too good for that. Since the family in Ireland had been involved with the East India Company, which used fast clippers to trade with the Far East, my theory was that this figure had been commissioned by a ship's captain or a merchant trader as a model to show Europeans what the Chinese looked like. After all, the West has been fascinated by oriental culture since the eighteenth century. I later learned that a similar, male, figure was on display at the Peabody Museum in Massachusetts, so mine may well have been one of a pair.

In Dublin the original asking price for my nodding mandarin had been £14,000. The Irish dealer and I chewed the fat for a bit and in the end he agreed to sell it to me for about £6,500. I spent a further £2,000 or so on some specialist restoration.

And so there I was, on the gala evening of the fair, enjoying a quiet drink before the invited guests turned up. I had just sold the mandarin figure at a preview for £19,000 to a very astute collector, and that was a very nice profit, as I told myself. As was customary, although the piece was reserved it remained on the stand for the opening day of the fair, and I had tucked it discreetly to one side. Suddenly I felt a hand on my back. Someone got hold of my glass and took it away. It was Victoria Borwick, the organizer of the fair.

'Victoria, what the hell – !' I started to say.

I thought she was having a bit of fun but she just nodded her head discreetly. I looked down the aisle and saw Princess Margaret approaching with her entourage of ladies-in-waiting and a couple of gentlemen courtiers.

The princess was tiny, and very pretty, with the most astonishing blue eyes.

Victoria greeted her with the words, 'Ma'am, may I introduce David Dickinson. He is one of our long-time exhibitors.'

'Your Royal Highness, how nice to meet you,' I said, bowing.

She glanced around with a genuinely interested air.

'What is this?' she asked.

'Ma'am, it is a Chinese vase from Canton –'

'And this?'

'Those, Ma'am, are a pair of Dresden porcelain candelabra that were made in Germany –'

She was smoking a cigarette in a long holder. The ash grew longer and she glanced around for an ashtray. There wasn't one in sight and I honestly thought she was going to flick the ash onto my nice clean carpet. But suddenly a courtier rushed forward, grovelled a bit and held out his cupped hands. My eyes widened. I thought, 'No, she can't! Surely she won't stub it out in his hand!' But, no, she flicked the ash into the man's cupped palm and he rushed off to empty it into one of the upright ashtrays that stood along the aisles.

Without missing a beat, she continued with her inspection of my stand. She spotted my star piece, the mandarin figure.

I turned around and said, 'Ma'am, may I point out to you this amazing female mandarin figure that I bought at a sale in Ireland –' and I launched into its history.

She listened intently, her huge blue eyes never leaving my face. No doubt about it, she was a corking good-looker and listener. I concluded by saying that I had already sold the figure. In fact, it had been snapped up so quickly that I thought maybe the price of £19,000 had been too low.

She laughed. 'And does it nod its head?' she asked.

'Blimey,' I thought, my mind racing, 'she knows what she's talking about.'

I was aware that she had recently been on a state visit to China and so perhaps she had come across similar figures in the Summer Palace or a museum.

'Have you seen any like it before?' I asked.

'Yes, I've seen them in china,' she said.

China! Summer Palace! Bloody hell, Dickie, you really have drawn the short straw here. Running through my mind was the thought that I could have sold it for a fortune.

'Ma'am, whereabouts in China did you see them?' I asked.

'No, I've seen them in china,' she repeated.

Now you don't actually touch these people, royalty, I mean, but I leaned forward and whispered deliberately into her ear, as if speaking to a child.

'As I said, Ma'am, it came from China in the late eighteenth century –'

She looked at me as if I'd lost my marbles, put her hands up as if to exclaim, 'Are you raving?' and said quite impatiently, 'No! I've seen them in china!'

The penny dropped. China was a posh word for porcelain. She was saying that she had seen similar little nodding porcelain figures. Meissen made them and it is more than likely that there would have been several in the royal homes.

I started gabbling, 'Oh, I beg your pardon, Ma'am –'

She looked at me with that quizzical look then she started to walk away.

No doubt at a dinner party she would later say, 'I met this batty northern gentleman who kept shouting in my ear as though I was deaf...'

The same year I had a very stylish art deco salon suite of furniture on my stand, made by Hilley and Co. in the Thirties. It was of satinwood and consisted of a large bergère-style settee, two armchairs, a cocktail cabinet and a display cabinet in Chinese Chippendale style with panels of chinoiserie (Chinese lacquer decoration), a pair of standard lamps, a table and mirrors. During the course of the show an interior decorator approached, inspected the suite and asked the price, which was £18,000. She said she thought it would be right for her client's New York apartment and off she went.

The following day, up bowls this little man in very short shorts and quite feminine, high-heeled, open shoes. Standing before me in the flesh was Rudolf Nureyev. He was very charming and chatted to me affably. He looked at the suite with great interest and I could see it disappearing off to New York, perhaps to play a role in some amazing sights and sounds in this charismatic man's apartment. It wasn't to be. Rudi decided this suite wasn't for him and I sold it instead to another fascinating and equally decorative man, my old chum Peter Stringfellow, who installed it in his offices at a new nightclub he was opening at the time, the Hippodrome. Now, that's a place for some amazing sights and sounds – and I bet a few drinks have been dispensed from that cocktail cabinet and quite a few dolly birds will have sat on those cushions. Peter is definitely what you would have to call 'a bit of a character'.

Extraordinary items often come my way, ones I never forget. One was a silver howdah. It might seem a strange place to look for good deals but I have discovered that they are often to be found in the shops in Mayfair. After all, even the poshest of dealers still has to turn over goods and make a profit, as I found when I bought my very first item in that rarefied world: the Little Admiral. And dealers will often accept a very slender profit margin if they are selling to a fellow professional.

I discovered the silver howdah in the Mayfair Galleries. It just jumped out at me, even though it was in a rather dirty condition, black, in fact, as silver gets when it hasn't been cleaned for a long time. A howdah is a large seat that sits on the back of an elephant. It usually has two tiers, the front for the maharaja and the back for a couple of servants, who hold up a large silk umbrella and perhaps a palm fan to protect their master from the heat; if it's a shooting party, they look after the guns. The howdah I had spotted had a wooden base, over which sheets of hand-beaten silver had been nailed. It was clearly marked with the arms, or emblem, of the Udaipur court in Rajasthan, and there was some text, not in English, on the back of one of the chairs. I assumed the howdah was nineteenth century.

With an eye for the unusual I bought it for about £10,000, though what a client would do it with it I had no idea. Perhaps they would place it in the centre of a marble hall in a villa-type property as a talking point, or maybe it could go in a grand hotel or Indian restaurant as a decorative item. Restoration took a great deal of time and money. The howdah was carefully gone over with toothbrushes and solvents, some of the missing silver was replaced and eventually it all came back gleaming. If I'd had the room I would have kept it. Instead, it was my prize exhibit at Olympia one year. It had only been on show for a couple of days when I was approached by David Nickerson, who was a very distinguished dealer from Mallets of Borden House. He's dead now but I always did like him. He was a most gentlemanly man.

'I like this,' he said. 'How much?'

I was asking £22,000 but I had spent a couple of thousand on restoration.

'Hmm, that's a bit high, let's chew the fat. What's your best on this, David?' he said.

While he was inspecting it another man, who I did not know, joined him and started a conversation. To be polite, I walked away. After a while I went back and the man was introduced to me as a director of S & J Phillips, a renowned Bond Street company that dealt in silver, jewellery and works of art. He and David Nickerson had decided to buy the howdah jointly. They offered £15,000. I asked for £20,000. I think we eventually settled for £18,000.

We did the business, drew up the invoice and signed the contract, then David Nickerson said, 'That is one of the best buys we've ever made, David.'

'Why?' I asked, my mind racing, wondering what I had missed.

'Well, it's platinum!'

For a second, my face drained. I stood there, rooted to the spot.

'Effing hell! I don't believe it! This must scrap at half a million quid!'

Suddenly the mist cleared as sanity reasserted itself. 'Hang on,' I thought, 'my restorer worked on this. Silver is quite soft and platinum would have been that much harder. He would have noticed at once.'

'Go on,' I said. 'Piss off!'

The two men walked away, chuckling. Shortly afterwards an elderly lady walked up to the stand. She was very well dressed, with a walking stick. She beckoned me.

'Young man, young man!'

'Yes, madam?'

'Do you know what this is?' she asked, pointing at the howdah with her stick.

'Yes,' I said, 'it's a howdah.' Being a little clever, I added, 'It belonged to the Sisodia dynasty that ruled Udaipur.'

'You are very well informed,' she said. 'I last saw this in use in 1920. My father was attached to some regiment there and was a friend to the maharaja. Every year these howdahs – and there were several of them, you know – were brought out for ceremonial parades through the cities – and the maharaja would be riding up there –' she knocked the side of the howdah with her stick. 'And see that thing at the back?' She pointed at the plaque. 'It tells the date. In our calendar it would have been eighteenth century.'

I thought, 'Blimey. My two chums had got a great deal, after all.' Being eighteenth century would make this that much more valuable.

'Do you know,' she mused, 'the elephant that carried this had an anklet around one of its legs with emeralds as big as eggs.'

It never ceases to amaze me the people who come out of the woodwork at these fairs, the most fascinating people, with the most fascinating stories to tell.

Dealers are a great lot when it comes to the crack and a good joke. Many of them had sneered a bit when they saw the howdah, and ribbed me that I had bought a fairground seat off a roller-coaster. So when a friend of mine, David Beadale, a well-known dealer from Cheshire, heard that I had sold it for a nice sum he went round the fair saying, 'You know Dickie? Well, hoo-dahs wins.'

When we gather together in the evenings to have a drink before they close the doors we always have a laugh about something that has happened in the course of the day's business. David Beadale told us once about someone who came to his stand, a really bumptious individual with a la-di-da voice. This man poked and prodded at everything with his nose in the air.

'Tell me about this, my man.'

'That, sir, is an eighteenth-century Chippendale table –'

Not pausing to listen, the man continued: 'What is that, laddie? – and that –'

Patiently, David obliged. 'This is a sixteenth-century Ming jardinière –'

'Provenance? Mmm? Provenance?'

'Yes, as you can see – I bought it in a castle on the Scottish borders. It's been there as far as I know for generations.'

The man pointed at a 12-foot rosewood Regency curtain pole.

'And this, laddie? The provenance? The provenance? Humbug, humbug, humbug –'

By now, David was getting thoroughly annoyed.

Looking the man squarely in the eyes, he said, 'Oh, you want to know the provenance, do you? Well, let me explain that I bought it out of the back of a K-Reg Volvo on a car park halfway down the M1.'

David smiled and walked away. The man got the message and skulked off the stand. I laughed. We all agreed that sometimes that is the only way to deal with people like that.

Donald Alison, a dealer from Preston, is another good chum, quite a card, who keeps us all entertained.

If you stroll along to his stand at Olympia on the second day and ask how he's doing, as we all do with each other, he will go, 'Oh, I sold a quarter of a million's worth on the first day – but hush-hush, say nothing.'

Everyone nods and says, 'Oh, right.'

Actually, he is a very good dealer but he does love to wind us up. A few years ago he used to share a stand with another friend, Tom Brindle, from Blackburn. Before one fair Tom, who is also quite a character, decided to have some signs made consisting of a round piece of cardboard with a written statement on it and a little hook that you could hang round your ear.

He handed them out to a little coterie of dealers in the know, saying, 'Nudge, nudge, wink, wink, let's wind up Don Alison.'

When Don toddled along to join us over drinks, we all went, 'Well, Don, how's it going?'

'Mmm, mmm – don't say anything, but yesterday someone came on the stand and we sold the lot!'

At a signal from Tom we all whipped out our little cards and hung them on our ears: 'Bullshit Deflector!'

We all roared with laughter – including Don. He took it in very good part but then he would. He's a good sort. And that's what makes Olympia for me. The fun we have, the new friends I make, and meeting old ones.

CHAPTER EIGHTEEN

•

My career in television started purely by accident. If I had planned it, it couldn't have been more cataclysmic, sudden and astonishing. At the end of 1996 my daughter, Catrina, who lives in Bramhall, invited me to a barbecue in the garden of her home. Lorne and I drove over and as always enjoyed being with Catrina and her daughters, Aimee and Lauren. We're a very close family, always getting together at the drop of a hat, and at the time we lived close to each other in Bramhall so we did see a lot of each other. As well as family there were lots of local people there, friends of my daughter. I was enjoying myself tending the barbecue, wielding a fork, poking the sausages, turning the steaks and chatting quite lightly about this and that to Catrina's next-door neighbour, who I had not met before.

Then he asked me, 'What do you do for a living, David?'

I thought, 'Strange question.' I said, 'I'm an antiques dealer. What do you do for a living?'

'I'm in television,' he said. 'I have a production company with a couple of others.'

'How interesting,' said I. 'What's your name?'

He told me that it was Alistair Much. We got into conversation on a slightly more personal level, and he told me a bit about television and I told him a bit about antiques. He appeared genuinely interested so I warmed to my theme, telling him stories, tales and many anecdotes.

'You know, David,' he said after a while, 'Talking to you and looking at you, you do remind me of that fictional character Lovejoy.'

'Well, there's not that strong a resemblance,' I retorted.

Now you could say there was a vague likeness between me and Ian McShane, the actor who played Lovejoy in the TV series, since we both have olive skin and dark hair – and we're even pretty close in age, having been born just a year apart. But I wouldn't say that I was the dead spit of him, and I would certainly not compare my approach to the antiques business with his, for while I am often very light-hearted about it and can spin out a yarn with the best of them, I have always taken it very seriously. No way would I get up to the scams and dubious deals of that fictional Jack-the-lad.

'You know, this antiques business is very interesting,' said Alistair. 'It would make a good series of perhaps six to eight parts. Come to my office and let's have a chat about it.'

'Me? What could I do?' I asked.

'I've got quite a few ideas,' he said, somewhat mysteriously. 'Let's discuss it further.'

We set a date and the following week I went along to his offices in Manchester. Alistair's partners, Ray Fitzwalter and Ray's wife, were there, and after introductions I got to hear about Ray's impressive track record. He had been in television for about 25 years and among many other things had steered the Granada programme *World in Action*, winning two BAFTA awards along the way. He was responsible for getting the Birmingham Six freed, proving beyond doubt that they were not the bombers they had been accused of being.

After the initial chit-chat was out of the way, I said, 'So, what's this all about? How do you think I can help you?'

They said that they had been discussing an outline for an eight-part series on antiques, which they would pitch to the major networks.

'We think you could present these programmes in some way,' they said.

I'm game for most things, and always willing to turn my hand to anything new and challenging, but this was something I had never considered in my wildest dreams.

'Sounds very interesting,' I found myself saying, with a great deal of assurance. 'Yes, I think I could give that a go.'

The proposal was written up and the idea duly pitched to all the major television networks. It fell on deaf ears, no one was interested. 'Well,' I thought, 'stick to the antiques, Dickie.'

A month or six weeks later, Alistair called me to say they had been commissioned to make a single episode of the *Modern Times* documentary series. This was a prime-time BBC 2 show, on at 8.30 p.m. each night, that covered a whole range of different contemporary issues and topics. The programme their company had proposed, and which had been accepted, was one on antiques, featuring me and two other prominent dealers.

One of these dealers was Keith Skeel, who had been in business for about 25 years, operating out of a highly successful warehouse in Camden Passage in north London. His main stock-in-trade was supplying antiques to American interior decorators. The other dealer was Lady Pigeon (formerly Mrs Pamela Howell), whom I have known for many years. She is always elegantly dressed and has a certain gracious manner. She and her Australian husband, a retired military officer, run a business from Great Brampton House, a very nice period mansion in Herefordshire. When she started her business it was way ahead of its time. She would arrange the most wonderful antiques in Great Brampton House, making it look like a family home (which, indeed, it was) and her clients could see the pieces *in situ*. You didn't have to imagine what the dining table would look like in a real dining room or how a four- poster bed would fit into a bedroom – she had done it for you. Not only that, but she was the first dealer to place full-page advertisements in lavish magazines like *Tatler* and *Vogue* rather than stick to the trade press as I had always done. That had been the making of her business, with the coffee-table set in England and overseas descending in droves.

So, we were the three dealers, all different. In my case I was the 'Lovejoy' character on the road, doing his stock-in-trade, covering hundreds of miles in my white Corvette, going through the whole process of buying goods for Olympia, restoring them, polishing them up to perfection and then selling them on my stand at that important fair.

A word about my cars. I started off with my dashing little red Mini, then gradually worked my way up with the E-types that Lorne and I used to drive on the Continent to her bookings, and the Corvette I bought from Peter Stringfellow. When I was about 40, like many men that age I thought to myself, 'Right, I'm going to get into one of those Rolls-Royces.' It seemed a landmark moment at the time to be able to own a second-hand Roller. I dressed in black and could often be seen with the white head of a marble statue sticking out of a back window. But you pass through that stage and, tiring of the image, I went back to a white Corvette. This was the car that featured in *Modern Times*, bombing up and down the motorways in search of rare and exotic pieces.

The job was done, we finished filming and I was paid a modest but reason-able fee. It wasn't a fortune but I was doing exactly what I did for a living anyway, so in terms of my daily round it didn't make that much difference to me that a camera crew were following hot on my heels, doing all the work. Then everyone disappeared and I heard nothing for a while. Eventually, the show was broadcast and that was a bit exciting. After that, again I heard nothing. 'Well,' I thought, 'it was nice while it lasted, on with your proper day job, Dickie.'

But things were happening behind the scenes. The *Modern Times* series had run for about 18 months. For our programme we had fitted in a shoot at the end, during a successful Olympia fair, where I had sold a lot of goods. The last deal was a Regency harp. A gentleman from Taiwan and an associate of his had looked at it on several occasions, then they had gone away, and had come back and were still thinking about it. This sense of 'will they, won't they?' worked out perfectly for the film. In the final minutes, they at last decided to buy it.

I encouraged them: 'Come on, gentlemen, let's get our hands out here, let's haggle, let's do it.'

Eventually, we reached a price of £5,000.

We slapped hands and I turned to the camera and said, 'That's another one done.' Then I made this remark: 'But I tell you what, you never know with Taiwan, there may be 5,000 of these harps sent out from Taiwan next year!'

And the closing titles came up.

I think this struck a chord with many viewers at home. It showed me as a wheeler-dealer cheekie chappie, not with a plummy accent but slightly down-market, a bit of a character. I think that perhaps the impact of that clicked with the public and perhaps with some television executive, which was why I got a telephone call from Mark Hill's office in Bristol asking if I would like to go down to meet with them and discuss the possibility of more television work.

Off I went. I met Mark Hill, an executive producer with the BBC, who was in overall charge of a big department, and the series producer, Jane Lomas. Mark told me that they had seen my work on *Modern Times* and liked it. They had been filming a new magazine format, *The Antiques Show*, for some time, which was destined to be another prime-time 8.30 p.m. series. On reviewing the tapes, however, they had sensed that something was missing.

'We feel it needs something more,' said Mark.

'Like what?' I asked.

'We were thinking of inserting an eight-minute segment in the "Buyer's Guide" slot, showing an in-depth report on various items by a working dealer. Do you think you could do it?'

'Sure,' I said.

Already on the show were the presenters: Francine Stock, a very smart and talented lady from *Newsnight,* who was a straight presenter and not versed in antiques as such, and Tim Wonnacot, a pal of mine whom I'd known for many years. Tim had been running the Sotheby's salesrooms in the Chester area for some considerable time. He is a very polished and knowledgeable auctioneer, very charming and dapper, a kind of very well-to-do, bow-tie, Terry Thomas character. Alongside him, I was the exact opposite.

It was explained that each week I would cover a different area. One week I would talk about chairs, another week it would be picture frames, then dining tables, clocks and so forth. We agreed a modest fee for ten episodes and away we went. Sally Norris was the young director of the first show. She proved very helpful to someone who was a relative novice and pointed me in the right direction. What they wanted was what the producers had originally seen in me, which was something that little bit different. I was not your normal television presenter. To start with, they didn't need to script me at all. They put a framework there, placed me in the right location, miked me up for sound and I busked the piece to camera, ad-libbing freely. Somehow I instinctively knew how long to talk. I don't want to give the impression that it was easy, a piece of cake – of course it wasn't – but I had my old confident way about me and knew I could do it.

The first shoot was me reporting on dining tables. I made my selection from the several chosen by the researchers, and away I went. It was fine. The second shoot was grandfather clocks and this was bad news from the start. There were two cocky young technicians, a cameraman and a sound man, and I can't say I have ever met guys like these before, or since, that episode. I stood in front of the camera and I seemed to hit a wall. The words were not flowing, I was stumbling, just not getting it together. Then I noticed that these two technicians were doing a little bit of impatient finger tapping, a lot of muttering, 'We're going to be here all bloody day, Charlie –' The more this went on, the more nervous I became and the more mistakes I made. Eventually, I lost it.

I turned round to these cocky young guys and said, 'Now look, do me a favour. Piss off. Give me a chance. I'm new at this game and you're not helping me.'

Sally stepped in.

'OK, stop right there,' she said.

We walked outside.

'Have a cigarette, David, just relax for a moment. Those boys were out of order and I'll tell them so.'

I lit a cigarette and smoked it, beginning to chill out a bit.

'Look,' Sally said quietly, 'you can really do this, David. You're good.'

It gave me a certain amount of confidence. After Sally had torn the guys off a strip in private, I returned, and although I struggled more than I liked, I did it. But if I hadn't been helped and guided gently, it might have got worse. I worked with Sally on quite a few episodes. There were other directors but she stood out. Some advice she gave me sounds like a cliché but it's so true.

She said, 'That camera sees all. If it likes you, it will really like you. But don't try to kid to it because it will see and know. If you kid to it, it will magnify that and make you look fake. Once you get used to working and living with that camera it will virtually disappear and what we will see is just you. Never be afraid to be just you.'

Another good bit of advice from Sally was, 'Don't try to copy anyone else.'

This rang true because when you first start off you do have your idols and try to borrow from them a bit. But what works for one person won't necessarily work for you. We're all individuals and unique, and that's the important thing in television – to be different.

Sally said, 'If that camera likes you it will have a great love affair with you. I can see you have a great potential style, which is very interesting. So go and do it your way, David.'

I think that those were some of the best pieces of advice I was ever given right at the start of my television career.

People said I was a natural but I don't know if that is so. I became very comfortable with the camera after two or three episodes and suddenly, out of the blue, I developed this very personalized style of talking directly to camera as though it was another person I was having a conversation with. I don't know how that came about. I wonder if subconsciously I was affected by *Alfie*. I have always liked that film, especially the parts where Michael Caine occasionally turns to camera and talks to it like a real person. He says things like, 'Did you see her over there? What a right little darling she is!' It wasn't a case of copying but it influenced me in some way. I felt as if I could talk to the camera and, through it, directly to the people at home.

'That's it!' I realized. I am talking through the camera, through the television, to an individual at home watching the programme. I can't see them but that's who I am addressing. Real people. Since that moment of truth, many people have come up to me in the street and said, 'I feel you're talking to me, David.' It's uncanny but that's exactly what I am doing.

One thing that did puzzle me was the activities of the researchers on the series. One week it would be mirrors, another week it would be chairs. Some very bright young researcher, probably with a wonderful degree in economics, or politics or English, who had moved from one type of programme to another and didn't know a great deal about anything in depth, would go off to a salesroom or several antique shops and make a selection of items for that week's topic, for me to talk about. But, sadly, they often hadn't a clue what was good and what was bad.

I remember on many occasions arriving, looking at the items of choice and saying, 'Well, this is the biggest load of crap I've ever seen in my life – who researched this?'

Some little voice would speak up, 'I did.'

'Well, why didn't someone with some professional knowledge do the research? I'm coming along to do pieces to camera about these mirrors. I'm not going to fudge or fake this, I'm not going to turn around to the people at home and tell them these pieces are great when they're no good or dodgy.'

I knew it wasn't the young researchers' fault. They were doing their job. Instead, I would speak my mind, to camera if necessary. This is when my catchphrases started to come out: 'This is a dodgy lot.' or 'This is a cracking lot'.

The Antiques Show was quite successful and got good ratings. People told me that my segment, 'Buyer's Guide', was part and parcel of that success. We were up against the highly successful *Antiques Roadshow*, a groundbreaking BBC1 series with a wonderful formula that has been running for 25 years. It is packed with top-flight experts who are specialists in their field, the best. Many of them have worked in, or are directors of, major salesrooms. On top of that there is the element of voyeurism the programme offers. Yes, of course we're all interested in the antiques that people bring along for evaluation, but the big cliffhanging question, the one we all anticipate, is – 'What is it worth?' When someone's piece is valuable and worth a ton of money you get that look of shock on their face, the hand clapped over the mouth. 'Goodness!' It doesn't always happen, but we are all waiting for that special look of excitement coupled with avarice. And then the viewers at home, who have been eavesdropping on this ostensibly private moment, instantly wonder if they've got anything themselves that could be as valuable. The programme is educational and exciting and run in a very sophisticated style, with wonderful presentation.

What is slightly different about me is here is a guy, a Lovejoy type of character, a working antiques dealer from the street level, who goes about his day-to- day business, buying, selling, wheeling and dealing, a regular guy with whom the public can feel a bit of an affinity. The others are a bit posh, with their bow ties and the glossy presentation, and they do it well because that's what they are and they're being true to themselves. Me, I'm a bit of an Arthur Negus, just being myself, warts and all. I wouldn't want it any different.

I used to go to the BBC studios in London to do voice-overs for *The Antiques Show* – these are added once the film has been cut and edited. One day Jane Lomas invited me to lunch in the BBC canteen and told me in as many words that I was surplus to requirements. She didn't give me a reason and I didn't ask. I left the show and nothing else was offered. Back to my day job.

Then I got a telephone call through Sally Norris, who by then was working in the features department at the BBC. I was asked if I would be interested in doing a pilot for Jane Lush, who was head of Factual. The show had an antiques theme. A researcher went into people's houses and found something they were not aware they had, or at least they weren't aware that it could be worth a bob or two. It was to be called *Under Your Nose*. A young woman involved in it, Alison Charman, was to figure in my television career in a considerable way as the years went by. I did the pilot and it was shown. It didn't make much of an impact and a series wasn't commissioned.

Sally said, 'They didn't like it, David, but they like you. Jane Lush wants to use you in *The Holiday Show*.'

I thought, 'Blimey, that sounds like a cracking job! It's just the job for Dickie.' I'd watched those programmes for many years and seen presenters swanning around the world and was very impressed. I mentioned it to Lorne, who didn't seem too keen. I could see her thinking, 'Hello, he's off in the sun and the surf and I'm sat here at home.'

I got the call for the first episode. My heart was beating.

'Hello, the Bahamas, is it?' I said.

'No, you're going to Devon.'

Devon? But I thoroughly enjoyed it. I zoomed down in my new car, a Mitsubishi Sports 2+2, a very high-powered vehicle, to report on 'thatched hotels'. All of them were small country inns, with perhaps four or six bedrooms. Some of them were fabulous, straight from the top of a chocolate box, with roses around the doors and hollyhocks, and the most charming interiors. I also reported on what was available locally, such as theme parks, sheep racing, that kind of bracing stuff. One thatched hotel I stayed at was called The Hoops. The landlady, a charming woman, pointed out the wrought-iron sign consisting of a series of small hoops that hung behind the bar. She told me that a few weeks earlier she'd been serving in the bar when a young man wearing a baseball cap came up and asked for a round of drinks.

He pointed at the hoops and asked pleasantly, 'Is that for sale?'

'No, I'm afraid not,' she said.

The man smiled and walked off with his drinks.

Another man at the bar said in an American accent, 'Do you know who that is?' When she shook her head, he said, 'Brad Pitt.'

She said, 'Who?'

All the young barmaids were swooning. Brad Pitt was there, having a drink with Gwyneth Paltrow. It seems that his nickname for her was 'Hoops' and he wanted the inn sign for her.

'I don't care who he is,' said the landlady. 'That's our inn sign and we're not selling it.'

Not many superstars get turned down but Brad Pitt took it in good part.

I was sent to Italy next, to Castellabate, a small near-vertical resort on the Amalfi coast, 500 feet above the shore, where I stayed in the castle. This was built in 1123 on the orders of Abbot San Costabile Gentilecore to fend off attacks by the Moors led by the ferocious red-headed pirate, Barbarossa. The lord of the castle, a descendant of the ancient family, was still in residence, having converted half of his home into a hotel. You need a head for heights and the legs of a mountain goat to stay in Castellabate, but despite that, I enjoyed myself doing the kind of things I would normally never do. I usually spend my holidays lazing around the pool with maybe the odd dip in the sea, but now I went to a factory where they made mozzarella cheese from buffalo milk, and explored the dazzling blue grottoes that Amalfi and Sorrento are famous for.

Now came the call I had been waiting for, the one that got my heart beating. I was to stay in a five-star hotel in Mauritius, the Residence. I had to break this to her indoors a little bit gently. I don't think she minded me doing a report on Wigan Pier, but Mauritius was a bit different. This was a cracking assignment, especially when I was upgraded to club class. (Yes, despite what people think, all BBC tickets are standard.) The hotel was fabulous. The general manager, Jean-Luc, had been head-hunted several times, going up the rung to grander and grander hotels until he landed up at the Residence. From all accounts he was head-hunted yet again to run the great Sandy Lane in Barbados which has recently been refurbished at a cost of 50 million quid.

We were setting up a particular shoot one day, with me sat under a palm tree, and the woman director kept coming across.

'Is everything all right David?' she'd say anxiously. 'Sorry to keep you waiting. Here's a cold drink.'

I remember thinking to myself, 'Is everything all right? I'm sat here in 80 degrees of heat, under a palm tree, doing a few pieces to camera, I'm staying in a luxury hotel in Mauritius, the food is fantastic, I've got a suite as big as the *Queen Mary* – and I'm being asked is everything all right? You bet your life it is. This is not digging roads, mate!'

The highlight of the trip was going big game fishing. I'm not sure why, but we had only two hours in which to film this, and the chances of catching any-thing bigger than a sardine were zero, so we had to cheat a little bit. Well, we had to cheat quite a lot, actually. The big tuna I caught with such a great deal of bravado was already dead. The people who hired out the boat had caught it on a previous trip and it was in one of their deep freezers. We went out and did our pieces to camera.

There was Dickie sighing, 'Size doesn't matter, does it? Well, it does in the fishing world!'

And suddenly I had a strike on my line.

'Whoops! Here we go!'

I struggled and fought with this giant tuna until finally I reeled it in to the side and guys with gaffs pulled it on board, shouting excitedly.

'Wow! David, you've caught a cracking size tuna!'

This five-foot-long helluva big fish, weighing some one and a half hundred-weight, bounced like a solid block of ice onto the planks. The camera caught every moment. Like several million people. I saw the finished programme, but I'm not sure if anyone at home was aware that when we pulled it in that fish was as stiff as a board, frozen solid.

Another assignment I was given was to go round London, doing what would appear to be very mundane things like riding on top of those open-air tourist buses. In fact, I was impressed with how interesting London is when you play the tourist; and as for those buses, the view from the top is stunning and I finally understood why visitors to the capital seem to like them so much. For £12 you get a ticket for a day, so you can hop on and off, diving into museums and galleries at will. It's a great day out and you see as much or as little as you want.

I had just finished for the day when the young director said, 'There's a party this evening. You're invited.'

It was a surprise party for Jane Lush, thrown to celebrate her promotion to head of Daytime. We went along to this very glamorous affair, with eye-popping celebrities at close quarters. Jill Dando and I nodded to each other and I bumped into Des Lynham, and Vanessa Feltz who had just signed a huge contract and looked very happy, as well she might. I was the new boy on the block. I stood to one side, taking it all in and nursing just a couple of drinks because I had to be up early the next day.

It was the first time I had met Jane Lush. I was introduced and had about ten minutes of conversation with her. I thought she was very astute – and quite a looker. She went on very rapidly to be head of Light Entertainment just a couple of years later. At the same time I also met Nicola Moody, who went on to be head of Factual; and, of course, the charming and very bright Lorraine Heggessey, who became controller of the BBC. Ladies were the new suits, rapidly climbing to the top of the tree at the BBC. It was a new hierarchy in the making, so it was all happening for them.

The team who made *The Holiday Show* made a nice presentation to Jane. Then 'the girls' – the programme's researchers and directors – started singing and dancing to Cliff Richard's song 'Summer Holiday', with new lyrics they had composed about Jane. We were all enjoying the performance when the surprise of the evening – Cliff Richard himself – appeared and joined in. He had been hiding in a back room until that moment. It was a very nice touch.

I don't know who took over after Jane Lush left but they didn't call me. Back to the old day job again. I was still out there in the antiques business, running about, buying pieces, going to sales, getting ready for the next Olympia, so I had plenty on my plate.

CHAPTER NINETEEN

·

Image and style have always played a very large part in my life. The style came first, with the textiles, the suits and then the antiques. All of those fitted neatly and almost coincidentally together, helping my career, helping me get ahead and helping me to forge a certain path though life. The combination of the apparel, as well as the type of antiques I chose to deal in, as well as the way in which I chose to present them – flamboyantly, tastefully – forged yet another career for me. When I got involved with television I was known as the real Lovejoy, a sharp dresser with an eye for quality. While this Lovejoy image boosted my career and launched me, I have moved away from it somewhat. I am now known for my wider image as well, one in which the nomenclature the 'Duke' seems to sit very well.

I am two people. I am David Dickinson, private persona; and I am also the Duke, that walking, talking, fashionably attired public name and image who has a commercial value as a media personality. I don't know where this latter persona will take me – so far some very surprising and unexpected things have occurred and, even as I write, continue to occur.

I often say that I was born under a lucky star and I thank my lucky stars that this is so. If the television and media work all ends tomorrow I won't cry. No one who has had as much fun as I have, who has learned so much, who gets to have not just one but at least four very different fulfilling careers, could ever complain if one of them ends. After all – who knows what is just around the corner? That's the endlessly exciting thing.

Where my style started was when, inwardly, I rebelled against the type of clothes at Prescott's, the local outfitters in Stockport where I was taken every year from the age of about nine or ten. My outfits, which I have to say I wasn't very happy with, though they were the best that Nanny could afford, consisted of a pair of shoes, a pair of gabardine slacks and a tweed sports jacket. That was my Sunday best and I really loathed the look. That was how every boy up and down the length and breadth of England was turned out. Normally I wore it on a Sunday or if I went to tea at someone's house. School was grey flannel shorts and a shirt, nice and neat, with long grey socks, polished shoes and a short back and sides, Brylcreemed haircut. Top to bottom, I was spick and span.

Nanny would insist on me polishing my shoes and that has stayed with me ever since. Shoes, clean shoes, cared-for shoes, have always been an important part of my image. I can still hear her voice: 'Never let your heels go down, David. You mustn't have down-at-heel shoes, it doesn't look very nice at all.' At the slightest sign of wear we sent them to the cobbler's.

That was how I was programmed to fit in with every other boy. But from a youthful age I didn't want to be typecast as a somewhat boring and drab grey flannels and tweed jacket type of a fellow. I think I always wanted to shine a little, to be different from the herd. I recognize that craving to be different in others, that sense of individuality and self. Whatever the current fad may be, when I see people taking on the fashions of the day I always say to them, 'Yeah, go for it!' because I remember those days when I was like that myself. I often go down the King's Road and if, for instance, I see a lad with one of those huge 'Mohican' haircuts, I never find it intimidating like some people do. Sometimes I even shout encouragement at the lad from across the street.

I remember what it was like to be young, to want to be different, to express yourself. I always say the same thing to the young people I meet up and down the country today: 'Respect your elders, but at the same time you've gotta go for it if you want to. You've got to go for whatever the look of the day is. Express yourself, be an individual. Be a leader, don't follow the herd.'

I went through the blue jeans and Marlon Brando T-shirts stage; but before that came a bit of a disaster, when my Christmas present one year was some perfectly frightful navy-blue fake jeans that looked like a pair of French work-man's pants. They were baggy and saggy and fitted in all the wrong places, and though I submerged myself and them in a cold bath time and time again, even in the depth of winter, those bloody things just wouldn't shrink. Fortunately, I moved on quickly to real Levi's, a DA hairdo, and a stylish black leather jacket bought with money I had earned myself.

Once I had got into the textile business, 'the look' started to become a bit more developed. I began buying fine suitings. I found a tailor, Chris Nicolaou. I wanted to have suits of my own, maybe because I wished to express myself and not to remain the boy from the working-class background. In a light-weight, worsted mohair mix, or a silk and mohair, I really felt 'the business'. And, of course, with the travelling, when I first went to France and the Conti-nent as a 16-year-old, I started to see a whole new world. I could appreciate the flair that Continental men had. Not only were they slick and elegant but people in England would never have dared to use some of the colours that they did. A lot of British men, especially when I was a boy, wore such dour, plain colours. I mean, charcoal grey was the colour of the day. Men just didn't take on brighter colours with perhaps lightweight fabrics. When I went abroad, especially to warm climates, I saw men wearing all manner of exaggerated clothing made of lightweight fabrics in bright colours, matching shirts that went with them and the ties – ooh la la! It was a riot. Everyone wears those bright, outrageous or clashing colours now from the Gucci or Versace palette – but back then it was unheard of.

At about that time we started to go and see Continental films by Fellini, a great film-maker, with stuff like *La Dolce Vita* with Marcello Mastroianni – what a hero! The good-looking Italian guy who got the girl. Who drove the Ferrari. And suddenly I decided I wanted to be like him, wear the shoes that guys like him wore. The loafers. It all rang bells with me and so when I went to my tailor I was demanding a different look to my suits. Chris Nicolaou was from Cyprus, he understood these things. Englishmen wore double-breasted suits, all very straight, all very conforming, whereas the Italians had different styles. They wore longer jackets, three or four buttons, cuffs on the sleeves, decorative buttons – and all this started to make an impression on me.

I remember when Chris Haworth and I used to go to France, we would be buying decorative shirts, casual shirts, very nice shorts, slacks, white trousers, coloured belts that went with our casual outfits and slip-on shoes. Well, I'd never seen a slip-on shoe before – all I'd seen was a bloody carpet slipper! And to see me wearing mules which were a half-shoe (not a sandal) that you put your toes into but where the backs were open, was an eye-opener around Cheadle Heath. They looked very dapper to me though I did get some strange looks at times. I didn't give a hoot but Chris, with his more conservative middle-class background, was always very nervous about togging up in his Parisian gear once he came home to Manchester.

All these ideas started to influence my later life pattern. All the decorative clothing that I wear today on television is a mixture of all those fashions from all those years as I grew and developed and experimented. I just tailored it to suit me, to make it mine, to formulate my style and image.

I remember being in Paris in the late Fifties and early Sixties and wandering into the great shopping streets off the Champs Elysées where the Elysée Palace is, streets like the rue St-Honoré, where the fashionable shops were. I'd look in the windows and would hardly be able to believe my eyes at the prices of some of those shirts and accessories. 'Boy,' I thought to myself, 'I'd love to get stuck in, Dickie!'

Where accessories are concerned, what I recall as a boy coming out of the war years, is that it was all slightly drab. This has driven me to be a little bit decadent, a little bit flamboyant and to explore all styles. I try to balance this by not going too far, with keeping it low-key and tasteful when required. It's a bit like life, isn't it? – horses for courses. Now, some can carry it off and some can't, but I always felt that I could. But even if I couldn't, my attitude has always been, fuck 'em. I'm going to go out and buy what I like. Maybe that's part and parcel of what students like about me. Perhaps they see that rebellious side.

An early daring purchase towards my new image was a couple of almost identical Cacharel ties, one grey, one blue, that I bought in Paris in the late Fifties – and I've still got them at home. Those ties are very individual, though a little dated now. I have never seen the likes of them anywhere. You know what they say: 'What comes around goes around', and yes, it's true. I even pulled one of these ties out the other day when I was invited to open an envelope on the *Top of the Pops* awards in Manchester.

Up there, in front of all those trendy kids, I was wearing one of these over 40-year-old Cacharel ties, the grey one. It is slim, not pencil. Three little button-hole-stitched vents come at the knot and on top of that are stitched three little black silk buttons peeping through. With the tie I wore a Cardin Italian slub silk suit that I had had made many years ago. When I got it out of the closet I realized that in the light it's a little OTT. I think if you were a Mafioso you'd look absolutely right in it but I don't think I've worn it but once or twice. When I knew I was going to *TOTP* I thought, 'That'll do, Dickie, get the old silk suit out.' Well, out it came and I put on a Versace black shirt and I fished this tie out of the wardrobe. On it went and it looked a treat.

I went to *TOTP* and all manner of pop stars were coming up and saying, 'Where did you get that tie?' And I tell you what – if I was manufacturing these ties today they would be a really big hit. And as for the rock and roll fashion memorabilia sales at Christie's in South Kensington, I have a feeling that if my two ties from Cacharel went in the sale they'd bring a few bob!

I used to buy hand-painted silk ties by Christian Dior in England at the House of Fraser, which did have some nice shops, to go with the lightweight mohair suits that Chris Nicolaou made for me. I've been with him since I was a precocious teenager and no matter what style comes and goes we just adapt and go with the flow. Sometimes it's a tighter peg-bottomed trouser; sometimes it's a bell-bottomed trouser like it was in the Seventies; sometimes it's with a turn-up and sometimes it's not. Sometimes the jackets are slightly waisted; and sometimes they have a large collar; or they have a similar collar to the lapel. Sometimes it's double-breasted style, sometimes it's a single. Sometimes single vent, sometimes double, and sometimes no vent. Sometimes it's a straight pencil line. As with the majority of men's suits there is a classical look that never really dates. I once saw a suit by Henri Mouglier, a French designer, in Bond Street. I sketched it and I was straight down to my tailor.

I showed him the sketch and said, 'I want that collar on my next suit.'

Chris understood at once what I meant.

With clothes, it's about being adventurous and finding what is right for you. I've always been into ties and from the Sixties I was buying expensive ones. Yes, they cost a few bob but I couldn't resist, because I knew they looked good. They lifted my outfits above the ordinary, I knew I wouldn't see many similar ones on people I bumped into, and what is more – I've still got them.

Ties do change in style with the years. Sometimes they become more narrow, like French ties, or sometimes they are wider, like a kipper. Fashion seems to come with the tie. It's done, then it's gone; but like I say, 'What goes around, comes around – and when it does, the Duke will have 'em to bring out!'

I go into all manner of stores and have a good nose about. It doesn't have to be a designer label, as long as it has a design that's fabulous and suits me. You'll often find me wandering around Harrods, where there are enough ties to tie the *Queen Mary* to the dock. I wander round everywhere. Up and down Jermyn Street, where you'll find a wonderful array of shirts and ties. You could be there for three days and you'd not see all the ties in Jermyn Street. Club ties, plain ties, silk ties, woven ties, any shape, any size, any colour, any fabric. You want a particular tie? Get yerself down to Jermyn Street!

I also tend to go into some of the exclusive boutiques on Sloane Street for the ties to be found there. They are unique. I know what people say: 'Too expensive, too much money, outrageous' and so on. But give those shops a whirl. You'll be very surprised. A particularly good time to go into them is when the sales are on. I've seen very good value for money buys in the sales in Gucci, or Versace, or Yves Saint Laurent. Yes, these are very posh shops, but they do have sales. And Dickie likes a bit of a bargain. I went into Valentino's and bought a couple of ties. Retail, they would have been asking for about £70 apiece, but they were in the sale for half price. I bought them both, two for the price of one – cheap as chips. I've worn them on TV, so keep your eyes open during those repeats and see if you can spot 'em. One has an oyster background with a pink and black stripe in it. It's stunning. Now if you look at an average tie at £30 from Tootal's, or a similar mass-production manufacturer, it hasn't got that oomph! about it. It hasn't got that whizz! about it. That whoa! Now that is a tie!

Some of my favourite ties are hand-painted in subtle colours by a woman called Teresa Ferracci, on sale in a Jermyn Street shop. These ties are individual, like none other. They are just beautiful and to me it is like they are works of art hanging around my neck. It just makes me feel good and that's what fashion and good quality clothing is all about – to feel good wearing it.

I remember looking at people like Roger Moore on television when they were doing the Bond series. I would look at the shirts, at the ties, at the blazer. They just jumped out at you. I knew that they were all supplied by famous stores along Jermyn Street and, given time, I could have pinpointed them all.

I must have about 60 or 80 ties but I still keep buying them. Recently, for a special present, Lorne bought me a tie by Brioni. It cost about £190 but it's fabulous.

When she showed it me, I said, 'What a tie! It's unbelievable!'

I was wandering around Harrods when I spotted a tie by Stephano Ricci that cost about £180. Ouch! But when you walk into a room wearing a very plain, elegant, blue-grey suit, with one of these luxurious ties on, it's like having a Ferrari round your neck. All eyes will be on it. It makes you feel good. It's not showing off. It's how you feel about your dress.

If I was to bring out a line of clothing I would certainly want to do shirts with my own style. I've been wearing hand-made shirts since I was about 18 but I didn't start out like that. I was in the textiles business, meeting the tailors of suits. Then I also started to meet shirt-makers in shops in Manchester. Like many tall men, I have long arms. I wanted to show half an inch of cuff outside my jacket and the normal out-of-the-box shirts didn't allow me to do that. So I started having my shirts hand-made and soon discovered that they cost only a few quid more than, say, a Van Heusen. For just a little extra money I could get myself a wonderful Sea Island cotton or voile shirt in any colour or pattern or combination I wanted. I could have the shirt white and the collar blue, or vice versa. I didn't invent these ideas. I just saw them and emulated them. Plain colours or mixed and matched. I experimented and found I could look very sharp with an individual suit and that's how I started. Now today my hand-made shirts cost me a bit more, maybe £80 or so. I don't even know the price of a good 'stock' shirt these days because I haven't bought one for 30-odd years. I suppose a nice one costs about £35 or £40. I'm paying twice the price but I've got the shirt that suits me.

And, by the way, I used to have the old D.D. initials on the chest pocket but in recent years they have gone on just one of the cuffs of the shirt. It's a touch that I saw 30 or 40 years ago on the Continent, which I've adopted. If I had my own range of clothing going into the stores, I would say, 'OK, boys and girls, have a shirt like the Duke. Come back in three days' time and your initials will be on the shirt that you just bought.' I think it would be a big hit.

My obsession with shoes, like all my taste in clothes, goes back to my days with Nanny. There was not a lot of money about. I was well turned out, well scrubbed, clean knees. I can still hear her voice. It was always, 'Wash behind your ears, press your trousers, David, never let anyone see you looking down-at-heel with your shoes. Soon as those heels start coming down we'll get them off to the cobbler and get them sorted out.' Nanny was quite a stickler for how she thought things should be. I had only one pair of shoes at a time so I had to wear them over and over until I grew out of them. If I scuffed the toes I learned how to polish them up so they looked nice and clean. I was always taught that clothes, like manners, maketh the man. Consequently, when I walk into a room today to meet a businessman I tend to look at his shoes. Are they in good condition? Are they down-at-heel? Same with his nails. Has he got unkempt fingernails? That goes back to Nanny again: 'Don't bite your finger-nails, David.' Nothing looks worse on men, or on women for that matter.

Back to Nanny again: 'Look a man in the eye when you first meet. Give him a firm handshake. Show the person you are meeting that you are a man who can hold his head up.' All these things Nanny used to teach me and they've stayed with me all my life, and I've passed them on to my son. There is nothing worse than a limp handshake from a grown man. I'm a man of the world and certainly not homophobic – if a lad's gay, fine, let him get on with it – but to me a weak handshake indicates a weak character.

As with my clothes, shopping for shoes was an annual event when I was a boy. My Uncle John was manager for England's shoe shop in Stockport. I would be taken down there to get my yearly allocation of shoes, usually a pair of plain black shoes, or brown, occasionally a brogue. I'm still partial to a brogue but those from England's were plain. They were made of leather, which was expensive then for a family like mine. But they did last. And last. Until I outgrew them, then it was back for another pair.

The first shoes I bought for myself were the heavy boots that went with my rock and roll blue jeans. Not the best thing in the world to dance in – heaven knows how John Travolta would have coped in *Grease* and *Saturday Night Fever* – but they were what all the young Turks in America and later in Britain were wearing. Once again it was going to the Continent that opened my eyes to a different kind of shoe. What I found, even at the age of 18 or 20, was that when you bought good shoes they lasted for a long time. I must have about 30 or 40 pairs of shoes, going back for years. As I've got older I've found that Gucci make superb shoes. Their loafers have become famous, of course, but they make all manner of shoes.

Shoes don't change a great deal. We've been through winklepickers and chisel toes but essentially they stay the same. I often go into Versace, especially when the sales are on. They often have 50 per cent off. I bought myself a pair of skin boots the other day which normally retail for £220, but I got them for half-price. In Bond Street I go to Cesare Paciotti. He makes shoes in suede or leather that you can fall in love with. Some of his stuff has a classic Italian look, some a seventeenth-century look to them. Normally they retail for about £200 but I always hotfoot it to the sales and it's down to 50 per cent off.

If you go into a chain store you pay £60 for a reasonable pair of shoes, anyway, and for the same amount you can buy the best and walk around feeling like a god. My favourite footwear, if it comes down to it, are by the Italian maker Artioli. You can't mistake his shoes. It's the difference between a Rolls-Royce and a Ford. You know the minute you spot a pair on someone.

I'm not saying it always has to be expensive designer shoes for me. I still go into some of the main chain stores like Russell and Bromley and I do find some very nice and comfortable shoes. At the end of the day, where your feet are concerned, it's not just looks – it's comfort, too. There is absolutely nothing worse than tight, painful shoes that pinch and make you hobble like a lame duck. Give me comfort and quality first, then style second. I like to go for unusual casual shoes in suede, like mules or basket weave, again something I first spotted in my early days of Continental travel when I saw them shuffling around the casino in Cannes.

Whenever I'm in Marbella I usually go down to the port where all the yachts are. Lorne and I go to the shops there and out comes the credit card. Gotta have it! I saw a pair of shorts and a top with a pattern of parrots and exotic leaves, by Leonard of Paris, in the boutique of a five-star hotel. They were for walking around the pool and taking your top of for a swim, and I saw myself swanning around in them. But when I saw the price I almost fainted. They were about £300.

I said, 'Christ! That's too much!'

I had a bit of a hangover at the time so I asked if they would take £200. No way José! But we did settle for about £220. It was outrageous but I just could not leave them there. I would walk down to breakfast with this matching pair of shorts and top on and I saw some admiring glances from guys who were international bankers, property dealers and millionaires, choosy, wealthy men. In their eyes I read, 'That lad doesn't half look smart in those.' And that's what it's all about. It's not about showing off. It's about your individuality, about how you feel about yourself.

I'm not being flash. Building your image takes work and dedication. We present ourselves in the best way we can to face the world. Some people are shy and like to hide behind a drab appearance; other people put on a front, as actors do, and face the world squarely. For people in the public eye, *appearance* is their bread and butter. It's about acquiring taste and skill in buying clothes, choosing the best you can. Some people read magazines, others discuss fashion with their friends, they window shop, or if they are very rich and very busy, they hire dressers to shop and select for them, and to look after their wardrobes. Come to think about it, actors have dressers, as do royalty. Me, I have learned over many years how to get my eye in. I have gradually absorbed what is good, what is quality, what works, exactly as I did when I started out to buy antiques.

In America I go down Rodeo Drive and I still look in at No. 420, the boutique of the great Bijan, that wonderful Iranian outfitter's. This is the single most expensive store in the world, where even movie stars must make an appointment in advance just to shop. This is where the average male customer spends $100,000 a visit on socks, which cost anything from $50 upwards, and suits at up to $15,000. You think the Duke is extravagant? I ain't got nothing on those big spenders! I don't go to Bijan's and buy their suits because why would I spend that much when I can get Chris to make mine for a great deal less? You see sets of luggage in Bijan's – and I'm talking Lear jet stuff, which is to die for.

Talking of luggage, I missed a good buy the other day. I was wandering around one of the fairs and there was a very nice Louis Vuitton case for £600. I offered £500 but the stallholder refused. I walked away, did a circuit, came back, and the bloody thing was sold. But between you and me, the Duke has got a graduated set of three Louis Vuitton cases. They look the business but they are not Vuitton. I had them made for about £300 in Thailand about ten years ago. I never send them down the chutes at airports where they would get damaged, but I use them in the car when Lorne and I go away to a hotel. Fake they may be but as soon as they come out we get some glances, I can tell you. It's all front, all show business, after all.

You can still get 'the look' at a price if you scour around. I often still look in all the great shops in London, like Rossini on Bond Street. They are really just a facsimiles, copies of the great Bijan. Still very pricy, true, but not so pricy that they won't consider cutting you a deal. I saw a bow tie in there about a year ago and I had to have it. I went in and got the plastic out.

'How much is that bow tie?' I said.

The salesman said, '£240, sir.'

'£240 for a bow tie?' I said. 'You must be joking! I am not a sheik.'

He didn't blink but quick as a flash, he said, 'What were you thinking of?'

'Well,' I said, 'if I had to push the boat out, £120.'

To which he said, 'Done.'

And what I realized here was that the margin of profit was so huge that this was one shop where you could negotiate, and if you could negotiate in one, then you could negotiate in many others. You'll often see me wandering around the designer section in Harrods' basement. This is where all the designer labels are. I go so often, they all know me – and they all know the Duchess. They always give a nod to me and make a comment about the programme. 'Saw it last night,' they'll say. There is a certain amount of backslapping that goes on when you're a celebrity, which is all very nice and it all helps. In the basement I look for nice things and will sometimes treat myself. Sometimes, too, I miss out on things, often because I think they are too expensive, and later I invariably look back and think, 'I should have bought that!'

A case in point was the Christmas we stayed with Blanche Blackwell in Nassau. At one of Sol Curzon's casinos, the Atlantis, where there are some wonderful shops, I saw a top in the Versace boutique that instantly appealed. It had short sleeves, was knitted but lightweight, and in all respects it was sensational. In fact, there were two – one was red, the other black. I asked the price. I thought I'd misheard when they said £500. My sensible side said, 'I can get a suit from Chris for £500.' I walked away. But I was tormented by visions of the black top. I had to have it! Two days later I went back and it was sold. Since then I have been in every Versace shop, from Rome to London. It was just a short series they had made for one season only. I missed it. Whenever I'm away on holiday I often think I should have bought it, perhaps I could have worn it in some five-star hotel and I would have looked a million dollars. That's what it's all about, looking good, feeling good. And if I had got five or ten years' wear out of it then surely I would be able to say I had my value for money.

A similar thing happened when I went into Valentino's once. I saw a had-to-have overcoat there – and again I walked away. It was a cashmere coat with a fur collar. It was the end of the season, spring was coming, and they were getting rid of winter stock. It had been £2,000 and was reduced to £1,300. But I thought it was just a bit too much money. I offered £1,000, but they refused. I didn't buy it and I've been gutted ever since. This year when I wandered into Gucci I saw another magnificent cashmere coat in a type of camel colour with a half-belt at the back. Instantly, I thought, 'I ain't missing this one, baby!'

'How much?' I asked.

'£1,000,' they said.

'You can wrap that up right now,' I said, handing over my plastic.

There was a matching scarf at about £199.

I said to Lorne, 'Do I need the scarf?'

She said, 'Don't be silly! The scarf goes with it! Get it bought!'

A lot of money, yes, but I'll get good use out of it on television this winter, so it's an investment. All part of the image.

So we've come a long way from being a lad in short trousers, and from going to France as a young boy, looking at fashions and learning. Every young person should get out there and learn their style. It states to the world who they are and what they are. It's all part of the process of growing up and gaining an identity. I would say to young people out there that it may not ultimately be your style, it may not suit you, but you should be adventurous. Start to buy things that will make you look good, make you feel good and, most importantly of all, will give you confidence in life. There's nothing like a bit of confidence when you go for that job interview. You go in and you've got on a nice crisp blazer and a nice pair of grey slacks, a starched white shirt and a quality tie that you treated yourself to in Jermyn Street. You walk in there and your future employer looks at you and thinks to himself, 'I like the cut of the jib of this lad. We need young men like him in our firm.'

I've found that someone's first appearance is what you remember about them. First impressions really do count. And by the way, if you got that first job was it that 60 quid's worth of silk tie worth it? You can bet your life it was!

CHAPTER TWENTY

I was on my stand at Olympia when I got the call on my mobile from the Ray Fitzwalter Organisation to say that Channel 5 had picked up on the original six- to eight-part series they had been offered a couple of years previously. They wanted to make it eight programmes, called *The Antique Hunter*, starring me. This was very good news and I felt like a million dollars.

The framework to the series was that I would go to the homes of couples – not necessarily husband and wife, they could be mother and daughter or flat-mates – and ask them what they were looking for in the antiques field. I would take them out into the world, to auctions or to country house sales, and advise them, help them and give them the benefit of my expertise. At the same time the viewer would get tips on what to look out for, what to buy and how to bid at an auction. The programmes were really a combination of entertainment and information.

The commissioning editor for Channel 5, Michael Attwell, came along to meet me on my stand at Olympia. He was a very nice, astute man, who gave me a coat of looking at without making me feel that I was auditioning for the part. Initially, I don't think they were sure whether I was going to be able to carry a series, fronting it as presenter. Michael told me that they were thinking of putting a young presenter with me, perhaps one of these bright up-and-coming girls at C5. I agreed that I didn't have a lot of experience, but had worked for about 18 months in all doing my segments in the 'Buyer's Guide' and reports for *The Holiday Show*.

Michael was very affable and said to me, 'I think you have got potential, David.'

For him to say that was a great morale booster and very encouraging for me. He gave the green light to a pilot with me presenting. At the time Lorne and I had been living for some years in the Weaver's Cottage at 77 Bramhall Lane South. It was a picturesque eighteenth-century house with a slate roof and white stucco walls that we had fallen in love with some 12 or 13 years previously when we were looking for a house to replace the Edwardian property we had lived in since our marriage in 1969. We had built an extension and made it bigger. The garden was especially charming. The director chosen for *The*

WHAT A BOBBY DAZZLER

Antique Hunter, David Fair, came to meet me at the Weaver's Cottage, bringing his wife and children for the day. We spent many hours going over the way he saw the programme while I put my tuppenceworth in.

I told him how I felt, how I would add to the series, in particular, because of what I had done on *Modern Times*, where I looked at individual pieces and offered tips on what to look out for and what to buy.

'It wasn't scripted,' I said. 'What I brought to that series was my expert, off-the-cuff commentary, which was very natural and flowed well.'

David Fair nodded. 'Then that is what we'll go for,' he said. 'You obviously know what you're talking about.'

We went ahead. I was told to 'do my thing' and I would go out and do it, putting my knowledge of 30 years to use. Again, my style developed as I spoke to camera, telling the viewers at home what they, too, should be looking out for if they wanted to buy a grandfather clock, a button-backed chair, a Persian carpet or an Edwardian garden seat.

'Now listen, Hunters at home,' I'd say, 'what I'm looking for is a nice chest of drawers, circa 1900 –'

And then I'd offer a few tips on how they should go about tracking one down, how to buy it when they had found it and what to look out for to make sure they didn't take home a dud.

What made my advice different was that in many antiques programmes the experts spoke in a very knowledgeable way but they used terms that only the professionals really understood. They would describe a bookcase as 'a superb example of a George III bookcase with a broken pediment'. They'd rattle off terms like cluster columns, ogees, Brahma locks, flame veneer and bombe this and curlicued that. I tried to break this down into a way more acceptable to the average person. I would say things like, 'We have this piece of furniture, it has boxwood stringing. This small inlaid line is called stringing. It is decoration.' I thought that this was the way forward to make antiques and collecting more accessible to members of the public. I tried to put everything into layman's words. If I was looking at a French writing table I'd say so. I wouldn't tell them that it was a *bonnes heures des yeux*, because what's the point of that if they haven't a clue what you're talking about? But neither would I talk down to them. I thought, 'Teach them, yes, but in a way they understand. There's no point in bewildering the people at home. Keep it simple, David. Make it fun. Inform in a light-hearted way. This is entertaining television with a touch of easily absorbed information, it's not a lecture hall.'

The Antique Hunter was very professionally directed by David Fair and had a first-rate cameraman, Peter Rance. It had a lot of charm and went out at 8.30 p.m. on Channel 5. This was four or five years ago, when Channel 5 was new and not getting great audiences. A top-line show would draw 1.5–1.6 million and we got just under the million, which wasn't bad at all. However, the head of the channel, Dawn Airey, who was bright and very intelligent and really knew her stuff, didn't recommission it. Perhaps it just didn't appeal to her. Michael Attwell telephoned me with the news.

'Sorry to say, David, we're not going ahead with a new series. I think it's a big mistake because this is well worth another series. One day, you're going to be a big star.'

I always remembered what he had said. Here was a senior television executive showing faith in me. It was a great encouragement. I'm an old-fashioned character and remember them that were good to me. I also remember them that weren't. As Ronald Reagan used to say, 'We know who our friends are and believe you me, we're onto our enemies.' You learn to judge who is for you and who agin you, and it all goes down in David's red book!

After Channel 5 there was a bit of a lull in my work for television and Lorne and I took the opportunity to move from the Weaver's Cottage. We had been very happy there for a number of years but things in our environment had changed and we weren't happy with what had happened. Opposite our garage, which was to the side of our house, there was a small community hall where people would go for Brownies and bring and buy sales, that sort of thing. They would park their cars there, but it wasn't too bad since the hall was to the side, not facing us. As the years passed the church gained planning permission to put up a larger purpose-built hall. More engagements and functions took place, every morning, noon and night. We could never get in or out of our garage. This became the bane of our existence. Eventually it wore us down and we sold the house in 1998. We rented a very nice restored barn on a year's lease while we looked around for a place to buy.

This barn was one of three next to a farmhouse on a hillside with beautiful views over a valley. Two had been converted, the third, at the top of the cluster and dating from 1750, was still in its original condition. It had huge, rickety barn doors, a dirt floor knee-high in cow muck, and the roof was falling in. It was both dreadful and spectacular.

When our search for the perfect house produced nothing, the farmer said, 'How about buying that big barn at the top, David? There's planning permission with it.'

I stared at the barn. All I saw was a headache. But after nine months, property prices were starting to move upwards, our lease was due to expire and we had still found nothing suitable. We bought the top barn. I hired an architect and then, when we looked around the place with restoration in mind, I wondered what on earth I had done. It was a traditional Derbyshire stone barn with double walls with a rubble infill, and was surrounded by dry stone walls. The 'grey slate' roof was, in fact, huge slabs of cut stone that weighed an astonishing 40 tons, all sitting on a massive oak beam construction. It was sagging a bit but had stood for 250 years against winter gales.

I hired two talented young men as builders, paying them by the hour, and we started work. One of them had a great deal of knowledge about the reconstruction of stone buildings. Then there was me. I was there a lot of the time, getting in the way as usual, but I did have a use: to save time and money. I ordered up all the materials from local builders' merchants and wholesalers so there was always enough on site.

Things went well. The roof was taken off bit by bit, the barn walls were underpinned, repointed and made good. The boys used all the old skills of dry stone walling on the walls that surrounded the property, without the aid of cement. About 250 tons of earth that had piled up inside and out over the centuries was removed, then the roof was replaced. The planners in their wisdom decided that the timbers that had stood the test of time for 250 years were not strong enough and we were told to install steel A-frames. My architect stood gazing upwards as these very heavy steel girders that cost thousands of extra pounds were swung into place.

'Well, David,' he said, 'if you ever have a fire, the steel frame holding up the roof will buckle and the lot will fall in. Whereas the oak timbers would probably just smoulder and remain intact under a layer of charcoal. But the planners know best.'

From reclamation yards I was able to buy about 30 huge pitch-pine beams, a foot thick from a dismantled Victorian mill. Some were 30 feet long, virtually a whole tree. I used these to hold up a middle floor so I could expose the ceilings. The sandblasters came in to give the old stone a dusting. We didn't want to over restore so it would look too new but, as with old furniture, we wanted to bring it to life while preserving its age and patina. While we were about it, we sandblasted the beams, which showed the grain and revealed a fantastic colour. The planners had asked us to retain the original huge barn door opening, so I had a frame constructed of hand-made and pegged Victorian pitch pine and put in a pair of double doors.

While all this was going on I was called to London to meet a young publisher, Trevor Dolby of Orion, to discuss writing a book. He had seen me on television, liked the cut of my jib and thought a book on how to buy antiques, the kind of advice I was offering on the programmes, would go down a treat. I had no agent, having always represented myself throughout all my negotiations with the television shows, and so I handled the publishing deal myself. I was a businessman, after all, and to me this was all show business. I always say that some's in it for the show, some's in it for the business. I also say the show is very nice but I will always be in it for the business.

I negotiated what seemed to me at the time to be a good deal for what was to be my first book, but looking back with the hindsight of experience I realized that I hadn't studied the small print too closely. A skilled literary agent would have pointed out a thing or two to this lad who was new to the ways of the book world, I can tell you. I do know that this book was and still is selling like hot cakes, but because of the way the deal was structured I ain't seeing any of it! I don't blame anyone – I did the deal myself – but I'll tell you what, once bitten, twice shy. Dickie is a quick learner.

I started work on the book while, all the while, work on the barn progressed. Eventually, the book was written and went off to the printers. I was given a publishing date and Trevor telephoned me to discuss a book-signing schedule.

'Very good, Trevor,' I said, 'now, if you'll excuse me, I've got to go and help the boys with the roof of that barn.'

In actual fact, six sturdy men were on the scaffolding with blocks and tackle, lifting the huge beams into position. One beam was gradually going up higher and higher. It was a tremendous weight and I could see them struggling. I was always about on the job, lending a hand here, a bit of advice there, whether required or not.

I was straight in there with a rallying cry, 'Come on lads, let's do the business.'

I ran up the ladder and starting tugging at this enormous beam. I don't know what happened. I think the scaffolding or the trestle or the position where the beam was to go was a bit amiss, but the next thing I knew I was hurtling head first down towards the ground, which I hit with an almighty bang. It knocked the steam out of me. When I opened my eyes, I saw workmen scuttling down the scaffolding towards me.

My first thought was, 'Christ! I hope I haven't broken my neck.'

Lorne was called. She came hurtling across the fence, shouting, 'Where is he? Oh, my God, what's happened?'

By now the men stood all around, too nervous to touch me.

Someone asked, 'Can you move, David?'

I was in a great deal of pain but it was all coming from the hand beneath me, which had taken the impact. Lorne cautiously pulled the heavy industrial glove off and it's amazing that she didn't scream. Two fingers were torn to the bone, the knuckles and fingers pushed right out of their sockets.

It's funny how the mind reacts in extreme pain. I looked at my hand pumping blood and thought, 'Dearie me, there goes the book-signing!'

Lorne says that once again my lucky star was shining over me. I had fallen 15 feet head first, straight down onto a stone floor and was able to walk. I'll draw a veil over the hospital visit and the treatment without anaesthetic. Let's just say this: it's a good thing I wasn't taken prisoner during World War II because if they had reset my knuckles the way those doctors did, believe you me, I would have talked.

A postscript to the barn story. Some months later, after we had moved in, I was interviewed by Jan Muir of the *Daily Telegraph*, who followed me around the Borough Street Market at the crack of one dawn. For her readers, she wanted to know what it was like to hunt for bargains. I showed her the ropes, discussed a few cracking items on this stall and that one, but apparently I also spent a great deal of time saying very enthusiastically, 'And do you know, I live in a barn.'

When the piece came out, the headline read: 'He's 60s bouffant (that's the hair) but he's in mint condition.' Then at the end came the punchline: 'He walks it, he talks it – and he lives in a barn.'

We knew it was just a good-spirited bit of leg-pulling, so Lorne and I wrote back, 'Thank you very much for your wonderful article. And by the way, still walking it, still talking it – and still living in a barn!' We still send Jan the odd postcard from around the world, ending with, 'Still living in a barn!'

The restored barn had slate floors, exposed beams, four bedrooms and three bathrooms, as well as three open-plan major reception rooms, ideal for display-ing wonderful pieces of antique furniture, objets d'art, jardinières and so forth. I even found an eighteenth-century water pump from an Irish village and a proper pump trough carved from a solid block of stone, with a hole at the bottom where a bit of bone went to allow the water to drain. With these stand-ing outside, the place took on a great deal of character and overall was a proper bobby dazzler.

Things worked out very well. With the barn finished and my first book out, I got a call early in 1999 to go down to Bristol to talk to Mark Hill, the man who had played such a big part at the start of my television career. Now here we were again, sat across the desk discussing the potential of a new series, a show to be called *Bargain Hunt*. I listened carefully to the structure and format of the proposed show. Two teams would be given £200 each to compete against each other to buy collectibles in an open-air type of informal broccante fair. Experts would accompany them to offer advice, but the choice would be down to the team players, who would hopefully make a profit when these items came up at an auction the following week.

Also at the meeting in Bristol I met the series producer, a lovely woman, Melanie Erickson, who played a big part in the promotion of my television career.

At the meeting she said, 'I've seen your previous work, David. I'd like to work with you and I think we can really do something here to make a success together.'

Melanie was the series producer for the first 18 months of the daytime *Bargain Hunt* and was also in charge of the first eight prime-time versions of the show. She was followed by another very charming producer, Susan McDermot, who was in turn replaced by the present daytime series producer, the very capable and delightful Linda Cleave, who had been a director on the show from the start.

It all sounded interesting, so wearing my agent Dickie Lazar hat, I negoti-ated a price and a contract for my services. Acting as my own agent can be quite entertaining. Taking a cue from the great Hollywood agent, Irving 'Swifty' Lazar, when a deal was offered, I'd say, 'I'll pass you over to Dickie

Lazar, let's see what he's got to say,' I'd listen, then, using the words of Colonel Tom Parker, Elvis's agent and another canny dealer, I'd say, 'Yes, that's interesting. That's all right for me, but what about the Duke, what are you gonna pay him?' (The colonel always used to say: 'That's all right for me – now what about mah boy?') I have a bit of fun with it. It's a spoofy way of breaking down the barrier. It's not easy negotiating on your own behalf because you have to talk about yourself. You have to say things like, 'He's doing fantastically at the moment, he's great –'and this sometimes sticks in the mouth a little bit. An agent is the perfect buffer. If, as has happened, negotiations get a bit rough, you'll find that personalities come out and personalities become upset and that's not necessarily a good thing. An artist should be to one side, always smiling and saying, 'That agent of mine, he's an absolute bastard.' I'm doing both because, in a nutshell, I did it for Lorne for years, and so far, no agent I've spoken to has told me what I want to hear – plus I'm saving 15–20 per cent commission. Get the idea?

We set to work on *Bargain Hunt*. The first few shows were a bit scrappy as we all found our feet within the designated framework. For my part, as is my style, I put my own stamp and image on the show. On the first half-dozen shows we'd go out, buy a few goods, then sell them at auction. I in turn would build in my tips on how to go about it in the salesroom or at the fair. It was similar to what I had done in *The Antique Hunter*.

One day David Fair rang me and said, 'Dave, this new series is working well, but you have rather nicked our ideas.'

I said, 'What do you mean?'

'Well, you're doing these pieces to camera, offering all these tips, addressing the audience at home.'

I agreed with him. 'That's *me*! That's what I do. It's my persona. That's what I brought to *The Antique Hunter*, and this is what in turn I am bringing to this particular series.'

He laughed and said, 'You're right. It is you, David. Good luck with it.'

He maybe felt he had a similar programme but it didn't have that competitive edge between two teams which made *Bargain Hunt* that bit more exciting. After six or eight shows, I rang Mark Hill.

'We have a problem here,' I said. 'The blueprint is back to front. We are buying goods in a semi-retail situation at the fairs. We are then bringing them back to a wholesale situation at auctions, where many of these pieces started life, and we're trying to get a profit on them. It doesn't often work.'

'Well, it's too late now,' he said. 'We can't change in midstream. Do your best to keep it upbeat. Win or lose, everyone seems to have fun and that's the thing.'

It's funny how a programme goes. The more we had losers, the more I made light of it. There didn't seem to be any other way to wrap the programme up. Originally, in the earlier shows, the summing up was done in a reasonably serious way until I thought, 'Hang on, you can't keep going on like this, it's getting beyond a joke.' So I made my closing comments more tongue in cheek.

At the finish, where I'd previously said, 'Have you had a nice day? The red team has lost 90 quid, the blue team has lost 120 quid –' I'd now just look at the camera and say, 'Well, we picked up a lot of old tat today –'

I think one of the things that makes the show work is that £200 is not a great deal of money to spend, and so the viewers at home can sit back in their seats and say, 'I could do better than that. I'd choose better stuff,' and I would encourage that. I would pull the contestants' legs in a light-hearted and humorous way but I would never go over the line where they were embarrassed. Without detracting from the work of the rest of the team, my frivolous and flamboyant approach worked and the ratings started to soar. At first it was 800,000 to 900,000 viewers at eleven-thirty in the morning. As the programme gained momentum the figure started to creep up to a million. Richard and Judy were still in their morning slot at about 1.6 million. We started to make inroads. Suddenly, we were saying, 'We can catch up with that magical Richard and Judy figure.' And within a matter of months we did. As they slipped down the scale, we climbed up, until we were getting three million – virtually unheard of for a daytime show.

I made it personal. I shared my finds with the viewers. I would spot something, and in confidential close-up I would whisper, 'This has an estimated price of £400. But it's a little corker and will probably go for £2,000 if anyone else gets on to it. I've a mind to bid for it myself and carry it home.' And when the bidding started to get hectic, as I had predicted, I would turn to the camera from my position at the back of the room and say, 'I was right, boys and girls. That piece is a real bobby dazzler.'

I don't often buy the things that I have pointed out as being special in the salesroom, but I may occasionally go for the odd find if I have a use for it, such as an Edwardian croquet set for my new lawn or some crockery for the wife. At one auction I came across a beautiful Victorian dinner set in perfect condition, complete with serving plates, tureens, bowls, dishes and plates of every size. There must have been about 72 pieces in all, and I said to the camera, 'For £250 you can buy all this. How much more will a modern set cost you? I'm going to throw my hat in the ring for this, boys and girls. Her indoors would love it.'

I don't usually look at jewellery stands at these fairs, but I once spied an extraordinary item in a showcase amongst some silverware and other small objects. It was a small oval cameo of a portrait, either of a Roman emperor or Homer, the Greek poet. I asked to look at it and, on further examination, I saw that it was carved by hand out of hardstone in such a way that various layers and colours were cut away to reveal the face, which had a different colour background to it. It had a pin at the back that enabled it to be used as a brooch. I asked the price.

'Seventy quid, guv.'

'What is it?' I said.

'A 1920s cameo brooch,' the dealer said.

My instinct told me that this was not a shell cameo but quality. It had been intended as a work of art. The concave shape indicated that it had been a ring at some time, not a brooch. My instinct kicked in, and I thought, 'This isn't 1920s at all. It's probably early nineteenth century, probably Regency.' In antiquity, men had worn these rings and the fashion returned in Georgian times from about the 1730s, when Herculaneum and Pompeii were discovered. I paid the £70 asking price and took the piece to a friend, Ian Harris, a jewellery expert who was often on *Antiques Roadshow*.

'What do you think?' I asked.

'Hmm, hardstone cameo, beautifully carved, obviously a ring, a gold brooch backing soldered on in the 1930s.'

'Age?'

Ian said, 'The good news, David, is it's late eighteenth century, up to 1790. What did you pay?'

'I got a good buy,' I said. 'Seventy quid.'

'You got a bloody good buy,' said Ian. 'It's two and a half thousand quid's worth.'

I reset it as a ring in a period Georgian setting and I wear it now. Watch my hand pointing out stuff, or caressing the patina on a fine piece of furniture, and you'll spot it. I bought it, and kept it, because it gives me sheer delight and pleasure to look at it – and that's what this business is all about.

On one *Bargain Hunt* show we had a couple of pilots and two members of the cabin staff from BA first class and Concorde competing against each other.

'If I turn up, don't forget the upgrade,' I joked, then I turned to the stewardess from Concorde and asked, 'What exciting people have you had on the aircraft?'

'I met Frank Sinatra,' she said. 'He was charming. I asked for his autograph and he obliged.'

'What about that infamous bodyguard of his, the Tank?' I said. 'Was he there?'

She laughed. 'No, I didn't see him. But on another occasion Princess Diana flew out with us to New York. We chatted a bit and she was delightful, so when we got her again on the way back I screwed up my courage and politely said, "Your Royal Highness, if it's not too forward, may I ask for your autograph?"'

Diana readily agreed and the stewardess went looking for something suitable for her to sign. She couldn't find anything in the galley area so she looked in the crew locker in the forward cabin. The only thing she found was a pack of cards, still in their box. She opened the box and offered the pack to Diana.

'Will these do?' she said.

Diana fanned out the cards, and with a smile, deliberately selected the queen of hearts and signed it. I believe the British press had already picked up on that epithet after her famous television interview on *Panorama*. When Martin Bashir asked her if she would regret never being Queen, Diana replied, no, she wanted to be the Queen of Hearts – of everyone's hearts.

I thought the story of the air stewardess was quite remarkable, and was instantly reminded of two other incidents that had taken place some time earlier on my stand at Olympia. One was when the fair that year was opened by Princess Diana. I met her and we chatted a while. She was absolutely charming and very lovely. She had the most incredible blue eyes, the same colour as all the royal ladies – Princess Margaret, the Queen and the Queen Mother – although I must say that Diana's eyes were startlingly beautiful. The second event was when I spotted Elton John moving at great speed along an aisle at Olympia, eyes cast to the ground, and I thought, 'What's wrong with him?' I realized that when he walked along, head up, eyes looking ahead, people found him approachable. By not making eye contact he was giving himself some space to do his own thing as a private individual. He came to my stand and had a look around. There was nothing that caught his attention but on the next stand, which was owned by a chum of mine, an oil painting caught his eye and he went over to look. He was there for some considerable time – about 30 minutes – studying it intently. It was the painting of a playing card: the queen of hearts. In the end he decided against it and moved on.

It struck me after I had talked to the air stewardess: I wonder if Elton John was looking at that as a gift for a princess? I knew that he and Diana were friends and it hit me forcibly that he could have been contemplating buying it for her. Some time later I learned that the Concorde stewardess was advised to enter her playing card into a sale in Sotheby's New York. It was catalogued, but before the event, she was approached by an English tabloid and they paid her, I believe, £65,000. Incredible. Many people have Diana's autograph, of course, but to have it on that particular playing card makes the item quite unique. Again, I am reminded that this business is fickle but in the end it always comes back to unique and individual items. They are the ones that hold their price and keep rising in value.

As the *Bargain Hunt* series grew in popularity I gained fans of all ages, from 12-year-olds to housewives and pensioners at home. I also have a huge student following. I get the most amazing letters posted on the website or sent to the BBC. They are very moving and charming and it makes me feel humble that so many people take the trouble to write in.

Before long I was being asked to appear on other people's shows: Ruby Wax; Gloria Hunniford; Johnny Vaughan; Frank Skinner; Dom Joly; BBC's *Diners*; *The Nation's Favourite Food*; *Shooting Stars*; *Dead Ringers*; *Have I Got News for You* – and Jonathan Ross, who in my opinion is 'the man'. The list, if you'll forgive me sounding too lovey, is long. I enjoy it all and even when I am endlessly teased about my flowing locks, or that suntan, I take it in good spirit. Jonathan Ross calls me 'the Orange One' and Terry Wogan was the one who introduced me on his show with the words: 'David Dickinson is like Peter Stringfellow's love child crossed with a mahogany hatstand.' Peter, that great style icon, and I have had a laugh about that, I can tell you.

When Peter appeared on *This Is Your Life* with me in the hot seat, he repeated it, then said, 'If you've got it – flaunt it!'

All I can say is, I agree with that, Peter. When you enter the world of show business you can't be a retiring, shy maiden aunt.

I got a great kick when *Through the Keyhole* came to our home and filmed me and Lorne there. I had watched those shows over the years and I had a quiet laugh when I recalled that newspaper feature: 'He walks it, he talks it – and he lives in a barn.'

I have requests for all manner of interviews and photo shoots from magazines like *Hello!* and *OK!* and topical hip magazines like *Loaded*. A big thrill was making the front page of the *Radio Times* I remember it so well as the big 'must have' magazine in millions of homes when I was younger – and to see my face on the front cover really did knock the socks off me. We had a bit of fun there. There I was on the front cover, and when you opened the magazine the centre spread was of me doing the full monty nudie shoot with a teddy bear strategically placed. It was all done in good taste and, because it was the *Radio Times*, I didn't have any hesitation. This shot went on to become a poster that was very much in demand. I was astonished. Dickie Dickinson, pin-up boy!

I've certainly done a lot of radio shows up and down the country, with major DJs, such as Steve Wright, Jonathan Ross and Chris Moyles. Chris has been a great supporter of mine; he used to mentioned *Bargain Hunt* quite frequently on his shows, thus gaining it a student audience. He's a lovely man from Leeds so we're both just a couple of provincial boys who are pretty outspoken and see eye to eye on many things.

I got a thrill when someone called me and said, 'Listen in to Chris Moyles's show at 5 p.m. They're covering the Glastonbury Festival.'

I tuned in and suddenly heard Chris Moyles saying, 'Here's the man – here's the Duke.'

A young music student had downloaded the theme music from *Bargain Hunt* and had added my catchphrases – my bobby dazzlers, my cheap as chips – and mixed it into a rap single. It was being played over the loudspeakers at the great Glastonbury Festival and, in turn, was picked up on Chris's show and relayed over the entire country.

Chris said to everyone who was listening to his show, 'Open your windows wide, wind down your car windows, turn it up!'

The rap song reverberated along the highways and byways, along the motorways and the city streets. It was an amazing moment. All I can tell you is, it made an old rocker very, very happy.

A highlight of 2002 was the National Television Awards, when *Bargain Hunt* was nominated as the most popular daytime programme. There were three other contenders in this category: GMTV's *This Morning*, which to me looked to be the favourite; the Australian soap *Home and Away*; and *Countdown*, a cult programme that has been on our screens for years and has been nominated many times before, though it has never won. Lorne and I were at the awards ceremony with some of the producers and executives from *Bargain Hunt*.

From the time I heard that we were nominated, did I think we had a chance? I thought we did, because I knew the show had three million viewers per day and we had a wonderful team.

Lorne was beaming. From the start of the evening she thought we in with a great chance. It gave me great pleasure to be nominated and we went to the ceremony just to enjoy the event. To be amongst the stars and to receive such flattering remarks from people I had long admired was quite something.

How wonderful to have Carol Vorderman coming up to you and saying, 'You're great, you are, and I think you've got a good chance.'

The stars of *EastEnders* and numerous other celebrities I'd seen on television at a distance and respected, all nodding, helloing, and saying, 'Cheers, go for it, have a good night,' was quite special.

The moment the envelope was opened and it was '*Bargain Hunt* – David Dickinson, come up here... ' Well, I've seen a replay of the tape and Lorne was so so excited. I went up and collected the award together with the producers and executive producers. I'm not normally tongue-tied but I felt a bit stuttery trying to remember to thank all the people who had made the show so terrific. It was an enormous thrill to be given the gong and it occupies pride of place on my coffee table.

Afterwards, well, you know what the Duke does – he celebrates. It was November, the tan was going a bit pale. I booked a couple of club class tickets on Emirates Airlines and we spent a wonderful week in the Ritz Carlton in the Emirates. We do like a bit of luxury, Lorne and I, and one's got to top the old tan up, of course.

It had been a thrilling period, but on a day-to-day level I do try to keep the old size elevens on the floor. This is not easy, when you are told, 'David Dickinson – This Is Your Life!'

That week I had been hosting a series of celebrity charity auctions with some fabulous guests to raise money for *Children in Need*. The last night took place in Folkestone. The show wrapped at eight-thirty in the evening and as soon as the live transmission finished they asked if I would make an announcement, which would be a recorded piece of film, to be used the next day in London at the BBC studios for a finale for *Children in Need*. I wasn't aware that this was just a bit of kidology – a ploy to hold me in position with the cameras while a certain person walked out with that red book.

Believe you me, I had no idea whatsoever. They had contacted Lorne several weeks before (she told me after the show) and spoken with her. She in turn mentioned people I had known, relatives and so on, and surreptitiously they gathered all these people together. Even on the day that I was approached by Michael Aspel with the red book I still had no idea. Sometimes Lorne travels with me while I film around the country and we had been together in Folkestone. A few weeks before, she had done a photo shoot for one of the national newspapers and she informed me that she had been offered another one of these shoots, so had to go in London that afternoon while I was working in Folkestone on the *Children in Need* auction. I was due to follow on afterwards in order to be in London the next morning for a live transmission.

I said, 'See you later,' and with a smile and a wave, off Lorne went.

At half past eight, as I was standing in the auction room making my little announcement, out of nowhere popped Michael Aspel with the old red book.

He tapped me on the shoulder and announced, 'I've got this book which I can offer you at a very reasonable price. It's a first edition of *David Dickinson – This Is Your Life.*'

Well, blow me down with a feather. It completely took me by surprise. I know they all say that, but it really did. Michael was everything you would expect him to be, a consummate professional and an absolute gentleman. I was whisked up to London to BBC Television Centre in a limousine. It was extraordinary to walk into the studios and to find them packed at such a late hour. It was like a cross-section of my entire life to date. Out there was the studio audience and this side of the limelights were friends and family. I didn't think I deserved it.

I even told the series producer, Jack Crawshaw, and the producer, Sue Green, 'There are many more people more deserving of this honour than I. There are lifeboat coxswains and people who clear landmines.'

I have to say I thoroughly enjoyed the evening. Jack and Sue, two wonderful people, made me feel so relaxed and were part and parcel of that memorable night, one I will never forget. After the show we had a party in an upstairs suite which eventually wound down in the early hours. You have to pinch yourself when something like that happens – but it's been an absolutely phenomenal year.

When you think of being presented with that big red book, of being told 'This is your life', in many ways you think it's all over. You've done it all, and this is the summing-up. But it's not all over. It's only the start. Believe you me – you ain't seen nothing yet, kid!

INDEX